LIVING THROUGH THE DEAD

STUDIES IN FUNERARY ARCHAEOLOGY

LIVING THROUGH THE DEAD
Burial and commemoration in the Classical world

Edited by
Maureen Carroll and Jane Rempel

with a preface by
John Drinkwater

OXBOW BOOKS
Oxford and Oakville

Published by
Oxbow Books, Oxford, UK

© Oxbow Books and the individual authors, 2011

ISBN 978-1-84217-376-3

This book is available direct from

Oxbow Books, Oxford, UK
(Phone: 01865-241249; Fax: 01865-794449)

and

The David Brown Book Company
PO Box 511, Oakville, CT 06779, USA
(Phone: 860-945-9329; Fax: 860-945-9468)

or from our website

www.oxbowbooks.com

Front cover image: Funerary Symposium, from the necropolis at Antioch (mosaic)
by Roman Worcester Art Museum, Massachusetts, USA/The Bridgeman Art Library

A CIP record for this book is available from the British Library

Library of Congress Cataloging-in-Publication Data

Living through the dead : burial and commemoration in the classical world / edited by Maureen Carroll
and Jane Rempel ; with a preface by John Drinkwater.
    p. cm. -- (Studies in funerary archaeology ; v.5)
Includes index.
  ISBN 978-1-84217-376-3 (pbk.)
  1. Burial--Greece. 2. Burial--Rome. 3. Funeral rites and ceremonies--Greece. 4. Funeral rites and
ceremonies--Rome. 5. Memorialization--Greece. 6. Memorialization--Rome. 7. Sepulchral monuments-
-Greece. 8. Sepulchral monuments--Rome. 9. Excavations (Archaeology)--Greece. 10. Excavations
(Archaeology)--Rome. I. Carroll, Maureen. II. Rempel, Jane.
  DE61.B87L59 2010
  393.0938--dc22
        2010050511

Printed and bound in Great Britain by
Hobbs the Printers Ltd, Totton, Hampshire

Contents

List of Contributors

MARTIN BOMMAS
Senior Lecturer in Egyptology
University of Birmingham

MAUREEN CARROLL
Reader in Roman Archaeology
University of Sheffield

JOHN DRINKWATER
Professor in Roman History
University of Nottingham

EMMA-JAYNE GRAHAM
Lecturer in Roman Archaeology
University of St. Andrews

CELINA GRAY
Assistant Professor of Classical Studies
Wesleyan University
Middletown

SÉBASTIEN LEPETZ
Centre National de la Recherche Scientifique
Paris
(UMR 5197)

POLLY LOW
Lecturer in Ancient History
University of Manchester

JOHN PEARCE
Lecturer in Archaeology
King's College London

JANE REMPEL
Lecturer in Classical Archaeology
University of Sheffield

SUSAN RUSSELL
Vice-Director
British School at Rome

WILLIAM VAN ANDRINGA
Professor in Archaeology
Université de Lille 3
(UMR 8164, CNRS – Malme-Ipel)

Acknowledgements

This volume grew out of an international conference on death and commemoration from Antiquity to the Eighteenth Century held in 2006 in the Department of Archaeology at the University of Sheffield. We gratefully acknowledge the sponsorship of the British Academy for that event, as well as the support of the Sheffield Centre for Historical Archaeology and our historical colleagues, Dawn Hadley, John Moreland and Hugh Willmott. Our thanks also go to our contributors, both those who were originally involved in the conference (Gray, Graham, Pearce, Russell) and those who wrote papers specifically for this volume (Bommas, Low, Lepetz and Van Andringa). Recurring health problems of both editors have resulted in delays in seeing this book through to completion; we appreciate the patience and forbearance of our authors. In particular, we are very grateful to John Drinkwater for his helpful comments and staunch support. It is our pleasure to acknowledge the assistance of a number of institutions and museums that have kindly allowed the reproduction of images. Thanks also are due to J. Willmott for Figure 4.11. Christine Baycroft's help in translating the paper by Lepetz and von Andringa from French into English was much appreciated. Finally, we are very grateful to Oxbow Books for taking up our idea for the book and to Clare Litt who supported our proposal to Oxbow.

Preface

John Drinkwater

The dead can do nothing for themselves. Their disposal is solely the concern of the living. But the character of this concern varies from age to age and from place to place. In the United Kingdom, for example, there has for centuries been a tradition of marginalising the dead:

> Beneath those rugged elms, that yew-tree's shade,
>   Where heaves the turf in many a mould'ring heap,
> Each in his narrow cell for ever laid,
>   The rude Forefathers of the hamlet sleep.
>   (Thomas Gray, *Elegy written in a Country Churchyard*)

The papers presented in this volume demonstrate that in the Ancient World the dead were not marginalised and forgotten but remained very much part and parcel of everyday life.

In line with current archaeological concern for what German scholars have neatly labelled *Sitten und Gebräuche*, 'customs and usages', contributors examine not just the material nature of funerary finds but their function in funerary ritual. In doing so, they point up many differences, but a common theme is that of ancient funerary practice as a means of intense commemoration, of keeping the memory of the deceased alive: who they were, what they did, even how they looked. As **Graham** notes, this was important in an age that was uncertain about the nature or the very existence of an afterlife (and, one may add, in an age in which, without photographs and voice recording, most people had very little chance of leaving their mark in the world). But commemoration needed a high level of interaction, and so the dead had to be placed close to the living and the living had regularly to make contact with them. Once closeness and contact were established, a new process could begin, as the living used the dead for their own purposes.

The broadest approach is found in **Bommas'** review of Egyptian funerary cult (he stresses – *not* religion, of which cult is just part), belief and practice from the later third millennium BC to the early fourth century AD Over this long period we can see significant continuity and change. The dead were always seen as living, in the sense that they had gone on to live a new life in the hereafter. This eventually generated the belief that these dead-living, if correctly handled (basically, solely through the agency of trained priests), might aid the living. Thus arose the notion of the "caring dead" who, if the living gave to them, might give to the living. Such feelings may easily have become crude reciprocity: 'you scratch my back …'. In their first phase, however, they gave the world of the living "social connectivity", the idea that 'what goes around comes around', and so the conviction that people should act prudently and justly: "the principle of Ma'at", of "something right", and hence the principle of truth and justice. Practitioners of Ma'at would be rewarded in this life and the next. Later, from the middle of the first millennium BC, the living sought a more personal relationship with the dead, sustaining them with gifts so that they might act as intermediaries between the living and the gods. In the Roman period this generated the desire for so great a degree of proximity that, for example, mummies were accommodated in the house, actually sharing the lives of the living.

Three papers treat Greek experience. I note two here, and return to the third at the end. **Gray's** study of immigrants from Miletus at Athens shows how burials could be used to express a community's experience of living as an ethnic minority. At first glance the Milesians' monuments appear very positive, reflecting their success as the predominant group of resident aliens in the city, and their ready adoption of Athenian ways. These monuments do so in themselves (they closely follow prevailing Athenian funerary fashion) and in what they communicate in their written messages and figurative decoration (e.g. the entry of their young men into the ephebate, and the marriage of their young women to Athenian citizens). However, there is also an underlying hint of the negative – of the realisation that, despite their aspirations and best efforts, the Milesians would never be fully integrated into Athenian society. This was because, even after the formal removal of legal obstacles to integration, Athenians remained viscerally opposed to its happening: there was a "glass ceiling". The gravestones' proclamation of Milesian citizenship thus reflects the group's continuing derivation of security from its older identity: one is bound to think of Jewish experience in Germany under the First Reich.

Rempel investigates the disposal of the dead in the Bosporan kingdom, a large and ethnically heterogeneous Hellenistic state in the north-eastern corner of the Black Sea. The Bosporan elites used burial to advertise and confirm their status. The dominant elite, headed by the Spartokid rulers, were laid to rest in style in great stone-chambered mounds, 'kurgans', with rich grave-goods. This elite evinced its strong Greek associations through the nature of these goods. However, other finds indicate the unabashed adoption of the fashionable chambered mound by other, clearly non-Greek, communities in the kingdom and, equally important, their adaptation of its use in line with their own cultural preconceptions and priorities. Furthermore, the very form of the kurgan pre-dates the Spartokids, and can be found in their time on the neighbouring steppe. A similar phenomenon of cultural cross-fertilisation is also visible in the less grand and more orthodox 'flat' burials of the area. Study of the dead thus identifies the complex processes of social interaction and integration that involved the living at the margins of the Greek world, and allows understanding of the cultural flexibility, and so the political strength, of the Bosporan kingdom. It also allows us to nuance and make positive the force of the otherwise potentially very negative phrase 'non-Greek' in this context.

Among the Roman papers, a fundamental difference between the ancient and modern treatment and experience of death, at least in the west, is pointed up by **Lepetz and van Andringa** in their study of a cemetery at Pompeii. Here, a wealthy and influential *parvenu*, Publius Veronius Phileros, muscled his way onto a prime burial site by the Porta Nocera. In shoehorning in his own, new, family memorial he respected some earlier graves but obscured others; and he aired his dirty linen by preventing the deposition of the remains of a close dependant, Faustus, originally promised burial there, and cursing him publicly. By modern standards, the place he thought so much of was small and crowded. A stone's throw from the city, it reflected all its life. Bodies were burned in the open on site. Families held regular funerary feasts, littering plots with uneaten food and broken crockery. Crude footpaths threaded the place, and dogs ran about leaving their mess. In short, it was cramped, noisy, smelly and vulgar.

Noise and vulgarity in a Roman funerary context is examined more specifically by **Carroll**. The unfortunate Faustus of Pompeii was not alone in being publicly vilified on what had been planned as his memorial. *Damnatio memoriae*, the practice of 'anti-commemoration', of condemning a person's memory or even of attempting to 'airbrush' him or her from history, is a well-known feature of political failure at the top of Roman society, usually involving the imperial family. Carroll, however, examines its occurrence among private citizens, in cases where names have clearly been deliberately excised from funeral monuments after their completion. She unveils a fascinating aspect of Roman everyday life as family discord – bitter rows between husbands and wives, parents and children, families and dependants, and among dependants – were recorded for all to see. As in the case of Faustus, monuments were even used as instruments of vindictive black magic, to curse, not to commemorate, the allegedly guilty parties. And, as in the case of the great, such practices, ostensibly meant to negate remembrance, actually intensify the curiosity of the observer. One begins to suspect that, in these all-absorbing soap operas of favourites fallen (and sometimes replaced), the principals actually wanted to keep the memory of their feuds alive for eternity.

However, not all Roman concerns were so secular. In the presence of death the living are in the presence of powerful and worrying unknown forces. The corpse of the newly deceased provokes both mourning and anxiety. Still in this world, it is no longer of it: it is different, alien, contaminating. These are aspects which have to be dealt with properly – from the point of view of religion, not personal expediency. Noted by **Lepetz and van Andringa**, they are followed up more closely by **Graham**, in an evaluation of the rite of *os resectum* – the holding back of a small part of a corpse (usually a finger joint) from cremation for religious use, before reuniting it with the other remains. She argues that this was not, as is commonly believed, exceptional, but standard practice: the joint was an essential element in ceremonies directed towards the ritual cleansing of the family of the deceased. Only then, after 'the deceased' had become 'the dead' could lives of the living return to normal, and proper remembrance of the dead begin. (Here one notes the difference between Roman and later Egyptian practice in this respect. Nero's attempt to retain the embalmed body of his beloved empress Poppaea in the imperial palace was regarded as yet another aspect of his insanity.) She further proposes that this same ritual, in focusing upon the deceased and his or her ancestors, may well have furnished a powerful means of remembering the dead quite distinct from, but as important as, commemoration by or at the grave. The importance of the *Sitten und Gebräuche* of non-monumental and non-epigraphic recollection of the omnipresent dead, especially for the illiterate and poor, is also touched on by **Bommas**, and is implicit in the funerary feasting noted by **Bommas** (as "binges") and **Lepetz and van Andringa**.

Pearce takes Roman treatment of the dead from the centre to the periphery of the Empire. Here, very much concerned with *Sitten und Gebräuche*, he is less concerned with particular funerary monuments and objects than with their general distribution. He suggests that if we look at Romano-British elite burials as a whole, we see that these turn to life – in this case, to the life of cities and some small towns, or to the highways that led to these. In other words, even at a distance, Romano-British elite burials respected urban settlements, looking towards them and designed to be seen and noted by those in or travelling between them. These burials should, therefore, not be regarded as 'rural', deliberately secluded on great estates that were the economic and social focus of the families that erected them, but "peri-urban", reflecting elite regard for city life.

An intriguing coda to the Roman experience is provided by **Russell**, in her study of the building activities of Pope Innocent X (1644-55), specifically his commissioning of the memorial church of Sant'Agnese in the Piazza Navona in Rome. In this, he went significantly beyond the usual classicising of the rich and fashionable seventeenth-century Italian nobility. The design of the structure, with its "central plan", shows him and his architects consciously copying Roman imperial and private tombs of the city and its region in order to project himself, his family (the Pamphilj) and the papacy as the true heirs of ancient Rome. His models were still impressive long after the original non-monumental *Sitten und Gebräuche* and so any personal commemoration of the deceased had ended – indeed, in most cases, long after their remains had vanished from their tombs. As with the pyramids of Egypt, it is ultimately brick and stone, not sentiment, that stand the test of time.

I would finish, however, by returning to the Greek world. Simonides' terse epitaph on the mass-grave of the Spartans who fell fighting the Persians at Thermopylae in 480 BC – 'the 300' – is justly famous:

> Go tell the Spartans, you who read,
> We took their orders, and are dead.

Low, however, asks after commemoration of the conflict and its dead in Sparta itself. The evidence is, as always, difficult, but she proposes that we can detect determined local efforts to keep memory alive based on regular festivals and on a range of monuments located through the city. She makes the point that, with the bodies of the slain far distant, state sentiments became more powerful than family grief. Mourning, in fact, yielded to celebration as the dead became "abstract entities, exemplars of Spartan heroism and glory". The power of this message was only intensified by the repatriation of the remains of Leonidas, killed at Thermopylae, and Pausanias, victor over the Persians at Plataea in 479 BC Writing this preface around November 11, Armistice Day, an occasion as usual made much of by all the media, I was moved by the realisation that in this respect nothing has changed. Ancient and modern treatments of 'our glorious dead' are virtually identical, as sophisticated record-keeping, and so the precise naming of the fallen, allows the power of personal sorrow to be tapped for state purposes. Anthony Peregrine remarks of the great monuments of the Somme battlefield:

> However, once I had stopped being moved, I had the fleeting notion, here as elsewhere, that bravery and suffering were being co-opted into national causes which – it might be argued – provoked the entire problem in the first place. All the vast complexity of four years of war, millions of men and numberless strategies seemed reduced to fine, nation-serving stones and sentiments … .
>
> *Daily Telegraph*, 8/11/08, T9

1

The power of the dead in classical Sparta: The case of Thermopylae[1]

Polly Low

The battle of Thermopylae, in 480 BC, was an atypical event in Spartan history – a conflict fought far beyond Sparta's normal sphere of influence or interest, at unusually uneven odds, and with an uncharacteristically (if not uniquely) lethal outcome: the remnants of a small Greek force consisting most famously (though not exclusively) of 300 Spartan citizens fought to the death in an attempt to thwart, or at least delay, the southward progress of a massive invading Persian army (Fig. 1.1). The afterlife of the battle is no less striking: the modern obsession with the event stretches back at least as far as the mid-eighteenth century (Macgregor Morris 2000), and its portrayal as a 'battle that changed the world' is still a prominent theme in contemporary scholarship (Cartledge 2006). As this chapter will attempt to show, this fascination is not purely a modern phenomenon. The battle of Thermopylae and the dead of Thermopylae occupy an unusually prominent position in the Spartan commemorative landscape throughout the classical period (480–323 BC), and beyond. Exploring the origins, changing shape, and wider implications of that prominent position is one of the chief concerns of this chapter.

But there is always a danger of making an unusual phenomenon into a unique and isolated one, and another, equally important, aim of this chapter is to show how the commemoration of the battle and its dead fits into the larger picture of Spartan funerary and commemorative practice. When seen as a whole, the commemoration of Thermopylae is certainly out of the ordinary in both form and scale, but its constituent elements are not entirely revolutionary. By placing this particular set of commemorative actions in their wider context, it is possible to say more (or at least to ask more questions) both about the reaction to Thermopylae, and about Spartan attitudes to burial, commemoration and monumentality at a more general level.

An important disclaimer must be made before proceeding any further. The evidence for classical Spartan commemorative practice, in general, and the commemoration of Thermopylae, in particular, is elusive in the extreme. A good deal of what follows is therefore devoted to the rather mundane task of attempting to unravel the matted clump of material which relates to the nature and location of some of the Spartan monuments and commemorative events associated with the battle and its dead. Even so, much

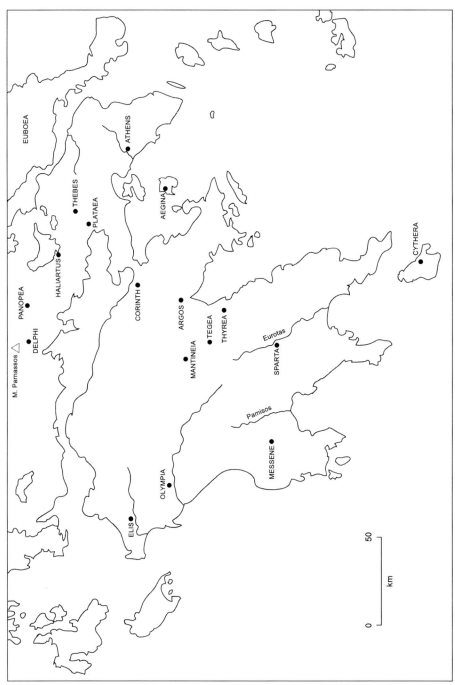

Figure 1.1 Map of central Greece and the Peloponnese with sites mentioned in the text. Thermopylae is located c. 30 km north of Delphi (map, Author).

remains extremely unclear, and a good deal of what is said here should be counted as extremely speculative. I would argue, however, that such speculation is nevertheless worthwhile, not least because it forces the questioning of a tendency, which stretches back at least as far as the late fifth-century BC (Thucydides 1.10), to claim that the Spartans had no interest in constructing the sort of ideologically or emotionally charged monumental landscapes that were characteristic of other Greek *poleis*.

Thermopylae and its dead

Only one thing is known for certain about the immediate fate of the Spartans who died at Thermopylae: 'they were buried on the spot where they fell, and a memorial was set up there to them' (Herodotus 7.228). This memorial included the epigram, attributed to the contemporary poet Simonides, which famously summed up the paradigmatically Spartan qualities of single-minded duty and patriotism up to and beyond the point of death in the service of the city: 'Foreigner, go tell the Spartans that we lie here obedient to their commands.'

Even this description is not entirely unproblematic. There is, for example, no obvious answer to the question of how exactly the burial was arranged. There were no Spartans left to look after their own dead, and the victorious Persians, far from being interested in following the usual Greek custom of allowing burial to a defeated enemy, went so far (according to Herodotus 7.238) as to mutilate the corpse of the Spartan king Leonidas. But even if the passage of the Spartan dead from battlefield to grave was probably a slower and more complicated process than Herodotus' brief notice suggests (Wade-Gery (1933, 72) argues for a gap of at least eighteen months between battle and burial) there is no reason to doubt the basic veracity of the story. Burial and commemoration at or near the site of the battle was standard Spartan practice (Pritchett 1985, 243–6) and Herodotus' description of the memorial is consistent with (though not identical to) the version later provided by Strabo (9.4.16; see Clairmont 1983, 223).

Up to this point, the treatment accorded to the dead of Thermopylae does not differ significantly from that which would be expected for the dead of any Greek battle, and their commemoration is comparable to that which the Spartans are known to have provided for their own dead elsewhere – the best-preserved example being the monumental grave constructed in the Athenian Kerameikos for those Spartans killed in the fighting in Athens in 404/3 BC (Fig. 1.2; Willemsen 1977).

The first hint at the existence of a more elaborate or sustained approach to the commemoration of the battle comes in Herodotus' (7.224.1) claim to have found out the names of all the Spartans killed at Thermopylae:

> Leonidas, proving himself extremely valiant, fell in that struggle and with him other famous Spartans, whose names I have found out, since they were worthy men. Indeed, I have discovered the names of all three hundred.

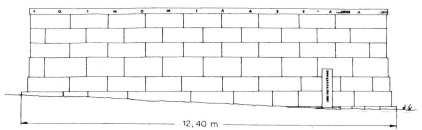

Figure 1.2 The tomb of the Lacedaemonians in Athens, 403 BC (after Knigge 1991, 161, fig. 156, drawing A. Kunanek).

Herodotus does not say how he came to discover this information, but, if it is safe to assume this claim to knowledge is not a bluff, then there seem to be two main possibilities: either he saw the names written on a commemorative stele (whether at Thermopylae or, perhaps more plausibly, at Sparta; see below pp. 5–6), or the list of names had become part of the oral tradition of the Spartans. These two options are not mutually exclusive: it is possible to hypothesise for Sparta (as for Athens (Ebbott 2000, 93–94)) a scenario in which oral performance of inscribed names formed a key part of a the preservation and cultivation of collective memory. The fact that Herodotus was able to discover these names might, therefore, point towards the existence of some sort of deliberate commemorative effort, focussed on the preservation of the memory of all those (not just the *axioi*, the 'worthy' or famous) who fought and died in 480 BC (Ball 1976).

Stronger evidence for the existence of a commemorative festival for the dead of Thermopylae comes in a fragment of Simonides (*fr.* 531) reported by Diodorus (11.11.6):

> Of those who perished at Thermopylae
> All glorious is the fortune, fair the doom;
> Their grave's an altar, ceaseless memory's theirs
> Instead of lamentation, and their fate
> Is chant of praise. Such winding-sheet as this
> Nor mould nor all-consuming time shall waste.
> This sepulchre of valiant men has taken
> The fair renown of Hellas for its inmate.
> And witness is Leonidas, once king
> Of Sparta, who hath left behind a crown
> Of valour mighty and undying fame.

Much is unclear about the form and purpose of this poem. The scale of the original work is unknown; it is possible that this passage formed only a part of a (perhaps much) longer piece (Flower 1998, 369). More importantly for the purpose of this discussion, there is considerable uncertainty as to the context which should be reconstructed for the poem's performance. It is not impossible that the work was intended for private, relatively informal performance, perhaps in the context of a symposium or (in Sparta) *syssition* (Podlecki 1968, 258–262). It seems more likely, however, that the poem was delivered (at least initially) in a more formal, civic context; the reference to 'this sepulchre' (*sekos*) implies that the poem was intended to be delivered at or near some form of shrine commemorating the dead of the battle (Flower 1998, 369; Molyneux 1992, 186). If this reading is correct, an obvious question follows: where was that shrine (and the commemorative festivals associated with it) located?

The possibility that some sort commemorative activity was focussed on the site of the battle (and burial) cannot be ruled out. But if such commemorations did take place, then it is striking that they – unlike, for example, the commemorations centred on the other major land-battle of the Persian Wars, the Battle of Plataea (Jung 2006, 225–297) – have left almost no trace in either the archaeological or literary record. Later sources suggest that Thermopylae retained its importance for the Locrians (Strabo 9.4.2), and perhaps also the Thespians (Stephanus of Byzantium, *s.v. Thespeia*), but later Spartan commemorative activity at the site is invisible, an absence which is all the more notable given Sparta's interests in the region in later years (most apparent in her efforts in the 420s BC to establish a colony at Heraclea Trachinia; see Thucydides 3.92–3). Simonides' poem seems to fit that general pattern of Spartan disengagement from the physical site of the battle. The fact that the location of the battle needs to be specified by name implies that the poem is being delivered somewhere else, perhaps at a panhellenic sanctuary or at Sparta itself (Bowra 1933, 279). Indeed, as Steiner (1999) persuasively argues, the poem as a whole can be seen as a representation or exploration of the consequences of commemorating the dead in a location that is distant from their physical remains. The tomb itself is replaced by the altar and, by extension, the commemorative festival which is centred on it. Physical markers of grieving and bereavement – the winding-sheet, the ritual lament – are overshadowed by rituals of praise and glory, and mourning for the dead is supplanted by praise and exhortation, 'transmuting grief into celebration' (Steiner 1999, 392).

This theme of the separation of commemoration from the physical remains of the dead can be pursued, and tied more closely to commemoration within Sparta itself, by turning to a much later piece of evidence: a brief comment made by the geographer Pausanias (3.14.1, late second century AD) in the course of his description of the monuments of central Sparta:

> Opposite the theatre are two tombs; the first is that of Pausanias, the general at Plataea, the second is that of Leonidas. Every year they deliver speeches over them, and hold a contest in which none may compete except Spartans. The bones of Leonidas were taken by Pausanias from Thermopylae forty years after the battle. There is set up a slab with the names, and their fathers' names, of those who endured the fight at Thermopylae against the Persians.

Pausanias' comments must, for obvious reasons, be treated with caution as evidence for the form (or even existence) of these monuments in the classical period (and there are, as will be discussed below, p. 8, specific problems with his account of the return of Leonidas' remains). Nevertheless, his reference to the existence of a *stele* listing the names of the Three Hundred does deserve some attention.

It is tempting to assume that the list of names Pausanias reports seeing must be a fifth-century BC monument (perhaps even the source of Herodotus' information; see above p. 3). However it is equally, perhaps more, likely that this *stele* was a later construction: the Roman-era fascination with the Persian Wars in general is well documented (Alcock 2002, 74–86), while a specific interest in lists of the dead is also now becoming apparent (a *stele* apparently listing the names of the Athenian dead of Marathon has recently been found at the villa of Herodes Atticus in Arcadia, although full details of the inscription (*SEG* 41.425) have not yet been published). But even if the list seen by Pausanias were not original, the fact that such a list existed (or could be created) so long after the battle must be significant, and gives further, albeit still circumstantial, support to the theory (outlined above) that deliberate effort was invested in remembering the names of the dead of Thermopylae.

More significantly, the existence of such a list supports the view that the commemoration of the battle allowed space for the remembering both of the collective – the 'Three Hundred' as a distinct and special group – and of the individuals who made up that collective. And – in a Spartan context – it is precisely this combination of collective and individualising commemoration which marks the treatment of the dead of Thermopylae as something unusual. Commemoration, in Sparta, of individual Spartan war dead is well attested: both literary (Plutarch, *Lycurgus* 27.1–2, *Moralia* 238d) and epigraphic evidence reveals that those who died in war were allowed an inscribed memorial in Sparta. But these monuments were irregular, scattered and probably associated with private or family commemoration. Where the Spartans are seen providing civic, collective commemoration to their war-dead, the memorials seem to focus, precisely, on the collective: the dead of the 'Battle of the Champions', for example, were reportedly commemorated with hymns sung at the annual Spartan 'festival of the naked youths' or Gymnopaedia (the testimonia, all late, are collected by Pettersson 1992, 43), but these dead are an anonymous mass – any scope for commemorating an individual has been effaced. Although, therefore, the scope for individualisation allowed by a simple list of names might seem limited, it was significantly greater than that which was typically available to the Spartan war dead.

In an important respect, however, the dead of Thermopylae remain just as marginal to Spartan life as the dead of any other battle; it is only their names, not their bodies, which find a place in the Spartan commemorative landscape. It is important not to underestimate the potential importance of that fact: the remains of the dead could have a significant role in the public life of the city (as will be discussed in the next section), but also have an important part to play in private mourning and commemorative rituals. The point might seem obvious, but is, I think worth making, because there is sometimes a tendency to attribute to the Spartans an almost emotionless attitude to

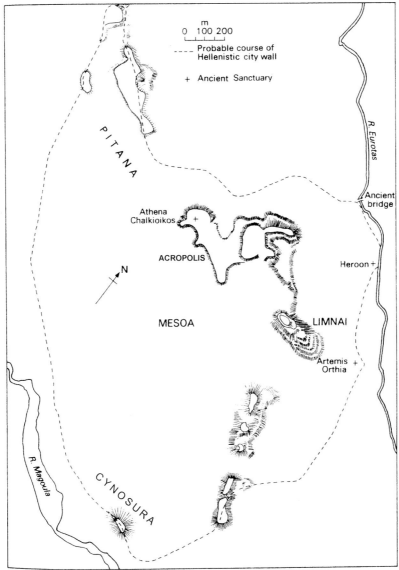

Figure 1.3 Sparta and its villages (after Cartledge, 2002, fig. 12).

the disposal of their dead (Parker 1989, 150). As Hodkinson (2000, 254) points out, such assumptions cannot be secure; the 'Lycurgan' restrictions on burial rites and grave markers reported by Plutarch (*Lycurgus* 27.1–2, *Moralia* 238d) are, precisely, restrictions not outright bans, and it is probable that there did exist in Sparta identifiable family burial grounds – probably located around the edges of the constituent villages of Sparta (see Fig. 1.3; Kourinou 2000, 215–219) – which could have acted as a focus for private mourning and commemoration. The body itself is likely to have been central to such mourning (Chaniotis 2006, 219–226), and its absence cannot be dismissed as a trivial matter. The absence of the physical remains of the dead of Thermopylae must have influenced the way in which they were commemorated in Sparta, and – though firm proof of the form that influence took is lacking – it does seem plausible that it will have contributed to the process of abstraction already identified in the Simonidean poem. Without a focus for individual mourning and grief, it becomes, perhaps, easier to treat the dead as more abstract entities, exemplars of Spartan heroism and glory.

Contextualising Thermopylae: Leonidas, Pausanias and the monuments to the Persian Wars

But there is, of course, one exception to that pattern of symbolic presence but physical absence: namely, the Spartan King Leonidas, whose remains were, if Pausanias' story is correct, singled out for special treatment and brought back to Sparta (above p. 6). As was noted above, Pausanias' version of events is not unproblematic. Something has gone wrong either with his chronology or his prosopography: there is no Spartan Pausanias who could plausibly have taken responsibility for the transfer of the bones in the middle of the fifth century BC, so it is necessary to correct either the time of the transfer (Corbett (1949) suggests a date at the turn of the fifth/fourth centuries BC) or the name of the person responsible (Connor 1979). In spite of these uncertainties, Pausanias' basic claim is inherently credible. Leonidas had been an exceptional case from the start: his body was singled out for special (mal)treatment by the Persians, and his glory was isolated for particular praise by Simonides. That a Spartan king's physical remains should be dealt with differently from those of an ordinary Spartan is also unsurprising; Herodotus (6.58) gives a detailed description of the peculiar concern taken by the Spartans to bury their kings with appropriate honours, and notes too the extraordinary honours given to those kings who died in war (Cartledge 1987, 331–343; the possible connection between Herodotus' account and the funeral of Leonidas is discussed by Schaefer 1957).

   It is, however, worth exploring the motivation for and consequences of the reburial in more detail. On the one hand, the chronological difficulties in Pausanias' account make it difficult to pinpoint the specific motivation for the repatriation of the bones. On the other hand, one of the reasons why the chronological question is so hard to resolve is that there is no shortage of moments in Spartan history when either the city as a whole, or a member of the Agiad royal house in particular, might have been keen to undertake such a task. The recovery of the bones could provide an ideal way either to boost a reputation, or to distract attention from a looming scandal (or both). The process of retrieval could be portrayed as providing recompense for the indignities inflicted by the Persians by bringing the bones safely into Spartan guardianship, and perhaps also as bringing Sparta itself under the protection of these special remains. The most obvious parallel for this sort of delayed repatriation is found in the stories of the return of the relics of exiled or reclaimed heroes, whether Orestes at Sparta (Herodotus 1.67–8) or, a closer parallel in date, Theseus at Athens (Plutarch, *Cimon* 8, *Theseus* 36).

The choice of site for Leonidas' body in central Sparta also suggests that more was at stake in the process of return than a simple wish to provide a standard royal burial. The usual burial site for Spartan kings of the Agiad house was in Pitana, on the north-western side of the city (Fig. 1.3; Pausanias 3.12.8). The selection of this different location for Leonidas' reburial must then be seen as a marked choice; if the particular importance attached to this body were not already suggested by the decision to find and repatriate it long after the battle, then its placement in the heart of Sparta surely makes the point unmissable.

But, as Pausanias' description also reveals, Leonidas' body was not the only one placed in this location. Another royal burial with Persian War connections could be found in the same place, namely that of Pausanias the Regent – hero of the great victory over Persia at the Battle of Plataea (479 BC), but villain of various tales of bribery and treachery in the years after that battle. This burial is also reported in another (and, reassuringly, more contemporary) source, namely Thucydides (1.134.4):

> The Spartans intended to throw Pausanias into the Kaiadas (where they throw criminals), but finally decided to bury him somewhere nearby. But, some time later, the god at Delphi ordered the Spartans to move Pausanias' tomb to the place where he had died – inscribed monuments show that he now lies in the *protemenisma* – and, because what had been done was a curse to them, to give back two bodies instead of one to the goddess of the Brazen House [Chalkioikos]. So they had two bronze statues made and dedicated them as a substitute for Pausanias.

The term Thucydides uses to locate the burial of Pausanias – *protemenisma* – is unusual, and its meaning is not entirely transparent. The *temenos* of Athena Chalkioikos probably covered most of the summit of the acropolis (Dickins 1906, 142), which makes the interpretation suggested by Förtsch (2001, 57, *n.* 493) seem most plausible: the burials, he proposes, were located on the south-eastern side of the acropolis, at the start of the approach to the Chalkioikos precinct (see Fig. 1.4). Even given the Spartans' attested fondness for relocating human remains, it seems unlikely that they would have moved Pausanias' body again once it had reached the location specifically insisted on by the Delphic Oracle. If that is the case, then it should follow that the grave seen by Pausanias, the geographer, and located alongside the burial of Leonidas, is the same as that described by Thucydides. (A location east of the theatre would also be consistent with Pausanias' route; when he sees the commemorative complex he is walking west from the agora towards the theatre, a route which would take him along the southern side of the acropolis.)

It cannot, surely, be a coincidence that these two heroes (or potential heroes) of the Agiad royal house end up in such close proximity. The suspicion that the relocation of

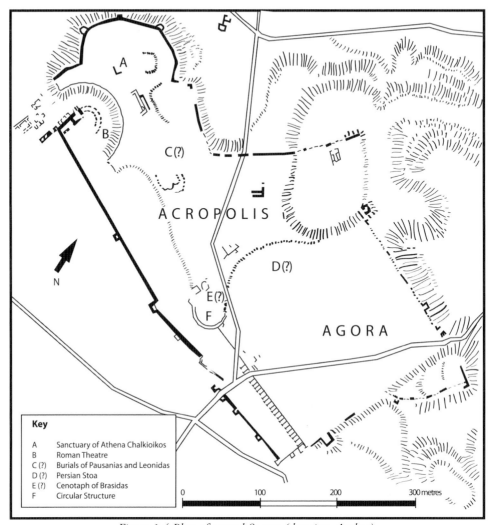

Figure 1.4 Plan of central Sparta (drawing, Author).

these two bodies is connected in some way is heightened by the fact that their arrival in this part of the city seems likely to have taken place within a relatively short period. Pausanias died some time between 470 and 465 BC (White 1964); Thucydides' account implies that there was a gap between his death and the arrival of his body at its final location, but also strongly suggests that it had reached that location by the start of the Peloponnesian War (431 BC). The precise date of Leonidas' repatriation is, as was noted above (p. 8), uncertain, although Connor's (1979) arguments in favour of a date of 440 BC are persuasive. But although it is impossible to say for certain which of the two bodies arrived first, it does seem reasonable to argue that the presence of one would act as a magnet for the other, and that the reputation of both Pausanias and the Agiad royal house stood to benefit from the creation of this shared commemorative site. The juxtaposition of these two royal burials plays on, and builds upon, a connection also gestured towards in the Herodotean picture of the Spartan (or Pausanian) reaction to the victory at Plataea. Pausanias is depicted as reprimanding a misguided Aeginetan (who is keen to encourage him to mutilate the corpse of the Persian Mardonius, as the Persians had mutilated Leonidas):

> 'I say that Leonidas, whom you are telling me to avenge, has been well avenged: he and all the dead at Thermopylae have been repaid in full with the lives of the countless men lying dead here' (Herodotus 9.79).

In this passage, we see an attempt to create an intrinsic link between the battles of Thermopylae and Plataea; losses suffered in the former encounter are avenged in the latter. The burials of Leonidas and Pausanias could surely be seen as a further manifestation of this claim: they represent in physical form the close and necessary connection between the self-sacrificing heroism of Thermopylae and its ultimate vindication, under Pausanias' leadership, at Plataea (Förtsch 2001, 55–60). Pausanias thus receives here a sort of post-mortem endorsement from his less compromised uncle. This mid-fifth-century BC reshaping of the commemoration of Thermopylae therefore has the important consequence not just of giving a much more prominent role to the physical of remains of the battle's general, but also of creating a much closer connection between the commemoration of Thermopylae and that of the Persian Wars more generally.

This wider contextualisation is visible, too, in the other commemorative monuments located in this central area of the city. Of these monuments, the most well-known, but also probably also most short-lived, is the so-called 'Leonidas' sculpture (Fig. 1.5), a larger than life-size marble statue of a helmeted and shield-bearing warrior, discovered, probably quite close to its original location, on the acropolis of Sparta, to the south-west of the sanctuary of Athena Chalkioikos (Woodward 1923–25, 253–266). The excavator's largely physiognomic arguments for identifying this statue as the hero of Thermopylae are too speculative to be safe (Woodward 1923–25, 260), but the general dating (on stylistic grounds) of this sculpture to the second quarter of the fifth century BC does seem more secure (and has more recently been supported by Palagia 1993, 169). If this dating is correct, then it is very hard to resist the conclusion that the erection on the Spartan acropolis, some time around the 470s BC, of a monumental statue of a military figure is very likely to have something to do with the commemoration of the Persian Wars.

This monument was no longer standing by the time Pausanias visited the city (its fragments of were found beneath building waste associated with the construction of the Roman theatre (Woodward 1923–25, 250, 258)), and may even have been destroyed very shortly after its construction (Palagia (1993, 268) suggests that it might have been destroyed in the earthquake of 464 BC). But another monument to the Persian Wars had greater longevity: that is, the 'Persian Stoa', praised by Pausanias (3.11.3) as 'the

Figure 1.5 So-called 'Leonidas' sculpture, Sparta, c. 475 BC (courtesy of the British School at Athens).

most striking feature in the agora.' The archaeological traces of this structure remain elusive, but it has recently been argued that they should be identified with the remains found on the north-west side of the agora (Kourinou 2000, 111–114; Waywell 1999, 14). If that identification is correct, then the building would have sat alongside the principal (perhaps only) route between agora and acropolis, and in close proximity to the site in which Pausanias and Leonidas were buried.

Another later commentator on Spartan monuments, Vitruvius (writing in the first century BC), places great emphasis on the hortatory force of the Persian Stoa. This is a monument which would encourage Spartans to risk anything for the sake of their city:

> Not less the Spartans under the command of Pausanias, son of Agesilas, having conquered with a small force an infinitely large army of Persians, gloriously celebrated a triumph with spoils and plunder, and, from the booty, built the Persian Colonnade to signify the merit and courage of the citizens and to be a trophy of victory to their descendants. There they placed statues of their captives in barbaric dress – punishing their pride with deserved insults – to support the roof, that their enemies might quake, fearing the workings of such bravery, and their fellow-citizens looking upon a pattern of manhood might by such glory be roused and prepared for the defence of freedom (Vitruvius, *De Architectura* 1.1.6).

Many of the decorations described here are very probably later elaborations (Pausanias 3.11.3), but Vitruvius' interpretation of the function of the building as a whole need not be anachronistic. (Compare, for example, Aeschines' (3.186–187) use of decorations in the Stoa Poikile in the Athenian agora as a source of paradigms for ideal Athenian behaviour.) But the reminder of the glories of Spartan history provided by the Persian Stoa becomes more complex, and more interesting, when considered alongside that of the monuments located further up the acropolis hill. If the Persian Stoa exemplified, in the most literal way possible, what Sparta had gained from the encounter, then the Persian War monuments in front of the Athena Chalkioikos sanctuary represented what Sparta had lost in that conflict – the life of one king, the reputation of another, hundreds of Spartan citizens.

The Persian Wars in Context

How, though, does this small section of commemorative space fit into the wider area in which it is located, and how do the Persian War monuments relate to other commemorative structures and activities in this part of the city? The monuments discussed so far are located in two key civic and religious spaces of the city – the agora and acropolis – and it is possible to see how they might have both contributed to, and drawn further resonances from, both of those environments.

The monuments on the approach to the acropolis are (as far as the extant evidence shows) somewhat unusual in form; this was not an area otherwise associated with military (or other) burials or cenotaphs. (The cenotaph of the fifth-century BC commander Brasidas was located in the same overall area, but rather further west on the road leading west from the agora to the theatre (Pausanias 3.14.1).) But they are not, I would suggest, radically different in their wider connotations, or possible intentions, from the other monuments located in this part of the city. The acropolis is to some extent a site of military commemoration: this role is visible (for a short time, at least)

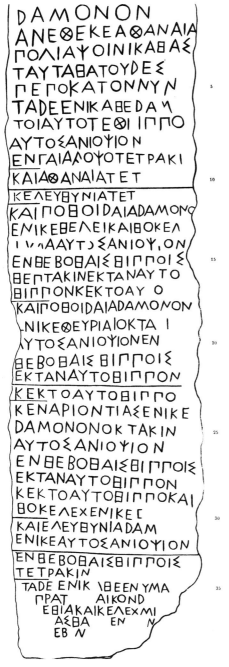

ΔΑΜΟΝΟΝ
ΑΝΕⓍΕΚΕΑⓍΑΝΑΙΑ
ΓΟΛΙΑΥΟΙΝΙΚΑΘΑΣ
ΤΑΥΤΑΒΑΤΟΥΔΕΣ
ΓΕΓΟΚΑΤΟΝΝΥΝ   5
ΤΑΔΕΕΝΙΚΑΘΕΔΑΜ
ΤΟΙΑΥΤΟΤΕⓍΙΙΓΓΟ
ΑΥΤΟΣΑΝΙΟΥΙΟΝ
ΕΝΓΑΙΑΛΟΥΟΤΕΤΡΑΚΙ
ΚΑΙΑⓍΑΝΑΙΑΤΕΤ   10
ΚΕΛΕΥΘΥΝΙΑΤΕΤ
ΚΑΙΓΟΘΟΙΔΑΙΑΔΑΜΟΝΟ
ΕΝΙΚΕΘΕΛΕΙΚΑΙΘΟΚΕΛ
ΙΝΛΑΑΥΤΣΣΑΝΙΟΥΙΟΝ
ΕΝΘΕΒΟΘΑΙΣΘΙΓΓΟΙΣ   15
ΘΕΓΤΑΚΙΝΕΚΤΑΝΑΥΤΟ
ΘΙΓΓΟΝΚΕΚΤΟΑΥ Ο
ΚΑΙΓΟΘΟΙΔΑΙΑΔΑΜΟΝΟΝ
ΝΙΚΕⓍΕΥΡΙΑΙΟΚΤΑ Ι
ΥΤΟΣΑΝΙΟΥΙΟΝΕΝ   20
ΘΕΒΟΘΑΙΣ ΘΙΓΓΟΙΣ
ΕΚΤΑΝΑΥΤΟΘΙΓΓΟΝ
ΚΕΚΤΟΑΥΤΟΘΙΓΓΟ
ΚΕΝΑΡΙΟΝΤΙΑΣΕΝΙΚΕ
ΔΑΜΟΝΟΝΟΚΤΑΚΙΝ   25
ΑΥΤΟΣΑΝΙΟΥΙΟΝ
ΕΝΘΕΒΟΘΑΙΣΘΙΓΓΟΙΣ
ΕΚΤΑΝΑΥΤΟΘΙΓΓΟΝ
ΚΕΚΤΟΑΥΤΟΘΙΓΓΟΚΑΙ
ΘΟΚΕΛΕΧΕΝΙΚΕΣ   30
ΚΑΙΕΛΕΥΘΥΝΙΑΔΑΜ
ΕΝΙΚΕΑΥΤΟΣΑΝΙΟΥΙΟΝ
ΕΝΘΕΒΟΘΑΙΣΘΙΓΓΟΙΣ
ΤΕΤΡΑΚΙΝ
ΤΑΔΕ ΕΝΙΚ ΙΘΕΕΝ ΥΜΑ   35
ΓΡΑΤ   ΑΙΚΟΝΔ
ΕΘΙΑΚΑΙΚΕΛΕΧΜΙ
ΑΣΘΑ   ΕΝ   Ν
ΕΒ Ν

Figure 1.6 The stele of Damonon (IG V.1 214). Detail of the inscribed part of the monument (Roehl, 1882, 31, no. 79).

in the warrior statue discussed above (pp. 11–12), and also in the dedications set up by the triumphant Lysander after the Peloponnesian War (two *Nikai*, according to Pausanias 3.17.4). Sparta's wider role, and powerful position, in the broader Greek world was also commemorated here: at least two major interstate documents were set up here in the fifth or early fourth centuries BC (the treaty which admits the Aetolians into the Peloponnesian League (Peek 1974), and a more fragmentary text (*IG* V.1 219) which seems to record donations, by an unknown party, to the Spartan state).

The material which dominates this area, however (and starts to do so even before the Persian Wars) celebrates a different sort of achievement. The epigraphic landscape of the acropolis is characterised above all by dedicatory inscriptions commemorating athletic victories, several of which are impressive both in the accomplishments they list and in the scale of monument they provoke. The *stele* of Damonon (Fig. 1.6; *IG* V.1 213), a mid-fifth or early-fourth-century BC inscription, topped with a relief depicting chariot racing and containing an extensive list of victories achieved, is the best-known example of this genre, and is somewhat unusual in both its scale and its decoration, but is not unique. Earlier examples include both individual victory dedications (such as the dedication of Eteoi(tas) (*SEG* 11.653) dated to the early fifth century BC) and longer – and probably publicly-erected – lists of victors (for example, the late sixth-century BC *SEG* 11.638, identified as a victor-list by Jeffery 1990, 194; further examples are discussed by Hodkinson 1999, 154–155). These monuments are a peculiarly Spartan phenomenon, and one which, it has been pointed out, fits well with what is known of the Spartan enthusiasm for the cultivation and celebration of agonistic activity (Hodkinson 1999; Whitley 1997, 647). The juxtaposition of these commemorations of agonistic culture with the military monuments of the acropolis makes particularly good sense in a Spartan context, in a city where the connection between athletic prowess and military strength seems often to have been emphasised, whether, for example, in the activities at festivals such as the Gymnopaedia (Pettersson 1992, 50), or in the custom of placing Olympic victors in a prestigious (and dangerous) point in the battle line (Plutarch, *Lycurgus* 22.4).

The Persian War burials and monuments would not, then, be entirely out of place in this part of the city, although this context would perhaps encourage a particular interpretation of their significance. Many of the monuments in this area are linked by a general concern to record, and celebrate, Spartan *andreia* or manliness. But there is some variety in the purposes for which that virtue is being commemorated: the inscribed records of individual athletic success place rather less emphasis on the importance of channelling that *andreia* in the service of the city, and for the benefit of the city's standing in the wider world, and give rather more weight to enhancing the standing of individual citizens (and their families) within Spartan society. Could the location of the Persian War burials, close to these other records of individual Spartan prowess, therefore have encouraged a reading of the monuments which promoted a focus on the commemoration of individual glory, rather than on the message of collective and self-denying sacrifice which is such a dominant theme in other representations of Spartan attitudes to warfare in general, and of Thermopylae in particular?

If such a reading were possible, however, it would clearly not be the only one available. The burials by the acropolis cannot be considered in isolation from the Persian War commemoration in the agora – or from the other monuments in that part of the city. Indeed, the different Persian War memorials might even have served to create a stronger link between those two spaces. Sparta's acropolis was always less spatially divorced from the rest of the city than that of other *poleis*, for the simple reason that it was not dramatically higher than its surroundings (a point noted, with disapproval, by Pausanias 3.17.1), but the placement of the Persian Stoa could be seen as a deliberate attempt to exploit and enhance the connection between these two spaces; the building, located alongside the route between agora and acropolis, could function as a sort of bridge between these places and the monuments they contained.

Someone moving from the burials of Leonidas and Pausanias, via the Persian Stoa, to the agora, could find in that key civic and religious space various suggestive echoes of the monuments of the Persian Wars. Above all, heroic burial is a recurring theme. According to Pausanias' (3.11.10–11) account, *heroa* and significant burials formed a conspicuous element of monumental landscape throughout the city (3.11.10), and burials in the agora included those of Orestes, the local hero Aphareus, and the Cretan prophet Epimenides (3.11.11). It is worth noting that all of these tombs could carry associations of political – and particularly interstate – contest, or even outright conflict. Epimenides' remains were also claimed by Sparta's local rival Argos (Pausanias 2.21.3), while Aphareus was in origin a Messenian hero, whose presence in Sparta cannot be separated from Sparta's more general annexation of, and assertion of power over, the Messenians. But it is in the tomb of Orestes that the strongest analogies with the Persian War burials might be seen. The way in which the recovery and repatriation of Leonidas' bones echoes the earlier treatment of Orestes' remains has already been pointed out, but there are further parallels in the part each hero plays in the history of Spartan military achievement. At least by the time of Herodotus, the story of the retrieval of Orestes' remains was closely associated with a narrative in which initial defeat turned to ultimate success; a story of Spartan military recovery, and of the expansion of Spartan hegemony through the Peloponnese (Herodotus 1.68).

By the Roman period, this area's focus on the heroised dead of past conflicts finds a clear analogue in the use of the space for activities aimed specifically at inculcating martial skills and values in the next generation of Spartans. The agora becomes a hub of ephebic activity in general (Marchetti 1996), and is also used as the site for the celebration of key elements of the festival of the Gymnopaedia, whose focal point, the choros or dancing ground, is often identified with the circular structure in the north-east corner of the agora (Kourinou 2000, 121–127). This festival had both prospective and retrospective military aspects: it included songs in praise of those killed in another costly (if glorious) engagement, the struggle for conquest of Thyrea (territory to the north-east of Laconia); and the festival also (according to Plato, *Laws* 1.633c) included 'tests of endurance' which were, allegedly, part of Lycurgus' grand design to enhance Spartan military preparedness (Pettersson 1992, 42–56). This area of the city therefore developed a strong association with both monuments and events focussed not just on remembering past political, and particularly military, successes, but also on actively instilling in future generations the civic and military virtues by which those victories were thought to have been achieved. The monuments to the Persian Wars would have formed a natural – even intrinsic – part of that landscape.

The date at which this intersection between burials, monuments and rituals became fully developed is disputed, but it does seem most likely that the Gymnopaedia's move to the agora took place only in the Hellenistic period (323–31 BC) or later (Kennell 1995, 67–69; *cf.* Ducat 2006, 266). But even if the specific trigger of the commemorative festival were absent in the classical period, it is, I think, still plausible that the connections and connotations of the monuments themselves did have some sort of impact even from an earlier date. That is, the political and civic business of the classical agora (rarely seen in our sources, but surely existent; see, for example, Xenophon, *Hellenica* 3.3.5; Kennell 1987) took place in an environment surrounded by memorials to and relics of Sparta's heroic dead – monuments which recorded, celebrated and encouraged emulation of actions which had enhanced the power and security of the Spartan *polis*.

Conclusion

The monuments to Thermopylae at Sparta have the potential to perform a number of roles. They commemorate and celebrate the achievement of individuals and, by extension, validate the importance of those individuals, and their descendents, to the life of the city. They show how the glory of the individual might bring benefit to the city as a whole, by fighting in defence of Sparta, or – in certain special cases – by elevation after death to the ranks of heroised protector of the city. They also combine with other sites of memory to evoke images of Sparta's role as a military and political force in the Peloponnese, and in Greece as a whole. What is, however, very hard to find evidence for – or perhaps even to envisage – is the use of these monuments as sites of mourning as well as sites of memory. It is of course true that evidence for mourning and lamentation – especially by private citizens – is even less likely to reach us than evidence of other Spartan activities, but I would nevertheless suggest that the gap here is perhaps likely to be a genuine one. From Simonides onwards, the idea that the dead of Thermopylae should be a focus for lament is progressively stripped away. The absence of the bodies of the majority of the dead and the depersonalising heroisation of the few which do return is both a further symptom of that Simonidean approach, and a contributory factor in its amplification.

Something further is missing from this picture, of course, and that is any positive proof that a classical Spartan would have responded to these monuments in the ways that I have suggested here, or made any of the connections whose possibility I have argued for. Literary evidence for this sort of monumental sensibility does not emerge until the Roman period, and we are lacking, too, the density of archaeological material which could point to the Persian War monuments having a positive impact on perceptions and uses of the spaces around them (as, for example, the Stoa of Zeus Eleutherios in Athens seems to have become a magnet for inscribed monuments marking other instances of Athenian commitment to the defence of liberty). I should, therefore, restate the disclaimer made at the start: much of what I have suggested here is only hypothesis. But I also repeat the claim of the importance of making such hypotheses: I am quite prepared to accept that it would be better to think about commemorative space in classical Sparta in different ways – to reconstruct different monuments, and to propose different interactions between them – but I do want to insist on the necessity of giving some thought to the question of how the space in which the Spartans spent their days might influence the way in which they perceived their roles in the city, and the role of their city in the wider Greek world.

Note
1   An earlier version of this chapter was delivered at the AIA/APA Annual Meeting in San Diego, 2007. I am grateful to Julia Shear for organising the panel at which the paper was presented, and to her, members of the panel and members of the audience for their helpful comments. I am indebted also to Felix Budelmann, who kindly shared with me his expertise on Simonides.

Bibliography

Abbreviations
IG   *Inscriptiones Graecae*
SEG   *Supplementum Epigraphicum Graecum*

Ancient Sources
Aeschines. *Orationes*. Ed. F. Blass; 2nd edn, corr., U. Schindel, 1976. Stuttgart, Teubner.
Diodorus Siculus. *The Library of History*, vol. 4 (Books ix – xii.40). Ed. and trans. C. H. Oldfather, 1946. Cambridge, Ma., Harvard University Press.
Herodotus. *Historiae*. Ed. K. Hude, 1926–27. Oxford, Clarendon Press.
Pausanias. *Description of Greece*, vol. 2 (Books iii – v). Ed. and trans. W. H. S. Jones and H. A. Ormerod, 1926. Cambridge, Ma., Harvard University Press.
Plato. *Opera,* vol.5 (*Minos, Leges, Epinomis, Epistulae, Definitiones, Spuria*). Ed. J. Burnet, 1907. Oxford, Clarendon Press.
Plutarch. *Lives*, vols 1 and 2. Ed and trans. B. Perrin, 1914. Cambridge, Ma., Harvard University Press.
Plutarch. *Moralia*, vol. 3. Ed. and trans. F. C. Babbit, 1931. Cambridge, Ma., Harvard University Press.
Simonides. *Greek Lyric*, vol. 3. Ed. and trans. D. A. Campbell, 1991. Cambridge, Ma., Harvard University Press.
Strabo. *Geography*, vol. 4 (Books viii – ix). Ed. and trans. H. L. Jones, 1927. Cambridge, Ma., Harvard University Press.
Stephanus of Byzantium. *Ethnicorum quae Supersunt*. Ed. A. Meineke, 1849. Berlin, G. Reimer.
Thucydides. *Historiae*. Ed. H. Stuart-Jones; emended edn rev., J. E. Powell, 1942. Oxford, Clarendon Press.
Vitruvius. *On Architecture*. Ed. and trans. F. Granger, 1931. Cambridge, Ma., Harvard University Press.
Xenophon. *Hellenica*. Ed. E. C. Marchant, 1901. Oxford, Clarendon Press.

Alcock, S. E. (2002) *Archaeologies of the Greek Past: Landscape, Monuments, and Memories.* Cambridge, Cambridge University Press.
Ball, R. (1976) Herodotos' list of the Spartans who died at Thermopylae. *Museum Africum* 5, 1–8.
Bowra, C. M. (1933) Simonides on the fallen of Thermopylae. *Classical Philology* 28, 277–281.
Cartledge, P. A. (1987) *Agesilaos and the Crisis of Sparta*. London, Duckworth.
Cartledge, P. A. (2002) *Sparta and Lakonia*. London, Routledge.
Cartledge, P. A. (2006) *Thermopylae: the Battle That Changed the World*. London, Macmillan.
Chaniotis, A. (2006) Rituals between norms and emotions: rituals as shared experience and memory. In E. Stavrianopoulou (ed.) *Ritual and Commnunication in the Greco-Roman World*, 211–238. Kernos Suppl. Liège, Centre international d'étude de la religion grecque antique.
Clairmont, C. W. (1983) *Patrios Nomos: Public Burial in Athens During the Fifth and Fourth Centuries B.C.: The Archaeological, Epigraphic-Literary, and Historical Evidence.* Oxford, British Archaeological Reports.
Connor, W. R. (1979) Pausanias 3.14.1: A sidelight on Spartan History, c. 440 B.C.? *Transactions of the American Philological Association* 109, 21–27.

Corbett, P. E. (1949) Λέων ἐπὶ Λεώνιδῃ. *Hesperia* 18, 104–107.

Dickins, G. (1906) The hieron of Athena Chalkioikos. *Annual of the British School at Athens* 13, 137–154.

Ducat, J. (2006) S*partan Education. Youth and Society in the Classical Period.* Swansea, Classical Press of Wales.

Ebbott, M. (2000) The list of the war dead in Aeschylus' "Persians". *Harvard Studies in Classical Philology* 100, 83–96.

Flower, M.A. (1998) Simonides, Ephorus, and Herodotus on the Battle of Thermopylae. *Classical Quarterly* 48, 365–379.

Förtsch, R. (2001) *Kunstverwendung und Kunstlegitimation im archaischen und frühklassischen Sparta.* Mainz am Rhein, Philipp von Zabern.

Hodkinson, S. (1999) An agonistic culture? Athletic competition in archaic and classical Spartan society. In S. Hodkinson and A. Powell (eds) *Sparta, New Perspectives,* 147–187. London, Duckworth and the Classical Press of Wales.

Hodkinson, S. (2000) *Property and Wealth in classical Sparta.* London, Duckworth.

Jeffery, L. H. (1990) *The Local Scripts of Archaic Greece.* Revised edition, with a supplement by A. W. Johnston. Oxford, Oxford University Press.

Jung, M. (2006) *Marathon und Plataiai: Zwei Perserschlachten als «lieux De Mémoire» im Antiken Griechenland.* Göttingen, Vandenhoeck & Ruprecht.

Kennell, N. M. (1987) Where was Sparta's Prytaneion? *American Journal of Archaeology* 91, 421–422.

Kennell, N. M. (1995) *The Gymnasium of Virtue: Education and Culture in Ancient Sparta.* Chapel Hill, University of North Carolina Press.

Knigge, U. (1991) *The Athenian Kerameikos.* Athens, Deutsches Archäologisches Institut.

Kourinou, E. (2000) Σπάρτη. Συμβολή στη μνημειακή τοπογραφία της. Athens, Megale Bibliotheke.

Macgregor Morris, I. (2000) 'To Make a New Thermopylae': Hellenism, Greek Liberation, and the Battle of Thermopylae. Gre*ece & Rome* 47, 211–230.

Marchetti, P. (1996) Le 'dromos' au coeur de l'agora de Sparte. Les dieux protecteurs de l'éducation en pays dorien. Points de vue nouveaux. *Kernos* 9, 155–170.

Molyneux, J. H. (1992) *Simonides: a Historical Study.* Wauconda, Ill., Bolchazy-Carducci.

Palagia, O. (1993) A marble Athena Promachos from the Acropolis of Sparta. In W. D. E. Coulson and O. Palagia (eds) *Sculpture from Arcadia and Laconia. Proceedings of an international conference held at the American School of Classical Studies at Athens, April 10–14, 1992,* 167–175. Oxford, Oxbow Books.

Parker, R. (1989) Spartan religion. In A. Powell (ed.) *Classical Sparta. Techniques behind her Success,* 147–172. London, Routledge.

Peek, W. (1974) *Ein neuer spartanischer Staatsvertrag.* Berlin, Akademie.

Pettersson, M. (1992) *Cults of Apollo at Sparta: the Hyakinthia, the Gymnopaidiai and the Karneia.* Stockholm, Svenska institutet i Athen.

Podlecki, A. J. (1968) Simonides: 480. *Historia* 17, 257–275.

Pritchett, W. K. (1985) *The Greek State at War.* Berkeley, Los Angeles, London, University of California Press.

Roehl, H. (1882) *Inscriptiones Graecae Antiquissimae.* Berlin, G. Reimer.

Schaefer, A. E. (1957) Das Eidolon des Leonidas. In K. Schauenburg (ed.) *Charites. Studium zur Altertumswissenschaft,* 223–233. Bonn, Athenaum-Verlag.

Steiner, D. (1999) To praise, not to bury: Simonides fr. 531P. *Classical Quarterly* 49, 383–395.

Wade-Gery, H. T. (1933) Classical epigrams and epitaphs: A study of the Kimonian age. *Journal of Hellenic Studies* 53, 71–104.

Waywell, G. (1999) Sparta and its topography. *Bulletin of the Institute of Classical Studies* 43, 1–26.

Whitley, J. (1997) Cretan laws and Cretan literacy. *American Journal of Archaeology* 101, 635–661.

Willemsen, F. (1977) Zu den Lakedämoniergräbern im Kerameikos. *Mitteilungen des Deutschen Archäologischen Instituts, Athenische Abteilung* 92, 117–157.

Woodward, A. M. (1923–25) Excavations at Sparta, 1924–25. The Acropolis. *Annual of the British School at Athens* 26, 240–276.

Burial in the Bosporan kingdom:
Local traditions in regional context(s)

Jane Rempel

In the larger realm of ancient history and Greek archaeology, the Classical period Black Sea state known as the Bosporan kingdom is perhaps best known for the monuments and actions of its Spartokid rulers: the Athenian law-court speeches and inscriptions that tell us about the deals Bosporan rulers made with the Athenians and the honours that they received in kind (*e.g.* Demosthenes 20.30–1; Dinarchus 1.43; *IG* II² 212; *IG* II² 653); and back at home, in the Taman[1] and Kerch Peninsulas of southern Ukraine and Russia, the inscriptions in which the Spartokids refer to themselves as both 'kings' and 'archons' (*e.g. CIRB* 6; *CIRB* 8; *CIRB* 974) and, perhaps most impressively, the monumental burial mounds with stone-built chambers that are assumed to be royal burials. This investigation takes these 'royal' burials as a starting point, from which to consider the variety and complexity of burial practices within the Bosporan kingdom. The focus will be primarily the fourth and third centuries BC, a time of considerable territorial expansion and consolidation, which saw the inclusion of a variety of populations under the aegis of the Bosporan state. The various burial traditions practiced, often in close proximity to each other, are considered with an emphasis on their local and broader regional cultural contexts.

The Bosporan kingdom

The state commonly known as the Bosporan kingdom was controlled by a dynasty of rulers, the Spartokids, from 438/7–108/7 BC. Its territory, at its greatest extent, covered the Taman and Kerch peninsulas, which dominate the Strait of Kerch, between the Black Sea and the Sea of Azov. This territory included not only the Greek colonies located on the shores of the strait (most notably, Pantikapaion, the capital, and Phanagoria) and on the Black Sea coast (from Theodosia in the west to Gorgippia in the east), but also numerous inland settlements, many occupied by sedentary Scythian, Sindian and Maeotian populations (Fig. 2.1). The first Spartokid ruler, Spartokos I, was based

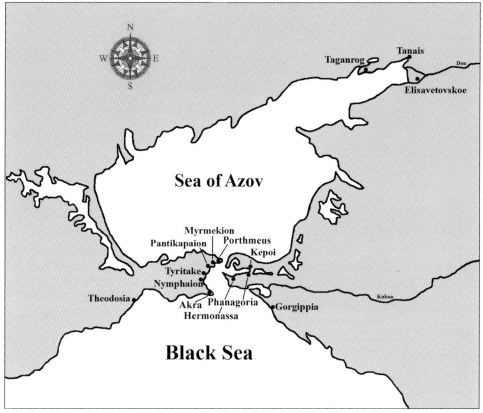

Figure 2.1 Principal Greek colonies and Bosporan settlements in the region of the Bosporan kingdom (map, Author).

in Pantikapaion and controlled many of the Greek colonies in the Strait of Kerch, including Kepoi, Myrmekion and Porthmeus. His successor, Satyros (433/2–389/8 BC), seized the colonies of Nymphaion and Phanagoria, and territorial expansion began in earnest with his son, Leukon I (389/8–349/8 BC). By the end of the first quarter of the fourth century BC, Leukon had conquered Theodosia, and in the next years of his reign proceeded to overcome the Sindians and some Maeotian tribes in the east. Paerisades, Leukon's successor, absorbed several more Maeotian tribes (Polyaenus 6.9; Gaidukevich 1949, 58–59, 498, n. 53; Gaidukevich 1971, 92–93; Burstein 1974, 412–3; Kuznetsov 2000).

Beginning in the fourth century BC, and continuing into the third and even second centuries BC, this expansion was followed by a *rastsvet*, 'flowering', of the rural landscape, marked by the foundation of numerous new settlements (Fig. 2.2; Paramov 1986, 1989; Maslennikov 1998) and the 'filling-in' of the landscape with new road networks and field systems. This was, in part at least, owed to the prosperity resulting from extensive

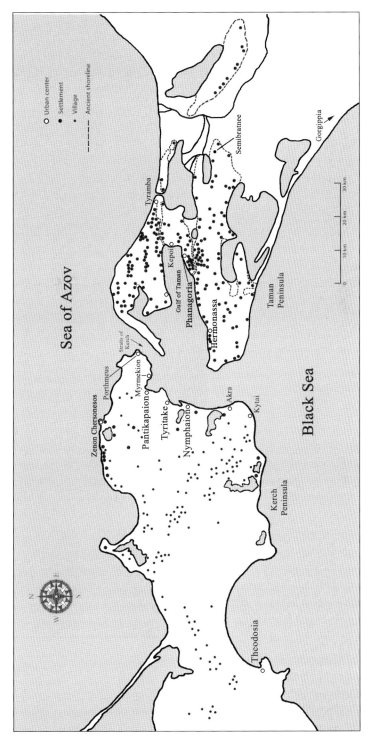

Figure 2.2 Fourth century BC settlements in the Bosporan kingdom (after Paromov 1986, 1989; Maslennikov 1998).

grain production in this period. The result was a large territorial state, with a markedly heterogeneous population, that was connected not only by economic and political ties, but also by a landscape that reflected these ties (Rempel 2004).

In line with the heterogeneous nature of the population of the Bosporan kingdom, the Spartokid rulers projected themselves in a variety of ways. They courted and celebrated Athenian honours, and adopted the title 'archon' to express their relationship to the population of the Greek colonies they ruled. At the same time, they called themselves 'kings' of the local non-Greek populations, and commemorated themselves in lavish burials, the form of which was related to other Black Sea and steppe traditions. It has long been noted that the dynastic names Spartokos and Paerisades were Thracian while Satyros and Leukon were rare aristocratic Greek names, and although onomastics are notoriously unreliable for determining cultural heritage or ethnicity it is likely that the Spartokid dynasty had some sort of Thracian connection, most likely to the dominant Odrysian kingdom.

Thus, the Spartokids and their Bosporan kingdom present a fascinating picture of a unique state at the margins of the Greek world, with a heterogeneous population and a culturally flexible ruling elite. The region is ripe for exploring questions of ethnicity, cultural interaction and social identities and it is difficult to describe, let alone understand, without reference to the larger regional and interregional cultural entities with which it interacted.

Local and regional interactions

Investigations of the margins of the ancient Greek world have traditionally focused on identifying commonalities and differences: commonalities with the larger Greek *oikoumene* and differences predicated on regionally specific contacts with various non-Greek populations (*e.g.* Boardman 1980; Cunliffe 1985, 12–37). While such comparisons are important, they implicitly constrain interpretation in a binary framework: ' Greek' and ' non-Greek'. More recently, the use of post-colonial approaches in understanding Greek colonisation, with emphasis on consumption, hybridisation, 'middle ground' and the possibility for transformation of cultural practices, has shifted attention to more specific contextual understandings that do not rely on straightforward Greek/non-Greek categorisation (Dietler 1995; Given 2004; Malkin 2004; Hodos 2006). As Dietler (2005, 63, italics added for emphasis) has argued, the colonial experience does not take place at a level of culture or abstract structures; rather "It is an active process of creative appropriation, manipulation, and transformation played out by individuals and social groups with a variety of competing interests and strategies of action embedded in *local political relations, cultural perceptions, and cosmologies.*"

With reference to burial in the Bosporan kingdom, this chapter investigates how and why certain regional and 'global' cultural forces were selectively adopted and

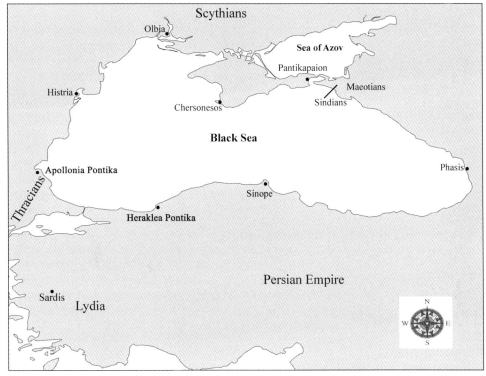

Figure 2.3 The Bosporan kingdom and its regional contexts with sites mentioned in the text (map, Author).

adapted by Bosporan elite groups, and what those choices meant in a local context. In particular, a close investigation of continuity, variability and innovation in burial traditions in the Bosporan kingdom in the fourth and first half of the third centuries BC is undertaken. The mortuary record is, at least in part, the direct result of conscious actions and of selections of symbolically invested objects, and therefore potentially informative for understanding social and cultural identities. Choice and social identity also play a large role in determining the treatment of the dead, producing variation in funerary ritual (Parker Pearson 2000, 33). Study of burial in the Bosporan kingdom may therefore reveal patterning within its heterogeneous population, and allow the tracing of connections to the larger Greek and steppe worlds.

First, however, it is important to define the regional frameworks that intersected in the Bosporan kingdom. *Pace* earlier criticism of the binary frameworks outlined above, this study situates the Bosporan kingdom primarily within the Greek *oikoumene*, but understands it as an extensive *oikoumene* – in which circulated a common, but regionally variable, vocabulary of Greekness – now expanding into the Balkans and Asia Minor. The inhabitants of the Bosporan kingdom participated in this dialogue, most obviously in the Greek colonies, *poleis* in their own right. The Greek world, however, did not constitute a 'global universe' for the Bosporan kingdom, far from it. By the fourth century BC, the kingdom was part of a number of several different political and/or cultural regional spheres: the Black Sea coast, and its Greek settlements; the Aegean Greek world; the Scythian steppe; the Thracian Balkans; and at something of a remove, the Persian empire (Fig. 2.3). And the Bosporan state was itself, as we have seen, a patchwork of peoples, making the 'local' context refer to the various communities that were united by the structures of that state. What drives this paper is the investigation of the ways in which those communities were transformed by their inclusion in the Bosporan kingdom.

Burial in the Bosporan kingdom: mounds

Perhaps the most well-known burials from the Bosporan kingdom are the large burial mounds ('kurgans') with stone-built chambers that first appeared at the end of the fifth century BC, and flourished during the fourth century and first half of the third centuries BC. They represent a new trajectory in elite burial practices in the kingdom. Although some of them are termed 'royal', variations in construction and burial ritual indicate that they were built for people from various communities within the state.

About seventeen mounds constructed in this period were truly monumental. In general, these burials consisted of stone-built chambers covered by an earthen mound, the largest of which were up to 20m in height, and 250m in circumference (Fig. 2.4). The chambers were usually rectangular (with the exception of the circular chamber in the Zolotoi kurgan) with corbelled roofs, and had long *dromoi,* or entrance-passageways, with step-vaulted roofs. The corpse was interred in a wooden sarcophagus or on a bench against the wall opposite the chamber door (Gaidukevich and Iakobson 1981, 6–54; Tsetskhladze 1998b). Unfortunately most of these mounds were robbed in the past, and only a few intact assemblages of grave goods have been excavated, for example at the Kul-Oba and Bolshaia Bliznitsa mounds and the Iuz-Oba group (Tsvetaeva 1968, 34). These assemblages are as impressive as the mounds themselves, including hundreds of gold objects, imported pottery, metal vessels and other luxury items.

Extant burials are usually divided into two categories: those with primarily Greek grave goods, and those with burials reflecting local customs. The majority of the former are located on the Kerch peninsula, in the vicinity of Pantikapaion, the Spartokid capital, and are commonly assumed to be burials of the Spartokids and their court. The 'local' burials are mostly located on the Taman peninsula and are connected with the Sindian elite (Fig. 2.6; Koshelenko, Kruglikova *et al.* 1984, 95–7; Tsetskhladze 1998b, 50; Ustinova 1999, 4).

The largest and most elaborate of the burial mounds are the Zolotoi and Tsarskii kurgans. Both date to the second half of the fourth century BC, and are located close

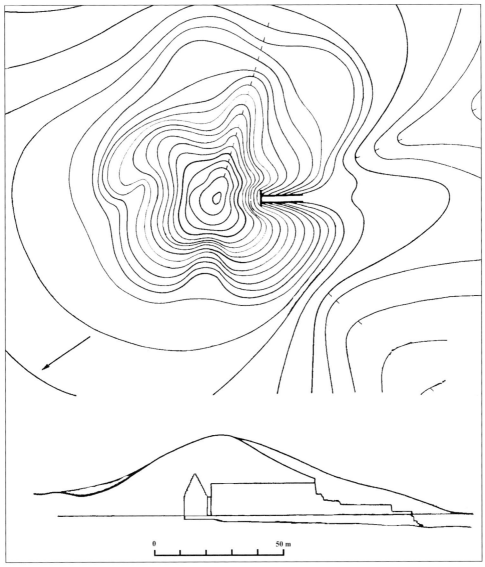

Figure 2.4 Plan and section of the Tsarskii kurgan, near Pantikapaion (second half of the fourth century BC) (after Gaidukevich 1981, 34, fig. 8).

to Pantikapaion (Fig. 2.5). The Tsarskii kurgan is the largest on the Kerch peninsula; its mound was 17 m high and 250 m in diameter and covered a large rectangular chamber with a corbelled dome (Fig. 2.4). Although looted in antiquity, its size and sophisticated construction suggest it was built for Spartokid rulers, perhaps Leukon I or Paerisades I (Minns 1913, 194; Tsvetaeva 1968, 39–42; Gaidukevich and Iakobson

Figure 2.5 Fourth century BC Bosporan burial mounds with chamber tombs located near Pantikapaion (after Tsvetaeva 1968: 37). 1. Tsarskii kurgan; 2. Zolotoi kurgan; 3. Patiniotti kurgan; 4. Kul-Oba kurgan; 5. Ak-Burunskii kurgan*; 6. Pavlovskii kurgan*; 7. Zmeinyi kurgan*; 8. Kekuvatskogo kurgan* (* kurgans in the Iuz-Oba cemetery).

1981, 25–45; Fedak 1990, 169; Tsetskhladze 1998b, 49). The Zolotoi kurgan is only slightly smaller than the Tsarskii, but it incorporated three different burial chambers. The two earlier ones, probably dating to the mid fourth century BC, were rectangular with corbelled roofs and originally each was covered by its own mound of earth. The third chamber, constructed in the late fourth century BC, was circular with a corbelled dome and was erected over the earlier mounds, and the entire complex was enclosed by a cyclopean retaining wall. These burials were also looted in antiquity, but the latest was "undoubtedly royal" (Minns 1913, 194–5; Tsvetaeva 1968, 36–9; Gaidukevich

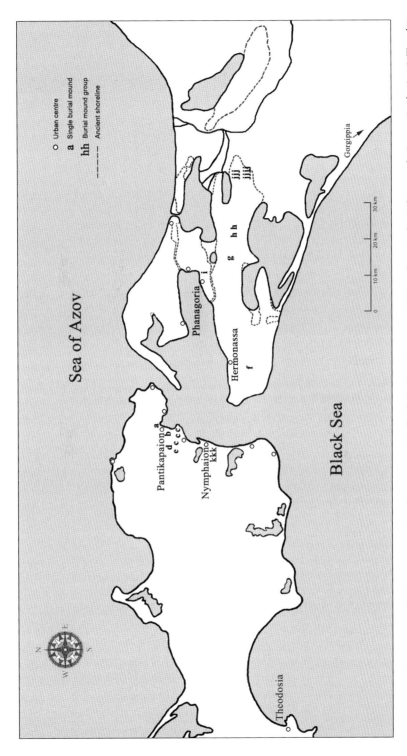

Figure 2.6 The territory of the Bosporan kingdom, second half of the fourth century BC and main burial mounds (map, Author): a) Tsarskii kurgan; b) Zolotoi kurgan; c) Iuz-Oba kurgans; d) Kukubatskii kurgan; e) Kul-Oba kurgan; f) Zelenskii kurgan; g) Vasiurinskii kurgan; h) Bolshaia and Malia Bliznitsii; i) Artiukhovskii kurgans; j) Semibratnie kurgans; k) Three Brothers kurgans.

and Iakobson 1981, 6–24; Fedak 1990, 168–9; Tsetskhladze 1998b, 49). It is likely that the earlier burials were also connected to the Spartokid dynasty, perhaps those of the parents of the ruler buried in the main chamber. While the connection of both great burial mounds with the Spartokid rulers seems entirely plausible, there is no direct archaeological evidence for it. Strabo (11.2.7), however, mentions a 'monument of Satyros' in his description of Pantikapaion (*cp.* Hind 1994, 506), and Diodorus Siculus (20.22–6), recounts the burial of Satyros II in a royal tomb. Neither mentions a burial mound, but it seems likely that they had in mind *tumuli* like the Zolotoi and Tsarskii kurgans.

Several smaller monumental burial mounds in the vicinity of Pantikapaion have been attributed to members of the Spartokid court. For example, the Iuz-Oba group, including the Kekuvatskii, Ak-Burunskii, Pavlovskii, and Zmeinyi kurgans, was located on a rocky range to the southwest of the city (Fig. 2.5). Most of these fourth century BC *tumuli* covered square chambers with vaulted roofs and *dromoi;* several of them had two or more chambers and are thought to indicate family groups. This cemetery is one of the richest discovered in the Bosporan kingdom, and most of the burials were excavated intact. The bodies were laid out in wooden sarcophagi, and were buried with quantities of fine gold jewellery and Attic pottery (including many of the famous Attic red-figure Kerch vases). Some of the male burials included weapons and armour, artefacts generally connected with elite burial traditions of the Eurasian steppe, prompting Ivanova (1953, 65) to comment that one example (the Kekuvatskii kurgan) was "a characteristic combination of Greek and Scythian goods in one burial" (see also Rostowzew 1931, 176–80; Gaidukevich 1949, 254–8; Ivanova 1953, 64–6; Tsvetaeva 1968, 50–60; Artamonov and Forman 1969, 72–3). Another burial of this type is the Melek-Chesmenskii kurgan, located in the plain to the north of Pantikapaion (Rostowzew 1931, 176–80; Gaidukevich 1949, 254–8; Ivanova 1953, 64–6; Tsvetaeva 1968, 50–60; Artamonov and Forman 1969, 72–3). There is also no direct evidence to connect these burials with the Spartokid court, but their construction techniques, wealth of grave goods and proximity to Pantikapaion make it a likely suggestion. In fact, it is assumed that the Zolotoi and Tsarskii kurgans originally contained similar assemblages of grave-goods, containing many Greek luxury goods and some evidence for steppe burial ritual.

Monumental burial mounds were not the exclusive preserve of the Spartokid elite. Indeed, the variation in chamber construction and burial ritual seen in monumental mounds throughout the kingdom are thought to reflect different constituent Spartokid, Scythian and Sindian elite groups. For example, the Kul-Oba kurgan, dated to the first half of the fourth century BC and located on a ridge 6.4 km to the west of Pantikapaion (Fig. 2.5), is assumed to have contained a member of the Scythian elite from the Crimea (Minns 1913, 195–206; Tsvetaeva 1968, 44–50; Tsetskhladze 1998b, 50). Its main chamber is similar to the 'Spartokid' burials, with a corbel-vaulted roof and *dromos.* The burial itself, however, was markedly different from those of the Iuz-Oba and Melek-

Chesmenskii mounds. The chamber contained three skeletons: a male resting in a large wooden coffin, and a female and another male lying on the ground beside the coffin (Fig. 2.7). Underneath the chamber was another pit burial, containing one body and 55 kilograms of gold artefacts. The main burial was also very rich in gold and electrum grave goods, and included many artefacts with Scythian imagery as well as Scythian weapons. In terms of burial ritual – including the burying of consorts and slaves – and grave goods, the Kul-Oba mound most resembles other Scythian kurgans in the lower Dnieper, such as the Chertomlyk kurgan (Skriver Tillisch 2008; *cp.* Herodotus, 4.71–2), though, as Minns (1913, 202) noted, Kul-Oba was atypical for Scythian elite burials in that it did not have side chambers for horse and groom burials "in the true Scythic style." The presence of a Scythian burial near Pantikapaion is not surprising; smaller Scythian mound burials from as early as the sixth century BC had been located in or near the *necropoleis* of Pantikapaion, Nymphaion and other colonies in the area (Maslennikov 1981; Vinogradov 1995; Tsetskhladze 1998a, 45; Ustinova 1999, 4; Vinogradov 2001). Unusual, however, is the size of Kul-Oba's mound and the stone-built chamber, as well as its location

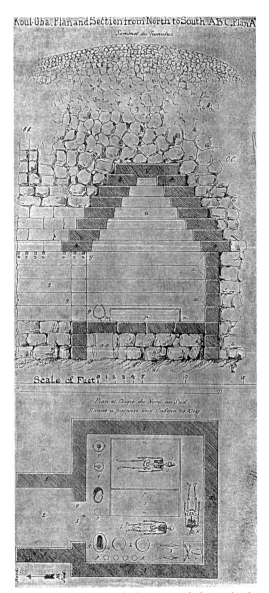

Figure 2.7 Plan and elevation of the Kul-Oba burials (from Minns 1913, 196, fig. 89).

outside Pantikapaion, which echo the Spartokid mounds described above. A similar, but smaller scale, example of this type of burial is the Three Brothers kurgan group located on the outskirts of Nymphaion (Fig. 2.6). Here, however, the three mounded burials all contained, in addition to Greek luxury goods and weapons, horse harnesses in Scythian style. The most famous of these burials, of a woman, consisted of a stone-

Figure 2.8 A nineteenth century drawing of the Semibratnie kurgans during excavation (after Gaidukevich 1971, fig. 7).

vaulted chamber with a limestone relief depicting the Greek goddess Demeter in a chariot (Zinko 2006, 298).

On the Taman peninsula, fewer monumental chamber tombs were constructed during the fourth century BC, perhaps because stone suitable for construction was more difficult to find in this area (Gaidukevich and Iakobson 1981, 51). Of those that were built, the most have been attributed to the local Sindian elite, by virtue of their locations and hybrid burial ritual (*e.g.* the Artiukovskii, Zelenskii, Vasiurinskii kurgans, and the Bliznitsi and Semibratnie groups; Fig. 2.6). The earliest are found in the Semibratnie kurgan group, located on a hill near the settlement of Semibratnee, the main Sindian settlement and seat of the Sindic rulers, at the eastern end of the Taman peninsula (Fig. 2.2, Fig. 2.8). These seven mounds (the 'Seven Brothers' after which the site is named) continued an established tradition of Sindian elite burial. The earliest date to the fifth century BC, and predate the incorporation of the Sindian territory into the Bosporan kingdom. They were most likely the burials of the Sindian rulers and their families. The latest date to the second half of the fourth century BC, long after the Spartokid takeover. Unlike the Pantikapaion examples described above, the Semibratnie mounds did not have stone-built burial chambers; the dead were interred in earthen pits. Burial ritual was also different from the Spartokid burials in that, alongside large quantities of gold grave goods and weapons, the Seminbratnie burials also contained horse harnesses. The burying of horses and tack with elite members of a community was common in Scythian burials on the steppe; in the Bosporan kingdom, the majority of the evidence for this practice comes from the Taman peninsula and is usually assumed to indicate Sindian burial. Despite the specific construction of the Semibratnie mounds, and the burial ritual evidenced within them, once Semibratnee and the Sindian territory was incorporated into the Bosporan kingdom (by the third quarter of the fourth century BC) they must be understood in the context of the new Spartokid monumental burials and indeed other new mounds on the Taman peninsula (described below). The preservation of this established location for elite Sindian burial even after the Sindians had been incorporated into the Bosporan state imbued these later kurgans with strong statements of Sindian identity and perhaps even rejection of

Bosporan authority. It is perhaps telling that the use of the Semibratnie mounds seemed to die out as new Bosporan mounds, with stone-built chambers, were constructed closer to Bosporan centres on the Taman peninsula.

From the second half of the fourth century BC, these new monumental burial mounds were constructed on the Taman peninsula, generally in closer proximity to the main Greek settlements on the Strait of Kerch. Many of these mounds have been attributed to Sindian elite, primarily because of specific features of ritual, usually involving the inclusion of horses or horse harnesses. For example, a third century BC kurgan on Mt. Vasiurina, to the south of Phanagoria, included four horse burials in the *dromos* of an otherwise empty tomb (Fig. 2.6; Gaidukevich 1949, 295). The specific association of these burials with a Sindian elite is, however, far from assured, given the use of stone-built chambers and of increasingly hybrid burial rituals.

The most elaborate burial mound on the Taman peninsula, the Bolshaia Bliznitsa *tumulus*, is located *c.* 8 km to the south west of Phanagoria (Fig. 2.6). The mound was large (15m high and 350m in circumference) and incorporated four stone burial chambers and probably an additional cremation burial dug into the mound. All the chamber burials date to the second half of the fourth century BC, and it has been proposed that all the deceased were members of the same family. The sole male burial contained a wooden coffin with ivory inlay, weapons and armour, gold jewellery (including a wreath) and imported pottery. All the female burials contained headdresses and jewellery associated with the Eleusinian mysteries (rites connected with the worship of Demeter and Persephone). The richest contained two sets of this religious jewellery, various other pieces of gold jewellery, a bronze mirror engraved with a picture of Eros and Aphrodite, imported pottery and decorative bronze parts of four horse harnesses. Most notably, the chamber was decorated with a painting of a female deity, often identified as Demeter, but now believed to be the Great Goddess of steppe religions (Artamonov and Foreman 1969; Rempel forthcoming). The Bolshaia Bliznitsa (and nearby Malaia Bliznitsa) burial mounds were quite similar to the fourth century BC mounds near Pantikapaion in terms of construction, size and some aspects of burial ritual (*i.e.* wooden sarcophagi, imported pottery); yet the inclusion of horse harnesses links them to Sindian burial practices and the Semibratnie kurgans described above.

Use of mounded burials for elite self-presentation was also made by other populations in the kingdom. The kurgan cemetery that developed on the outskirts of Hermonassa is a good example. During the fourth century BC, a cemetery of smaller mound burials was established on the outskirts of this settlement, which was originally a Greek colony (Fig. 2.2). These burials were located on a ridge that followed the main road leading into the city, *c.* 2 km from the centre. In this location, the kurgans served to define the territory of the Hermonassa and to mark the point of access to it. Paromov (2002) has suggested that they contained the elite of the city. Although not as monumental as the ones discussed above, they are also characterized by stone-built chambers and wooden sarcophagi. In grave ritual, however, they preserve a variety of undeniably hybrid assemblages. Some burials had largely Greek pottery and luxury goods, while others included weapons, horse harnesses, and religious imagery akin to that found in the Bolshaia Bliznitsa burials (Paromov 2002). It seems clear that at least some of the Hermonassa elite subscribed to the same basic notions of funerary display as those of other elite groups in the state, including the ruling Spartokids. Indeed, the variation in grave-good assemblages seen in these burials seems to suggest that for them it was the mound and stone chamber, along with a wealth of grave goods, that were the primary indicators of status, rather than any specific burial ritual.

Mounded burial in the Bosporan kingdom was not the preserve of the ruling elite groups. As mentioned above, non-monumental mounded burial had been practised by Scythians in the territory of the Bosporan kingdom since the sixth century BC. In the fourth and third centuries BC, a new tradition of mounded burial was established by a newly sedentarised Scythic population. One of the most remarkable phenomena of the fourth century BC 'flowering' of the rural landscape was the proliferation of small villages (*selishcha*) in the western part of the kingdom, mainly to the north of the Theodosia and in the interior of the Kerch peninsula (Fig. 2.2). Almost 300 of these villages have been found to date, although unfortunately only a handful has been excavated (*e.g.* Koshara, Aktashskoe, and Zolotoe Platau; Maslennikov 1998, 76*ff*). They were not evenly distributed throughout peninsula, but were located on fertile land and near water sources and often situated on the south slope of a hill, or on a plateau. All of the *selishcha* date from between the second quarter of the fourth century BC and the 270s BC, with the majority established around the middle of the fourth century BC (Kruglikova 1975, 72–83; Maslennikov 1998, 86–88; Maslennikov 2001a, 91). These villages are notable for occupying a region that had previously been controlled by largely nomadic Scythians and they represent the first permanent settlements in this part of the Kerch peninsula since the eighth century BC.

Archaeological survey has shown the *selishcha* to be grouped in clusters, which may or may not represent administrative units. They are thought to have accommodated a new Tauric-Scythian population that settled down to an agrarian lifestyle in the central and western parts of the Kerch peninsula in conjunction with the formalisation of the Bosporan state (Masslenikov 1998). The clusters of villages were usually arranged around contemporaneous groups of kurgans that are similar in character to Scythian kurgans from the steppe to the north. These mounds are relatively small, covering pit or cist burials. The burials are poor, but in construction and ritual they are clearly associated with wider Scythian mortuary practice. The small clusters of kurgans may indicate the presence of larger kin groups that became important as the population sedentarised (Gavrilov 2004, 148) and became economically entwined with the Bosporan state.

Although these *selishcha* kurgans are quite different from the monumental Spartokid burials near Pantikapaion or the Sindian mounds on the Taman peninsula, they must be considered in the general context of a new mode of elite burial in the Bosporan kingdom that deployed large burial mounds and stone-built chambers as key indicators of status, but tolerated a great deal of variety in terms of burial ritual within the mounds. The particular cultural imperatives of different elite groups, be they Spartokid, Scythian or Sindian, could be accommodated by this rubric without compromising it.

Burial in the Bosporan kingdom: flat burials and burial markers

In their study of the *necropolis* located immediately on the outskirts of Pantikapaion, Fless and Lorenz (2005; Fless 2002) express a similar idea, suggesting that elite status in this city was projected through the quantity and quality of grave goods in burials, rather than by ethnic differentiations in their external appearance. In the *necropoleis* of the *poleis* of the Bosporan kingdom, flat cist burials associated with the Greek population were located alongside small *tumuli*. In Pantikapaion, at least, there is no clear spatial segregation between mounded and flat burials or between burials with distinct cultural connections (Fless 2002). Indeed, flat burials in the Bosporan kingdom and *stelae* used to mark them provide another important facet of local expressions of identity that developed in the fourth century BC. Unfortunately, excavations of non-monumental burials in the Bosporan kingdom have not traditionally been a priority and as Maslennikov (2001b, 189) states: "Much about the ethnocultural characteristics of the region that concerns us could be provided by the excavation of kurgans and flat cemeteries, but unfortunately this has only been undertaken in limited numbers."

Nonetheless, excavated examples of flat burials in the *necropoleis* associated with the original Greek colonies indicate that they reflect connections to established Greek funerary ritual while exhibiting specifically local variations. While there was variation in burial ritual throughout the Greek world, in the Classical period Greek burials were typified by individual inhumation or cremation burials marked with decorated grave *stelae*. Grave assemblages included pottery, jewellery and mirrors for women, and strigils for men. While Athens does not necessarily represent the norm, Attic grave *stelae* from the fourth century BC were often decorated with relief sculpture showing the deceased, increasingly in family groupings, in a variety of established idealised representations (*e.g.* matron, heroic male youth, wise older man; Leader 1997). Excavated flat burials from the Pantikapaion *necropolis* have revealed burials that roughly follow these established Greek conventions of burial: burials were placed in slab stone chambers, and included wooden sarcophagi. The assemblages were usually dominated by traditionally Greek grave goods: Greek pottery, mirrors and jewellery for women and strigils and alabastra (metal scrapers and oil flasks, equipment associated with exercising at the gymnasium) for men (Zinko 2001; Fless 2002; Fless and Lorenz 2005). Nonetheless, the quantity of grave goods and the proportion of gold and silver artefacts within the Pantikapaion assemblages are markedly greater than elsewhere in the Greek world. The quantity of such goods continued to increase in the fourth century BC, perhaps reflecting the profits of the grain trade. In the *necropolis* of Theodosia, where the burials were primarily cremations, the quantity and quality of grave goods also increased in the fourth century BC (Gavrilov 2004, 150). Although there is generally a great deal of variability in burial ritual in Greek *poleis* in the Black Sea region (Damyanov 2005), according to Fless (2002) the importance of grave goods for marking social status and gender in these burials is in marked contrast to other Greek cities on the north coast of the Black Sea; the use of the pelike, a two-handled, open-necked pottery vessel, as a grave good is also out of line with mortuary practice in the Aegean Greek world. More orthodox are, for example, burials from Apollonia Pontika, a Greek colony on the east coast of the Black Sea, where flat inhumation burials are more typically Greek (although it should be noted that nearby the *necropolis* were *tumuli* clusters that are thought to represent Thracian elements in the community) (Panayotova 1997; Nedev and Panayotova 2003; Petersen 2004).

Grave *stelae* from the Bosporan kingdom are rarely found *in situ*, but seem to have been used to mark mounded and flat burials alike. Bosporan *stelae* in Greek style are relatively common and are assumed to have marked flat burials like those outlined above. The simplest were decorated with a palmette and usually only the name and patronymic of the deceased (Fig. 2.9b); more elaborate relief scenes and painted images are also found (Kreuz 2005). There is evidence of a sporadic import of Attic grave markers, and imitation of Attic styles in local stone (Fless 2002), but apart from these limited examples it seems that the *stela* itself was not used as a marker for conspicuous displays of status or wealth.

The inscriptions on Greek-style *stelae* occasionally included *polis* ethnics along with names and patronymics, and these cases document a certain amount of mobility in the Black Sea region. For example, grave markers from Pantikapaion record people originally from Chersonesos and Theodosia, while the *necropolis* of Nymphaion has a grave marker of a citizen of Heraklea Pontika (all dating to the first half of the fourth century BC; Molev 2003, 211; Bekker-Nielsen 2003, 301). In addition, *stelae*-inscriptions give some insight into the incorporation of non-Greeks into the *polis* communities. On one such example, Tokhtasiev (2006) has identified a Paphlagonian from Sinope in the *necropolis* of Myrmekion, and connects the burial to larger 'superficially Hellenized' immigrant groups in the Bosporan cities. Another inscription suggests that a man with a Sindian name married a woman from Pantikapaion (*CIRB* 709, Bekker-Nielsen 2003, 301).

Grave *stelae* in the Bosporan kingdom, however, were not only in the Greek style. Two types of anthropomorphic *stelae* were also in use in the fourth century BC: a plain, aniconic type of *stela,* which had a long history in the steppe region and is found typically on the Kerch peninsula in association with Scythian burials (Fig. 2.9a; Telehin 1994); and roughly sculpted half-statues of draped figures, which are usually found on the Taman peninsula and associated with non-monumental Sindian burials (Sokolskii 1976). These types of *stelae* appear to have marked flat and mounded burials alike and were widely used in their respective areas of the kingdom.

A rural cemetery on Cape Tuzla at the western tip of the Taman peninsula (Fig.

2.2), provides an evocative example of the ways in which different burial styles and markers were deployed within a distinctly Bosporan context. Archaeologists first began investigating this cemetery in the mid-nineteenth century, and to date it has produced a wealth of burials dating from the sixth century BC to the Roman period, including several fifth-century BC Scythian kurgans (Vinogradov 2001). In the mid-1990s, rescue excavations in the cemetery unearthed several new burials from the fourth century BC, as well as grave markers from this period that had been reused in later burials. These burials, all flat inhumations in pit graves with wooden covers, were not particularly different from one another in terms of body placement or grave goods (which were generally jugs and plates), but some were marked with Greek-style stone *stelae*, while others were marked with anthropomorphic slab markers (Tsetskhladze and Kondrashev 2001). Interestingly enough, even though the Tuzla cemetery is located on the Taman peninsula, it is the aniconic anthropomorphic *stela* (a type

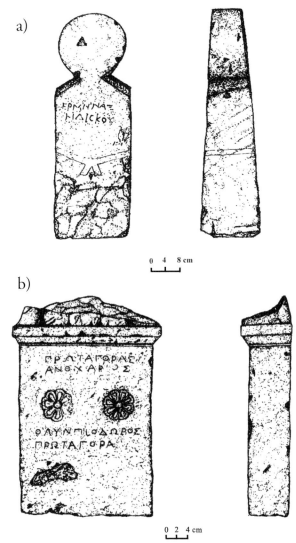

Figure 2.9 Grave stelae from the Tuzla necropolis, second half of the fourth century BC: a) aniconic grave marker with the inscription 'Erminax, son of Eliskos'; b) Greek style stela with the inscriptions 'Protagoras, son of Anoxarios' and 'Olynpiodoros, son of Protagoras' (after Tsetskhladze and Kondrashev 2001, figs 7, 9).

more usually found on the Kerch peninsula) that was most commonly used there.

Two burial markers were found together, probably reused in the fill of a later single burial (Fig. 2.9a and b). The pair provides a useful illustration of the ways in which, by the fourth century BC, burial in the Bosporan kingdom could draw on a varied set of traditions. Both markers have been stylistically dated to the second half of the fourth century BC, and both were carved out of the local limestone. The first can be safely situated within a Greek tradition of burial markers, with its architectural pediment, incised rosettes and inscriptions of the names of a father and son (Fig. 2.9b). These names – Protagoras and Olynpiodoros – are attested to elsewhere in Bosporan inscriptions. The second marker is an anthropomorphic *stela* that *prima facie* fits well with the Kerch tradition of anthropomorphic gravestones (Fig. 2.9a). Specific details, however, such as the belt, connect it to Scythian burial markers from the Crimea. Cape Tuzla had, in fact, long been an important point of crossing the Strait of Kerch, and as late as the second to third century AD was still known as a 'barbarian road' (*CIRB* 837). Despite this 'Scythian belt', the name of the deceased is inscribed in Greek, although his name, Erminax, son of Eliskos, is unknown elsewhere in Bosporan epigraphy (Tsetskhladze and Kondrashev 2001).

Each of these burial markers articulated specific cultural traditions, one the Greek world of the *poleis* and the other the Scythian world of the steppe. Nonetheless, based on evidence from intact burials excavated nearby, it is likely that in terms of ritual and grave goods the burials would have been quite similar. In addition, the markers were carved from the same local stone at roughly the same time, and were used to mark burials in close proximity to each other. Although traditional interpretations use these types of burial markers to identify the ethnicity of the deceased, this may be imprudent. By the fourth century BC, such claims to primarily Greek or indigenous traditions in burial practices might reflect social divisions on a number of axes (rank, status, even gender). Rather, aspects of Greek, Scythian and Sindian cultural heritage may have been deployed in new and varied ways. Erminax's local-style marker was decorated with Scythian iconography and inscribed with a Greek text. Its particular claims – to a particular part of the kingdom, to steppe connections, even to literacy – gain significance when set against the statements made by the neighbouring Greek-style *stela*, because they suggest a choice rather than an ethnic imperative. For it is clear that these burial markers existed as part of a discrete and coherent social system within the Tuzla *necropolis*: in this context, they were both legitimate and potent modes of expressing one's place in the world, yet resonated with each another by virtue of their proximity.

Regional and local contexts

Up to this point, this paper has considered examples of new modes and styles of burial that developed in the Bosporan kingdom during the fourth and first half of the third centuries BC and has suggested that this variety of burial practices constituted a dialogue of status and wealth. That is to say, the monumental mounded burial traditions, whether

Spartokid, Sindian or Scythian in style, were expressions of elite power and wealth that made sense within a Bosporan context. Smaller mounded burials similarly connected themselves to this Bosporan dialogue, either through the inclusion of stone chambers (like at Hermonassa) or simply by virtue of being mounded (*e.g.* the *selishcha* kurgans in the western part of the kingdom). Greek-style flat burials may be seen as part of the same discourse in their conspicuous display of wealth in the form of large quantities of grave goods. Perhaps more telling is the development of hybrid styles of burial, as in the Bolshaia Bliznitsa burials or the more humble fourth century BC burials at the Tuzla *necropolis*, which draw on a variety of burial traditions and enter the larger Bosporan sphere in new ways.

With this happening at the local level, it is necessary to ask after the larger regional imperatives behind the development of new burial practices. The monumental mounded burials with stone-built chambers provide the starting point for this regional investigation because of their connection with the Spartokid elite, and the apparent appeal of the burial style to other elite groups in the kingdom. Mounded burials have a long history in the north coast of the Black Sea. Major trade routes running west to east across the Strait of Kerch had been marked with kurgans from the Bronze Age and Early Iron Age, often following the east-west ridges of the landscape. These routes are sometimes referred to as 'Kurgan Alleys' because they were lined by hundreds of burial mounds (Paromov 1986, 71; Maslennikov 1998, 28–9; Smekalova and Smekalov 2006, 229–233). The fourth century BC monumental mounded burials around Pantikapaion were set in this pre-colonial kurgan landscape (Fig. 2.5). In the Bosporan kingdom, mounded burial was thus firmly connected to a primarily Scythian steppe world and linked to past markers of ownership or control in the landscape.

Given the political situation in the Bosporan kingdom during the fourth century BC, with the creation of a large and culturally heterogenous state, it is understandable that the Spartokids chose to commemorate their dead using mounded burials, thereby legitimating their authority through claims to historicity or tradition (a process similar, perhaps, to the Anglo-Saxon reuse of Bronze Age burial mounds in England; Williams 1998). By referencing the past landscape, the Spartokid burials habituated the Bosporan viewers to 'ancestral' connections that served Spartokid political interests, and in order to surpass the symbolic power of the old mounds they built much larger, more dominant ones (*cp*. Cannon 2002). The 'ancestoral history' being referenced was entirely fictitious (there is nothing to suggest that the Spartokids had Scythian heritage), but would nonetheless have served to acknowledge and include the new non-Greek populations of the state.

But the massive size and stone-built chambers of the Spartokid mounds represent an entirely new tradition in this region. The architectural origins of the Bosporan chamber tombs have been much debated (Gaidukevich and Iakobson 1981; Fedak 1990). Tsetskhladze (1998b and 1998c) has proposed an Anatolian inspiration, suggesting that the idea was brought to the steppe by Ionian colonists in the Bosporan kingdom.

Jane Rempel

Figure 2.10 A royal Scythian kurgan at Nachaeva, lower Dneiper region (Ukraine), fourth century BC, with a World War II monument in the foreground (photo, Author).

It must be noted, however, that the Bosporan mounds share many similarities with the royal chamber tombs in Thrace, where the earliest examples date from the mid-fifth century BC (Archibald 1998; Kitov 1997/8) and it is clear that the Bosporan mounds sit comfortably within a new steppe tradition of monumental mounded burial, which included the Thracian royal tombs and also the Scythian royal kurgans.

Comparable burial mounds with stone chambers and *dromoi* also flourished during the fourth century BC in Scythian territories (Fig. 2.10). The burials in the lower Don and the Crimea, territories adjacent to the Bosporan kingdom, were more similar to the Bosporan and Thracian tombs than those in the lower Dnieper (where the mounds tended to have wooden chambers), suggesting close contact with Bosporan elite. Certain aspects of burial ritual (such as the location of the body) are also found in all three regions. Despite the fact that the Thracian, Bosporan and Scythian mounds clearly represent culturally distinct traditions (Tsetskhladze 1998b, 51–2), these similarities indicate the development of a new interregional dialogue of elite display. The Spartokid elite was participating in this dialogue and the construction of a ruling elite identity within the kingdom was informed by it.

The Kul-Oba mound, described above (Fig. 2.7), with its Scythian burial ritual and stone-built chamber, may be viewed as an example of the close interaction between Bosporan and Scythian elite in this period, as well as a potent reminder of the continued importance of Pantikapaion as both a crossing point and the seat of Spartokid power. The Kul-Oba kurgan picks up the twin connotations of the Spartokid mounded burials, aligning itself with the earlier Scythian kurgans that marked the crossing, as well as resonating with the more recent statements made by the Spartokid burials nearby and the Scythian royal kurgans further to the west (Tsetskhladze 1998b, 53; Vinogradov 2001). This flexibility must shape our interpretation of all of the fourth century BC monumental mounded burials in the Bosporan kingdom. The Spartokid rubric of elite display and self-presentation, through mounumental mounded burials, was accessible to other elite groups in the kingdom precisely because it referenced a regionally varied practice. It was both Bosporan and specific to local communities. It could therefore accommodate the cultural imperatives of different elite groups, Spartokid, Scythian or Sindian, without compromising them. Each claim to this Bosporan construction of elite power confirmed local and state identity and status.

For a potential parallel, we can turn to Achaemenid Sardis, the ancient capital of Lydia in Asia Minor (Fig. 2.3). Dusinberre (2003) has shown that various elite groups in Sardis (including Achaemenid Persians as well as the local Sardians) signalled status by drawing on a newly developed iconographic and stylistic system that indicated wealth but *not* ethnicity, and advertised inclusion in the empire-wide elite. At the same time, however, the Sardian elite sometimes chose to bury their dead in different tomb types based on differing traditions, probably to claim particular aspects of 'Lydian-ness' or 'Persian-ness' as their own and to differentiate themselves – perhaps in a consciously ethnic way – by altering aspects of the established Achaemenid patterns. In addition, in this period there was a revival of a mounded burial tradition, located around three pre-Achaemenid Lydian monumental *tumuli*. Dusinberre (2003) has postulated that these burials may have represented a conscious expression of Lydian identity by virtue of their form, but notes that their burial assemblages contained large quantities of Achaemenid Persian luxury goods. At Achaemenid Sardis, then, the mortuary evidence seems to indicate a society organized not along ethnic lines, but rather along lines of status, where the elite consisted of people of many backgrounds.

Without suggesting any specific connection between the Spartokid elite and the Achaemenid elite at Sardis, it is tempting to draw comparisons with the cultural processes seen in the Sardian burial practices. The Spartokid elite established a mortuary vocabulary that was informed by larger regional practices but deployed in specifically local ways; the other elite groups in the Bosporan kingdom were able to access this vocabulary, and change it to suit their needs, precisely because it was not organised along cultural lines.

Acceptance of this interpretation invites reconsideration of other modes of burial ritual that were in use at this time in the Bosporan kingdom. For example, although the rich assemblages in the smaller burial mounds around Hermonassa, as well as in mounded slab burials recently excavated near Pantikapaion and the less rich slab burials from the *necropolis* at Nymphaeum (Zinko 2001, 295–6, 313–4), may not have been conscious emulation of Spartokid burial practices, the statements they made – including their mounded form – echoed the expressions of power, prestige and wealth made by the large Bosporan chamber tombs. Thus local communities could adapt a particularly Bosporan mode of burial and display to their own needs precisely because it carried no particular cultural or ethnic connotations. Similarly, the people of the *selishcha* in the Kerch peninsula also connected with these larger statements of power, prestige and wealth. This sedentary Scythian population, with its simple kurgan burials, was not just engaging in longstanding burial traditions, but was also participating in the dialogue of the Bosporan landscape, reflecting and validating the new elite vocabulary of prestige and power, and in turn finding validation for its own cultural traditions. They did not look to the Spartokids or the heart of the Bosporan kingdom for their choice of burial traditions, which clearly derived from a direct cultural connection to the steppe region, but it is important to recognize that they would have understood their kurgans in the context of the Bosporan elite burials, and the powerful statements that burial mounds could make in the Bosporan kingdom.

Even the *necropoleis* of the Bosporan cities, with their burials with predominantly Greek grave assemblages, can also be placed within this larger Bosporan elite dialogue. Clearly these burials, by virtue of their burial ritual as well as their imported Greek goods, were connected to, and informed by, the larger Greek world, and this regional connection was an important element of the identities they expressed. Equally important, however, are the ways in which these Greek-style burials access local Bosporan vocabularies of elite display. For example, the flat burials in the *necropoleis* of Pantikapaion and Theodosia were characterized by more conspicuous displays of wealth, including more frequent inclusion of gold and silver artefacts in the fourth century BC. This increase in grave goods undoubtedly reflected the general prosperity in the kingdom during the fourth century BC; it also must be understood, however, in the context of the large Bosporan mounds, which included conspicuous displays of wealth as part of a new way of expressing elite status. Similarly, acceptance of the existence of a Spartokid-led, but nonetheless Bosporan, framework of elite display allows for a more nuanced understanding of the close proximity of both flat Greek-style burials and Scythian mounded burials in the *necropoleis* of the Greek cities in the kingdom, or indeed of the more humble burials from the Tuzla *necropolis*.

Conclusion

Burial practices in the Bosporan kingdom during the fourth and third centuries BC were varied and variable. They had a range of regional cultural connections, and often multiple regional resonances; at the same time, they were deployed on a local or community level within the Bosporan kingdom. These local expressions, however, responded to and were implicated in a dominant Bosporan mode of elite commemoration and display, and it is this Bosporan rubric that can help us to understand the social force of particular cultural appropriations.

Note
1 Russian transliteration follows the conventions outlined in *Ancient West and East* (2002) 1: 234–5; for proper names, however, the most commonly established transliteration is used unless in reference to a Russian text. Russian translations are the author's own.

Bibliography

Abbreviations
CIRB   *Corpus Inscriptorum Regni Bosporani = Korpus bosporskikh nadpisei* (Struve 1965)
IG   *Inscriptiones Gracae*

Ancient Sources
Demosthenes. *Olynthiacs, Philippics, Minor Public Speeches, Speech Against Leptines.* Trans., J. H. Vince, 1930. New York, G.P. Putnam's Sons.
Diodorus Siculus. *Library of History,* vol. 10. Trans., R. M. Geer, 1954. Cambridge, MA, Harvard University Press.
Herodotus. *The Persian Wars*, vol. 2. Trans., A. D. Godley, 1921. Cambridge, MA, Harvard University Press.
Polyaenus. *Stratagems of War*. Trans., R. Shepherd, 1974. Chicago, Ares.
Strabo. *Geography,* vol. 5. Trans., H. L. Jones, 1928. Cambridge, MA, Harvard University Press.

Archibald, Z. (1998) *The Odrysian Kingdom of Thrace: Orpheus Unmasked*. Oxford; New York, Clarendon Press; Oxford University Press.
Artamonov, M. I. and Forman, W. (1969) *The Splendor of Scythian Art; Treasures from Scythian Tombs*. New York, F. A. Praeger.
Bekker-Nielsen, T. 2003. Mobility, ethnicity and identity: the evidence of the funerary inscriptions from Pantikapaion. In V. N. Zinko (ed.) *Bospor Kimmeriskii i varvarskii mir*, 299–302. Kerch.
Boardman, J. (1980) *The Greeks Overseas. The archaeology of their early colonies and trade*. London, Thames and Hudson.
Burstein, S. M. (1974) The war between Heraclea Pontica and Leukon I of Bosporus. *Historia* 23, 401–416.
Cannon, A. (2002) Spatial narratives of death, memory and transcendence. *Archeological Papers of the American Anthropological Association* 11.1, 191–199.
Cunliffe, B. (1988) *Greeks, Romans and Barbarians: spheres of interaction*. New York, Methuen.
Damyanov, M. (2005) Necropoleis and Ionian colonisation in the Black Sea. *Ancient West and East* 4(1): 77–97.
Dietler, M. (1995) The Cup of Gyptis: Rethinking the colonial encounter in Early Iron Age Western Europe and the relevance of World-Systems models. *Journal of European Archaeology* 3(2): 89–111.
Dietler, M. (2005) The archaeology of colonization and the colonization of archaeology. In G. J. Stein (ed.) *The Archaeology of Colonial Encounters: Comparative Perspectives*, 33–68. Santa Fe, School of American Research Press; Oxford, James Currey.

Dusinberre, E. R. M. (2003) *Aspects of Empire in Achaemenid Sardis*. Cambridge; New York, Cambridge University Press.

Fedak, J. (1990) *Monumental Tombs of the Hellenistic Age: A Study of Selected Tombs from the Pre-Classical to the Early Imperial Era*. Toronto; Buffalo, University of Toronto Press.

Fless, F. (2002) The necropolis of Pantikapaion (Kerch, Crimea). www.pontos.dk/e_pub/FlessPantikapaion_1.html (last accessed 14/5/08).

Fless, F. and Lorenz, A. (2005) Die Nekropolen Pantikapaions im 4. Jh. v. Chr. In F. Fless and M. Treister (eds) *Bilder und Objekte als Träger kultureller Identität und interkultureller Kommunikation im Schwarzmeergebiet*, 17–26. Rahden/Westf.,Verlag Marie Leidorf.

Gaidukevich, V. F. (1949) *Bosporskoe tsarstvo*. Moscow, Izd-vo Akademii nauk SSSR.

Gaidukevich, V. F. (1971) *Das Bosporanische Reich*. Berlin, Akademie-Verl.

Gaidukevich, V. F. and Iakobson, A. L. (1981) *Bosporskie goroda: ustupchatye sklepy, ellinisticheskaia usad'ba, Ilurat*. Leningrad, Nauka.

Gavrilov, A. V. (2004) *Okruga antichnoi Feodosii*. Simperopol, Azbuka.

Given, M. (2004) *The Archaeology of the Colonized*. London, Routledge.

Hind, J. (1994) The Bosporan Kingdom. In *Cambridge Ancient History* VI[2], 476–511. Cambridge, Cambridge University Press.

Hodos, T. (2006) *Local Responses to Colonisation in the Iron Age Mediterranean*. London, Routledge.

Ivanova, A. P. (1953) *Iskusstvo antichnykh gorodov severnogo Prichernomor'ia*. Leningrad.

Kitov, G. (1997/8) The valley of the Thracian kings. *Il Mar Nero* III, 9–35.

Koshelenko, G. A., Kruglikova, I. T., *et al.* (1984) *Antichnye gosudarstva Severnogo Prichernomor'ia*. Moscow, Nauka.

Kreuz, P.-A. (2005) Grabstelen klassischer und frühhellenistischer Zeit aus den Städten des Bosporanischen Reichs und das Relief aus dem Drei-Brüder-Kurgan bei Nymphaion. In F. Fless and M. Treister (eds) *Bilder und Objekte als Träger kultureller Identität und interkultureller Kommunikation im Schwarzmeergebiet*, 43–52. Rahden/Westf.,Verlag Marie Leidorf.

Kruglikova, I. T. (1975) *Sel'skoe khoziaistvo Bospora*. Moscow, Nauka.

Kuznetsov, V. D. (2000) Afiny i Bospor: khlebnaia torgovlia. *Rossiiskaia arkheologiia*, 2000.1, 107–20.

Leader, R. (1997) In death not divided: gender, family, and state on Classical Athenian grave stelae. *American Journal of Archaeology* 101(4): 683–99.

Malkin, I. (2004) Postcolonial concepts and ancient Greek colonisation. *Modern Language Quarterly* 65.3, 341–364.

Maslennikov, A. A. (1981) *Naselenie Bosporskogo gosudarstva v VI–II vv. do n.e.* Moscow, Nauka.

Maslennikov, A. A. (1998) *Ellinskaia khora na kraiu Oikumeny*. Moscow, Indrik.

Maslennikov, A. A. (2001a) Some questions concerning the early history of the Bosporan state in light of recent archaeological investigations in the eastern Crimea. In G. R. Tsetskhladze (ed.) *North Pontic Archaeology*, 247–60. Leiden: Brill.

Maslennikov, A. A. (2001b) "Tsarskaia" khora Bospora na rubezhe V–IV vv. do n.e. *Vestnik drevnei istorii* 1: 178–190.

Minns, E. H. (1913) *Scythians and Greeks; A Survey of Ancient History and Archaeology on the North Coast of the Euxine from the Danube to the Caneasus*. Cambridge, University Press.

Molev, E. A. (2003) Bosporos and Chersonesos in the 4th–2nd centuries BC. In P. Guldager Bilde, J. Munk Højte and V. F. Stolba (eds) *The Cauldron of Ariantas*, 209–216. Aarhus, Aarhus University Press.

Morgunova, N. L. and Khokhlova, O. S. (2006) Kurgans and nomads: new investigations of mound burials in the southern Urals. *Antiquity* 80, 303–317.

Nedev, D. and Panayotova, K. (2003) Apollonia Pontica (end of the 7th–1st centuries BC). In D. V. Grammenos and E. K. Petropoulos (eds) *Ancient Greek Colonies in the Black Sea*, Vol. 1, 95–155. Thessaloniki, Greek Ministry of Culture.

Panayotova, K. (1997) Apollonia Pontica: Recent discoveries in the necropolis. In G. R. Tsetskhladze (ed.) *Greek Colonisation of the Black Sea Area. Historical Interpretation of Archaeology,* 97–113. Stuttgart, Franz Steiner.

Parker Pearson, M. (2000) *The Archaeology of Death and Burial*. College Station, Texas A&M University Press.

Paromov, I. M. (1986) Obsledovanie arkheologicheskikh pamiatnikov tamanskogo poluostrova v 1981–1983 gg. *Kratkie soobshcheniia, Institute arkheologii* 188, 69–76.

Paromov, I. M. (1989) Obsledovanie arkheologicheskikh pamiatnikov tamanskogo poluostrova v 1984–1985 gg. *Kratkie soobshcheniia, Institute arkheologii* 196, 72–8.

Paromov, I. M. (2002) Kurgannyi nekropol' Germonassy. *Drevnosti Bospora* 5, 192–206.

Petersen, J. H. (2004) Greek or native? A case study of burial customs in the northern and western Black Sea region: Olbia and Apollonia Pontika. http://www.pontos.dk/e_pub/ JHP_Stockholm-foredrag.pdf (last accessed 14/5/08).

Rempel, J. E. (2004) *Rural Settlement and Elite Representation: Social Change in the Bosporan Kingdom in the Fourth Century BC*. PhD thesis, University of Michigan, Ann Arbor.

Rempel, J. E. (forthcoming). Where are the Greeks? Understanding cultural categories in the Bosporan Kingdom. In G. R. Tsetskhladze (ed.) *Proceedings of the Second International Congress on Black Sea Antiquities*. Oxford, British Archaeological Reports.

Rostowzew, M. I. (1931) *Skythien und der Bosporus*. Berlin, H. Schoetz.

Skriver Tillisch, S. (2008) *"Scythians is a Name Given Them by the Greeks." An Analysis of Six Barrow Burials on the West Eurasian Steppe*. BAR 1784. Oxford, Archaeopress.

Sokolskii, N. I. (1976) Vopros Sindskoi skul'pturyi. In N. I. Sokolskii *et al.* (eds) *Khudozhestvennaia kul'tura i arkheologiia antichnogo mira,* 187–98. Moscow, Nauka.

Smekalova, T. N. and Smekalov, S. J. (2006) Ancient roads and land division in the *chorai* of the European Bosporos and Chersonesos on the evidence of air photographs, mapping and surface surveys. In P. Guldager Bilde and V. F. Stolba (eds) *Surveying the Greek Chora: Black Sea Region in a Comparative Perspective*, 207–248. Aarhus, Aarhus University Press.

Struve, V. V. (1965) *Korpus bosporskikh nadpisei*. Leningrad, Nauka.

Telehin, D. A. I. (1994) *The anthropomorphic stelae of the Ukraine: the early iconography of the Indo-Europeans. Journal of Indo-European Studies,* Monograph 11. Washington, Institute for the Study of Man.

Tokhtasiev, S. R. (2006) Tomb stone of the sons of Attes from Myrmekion. *Ancient Civilizations* 12(3), 181–192.

Tsetskhladze, G. R. (1998a) Greek colonisation of the Black Sea area: stages, models, and native populations. In G. R. Tsetskhladze (ed.) *The Greek Colonisation of the Black Sea Area: Historical Interpretation of Archaeology*, 9–68. Stuttgart, F. Steiner.

Tsetskhladze, G. R. (1998b) More on Bosporan chamber tombs. In S. L. Solovyov (ed.) *Tamanskaia Starina,* i, 48–61. St. Petersburg.

Tsetskhladze, G. R. (1998c) Who built the Scythian and Thracian royal and elite tombs? *Oxford Journal of Archaeology* 17.1, 55–92.

Tsetskhladze, G. R. and Kondrashev, A. V. (2001) Notes on the rescue excavation of the Tuzla necropolis (1995–1997). In G. R. Tsetskhladze (ed.) *North Pontic Archaeology*, 345–363. Leiden, Brill.

Tsvetaeva, G. A. (1968) *Sokrovishcha Prichernomorskikh kurganov*. Moscow, Nauka.

Ustinova, Y. (1999) *The Supreme Gods of the Bosporan Kingdom: Celestial Aphrodite and the Most High God.* Leiden; Boston, Brill.

Vinogradov, I. A. (2001) Kurgany varvarskoi znati V v. do n.e. v raione Bospora Kimmeriiskogo. *Vestnik Drevnei Istorii* 4, 77–87.

Vinogradov, I. G. (1995) Nekotorye diskussionnye problemy grecheskov kolonizatzii Bospora Kimmeriyskogo. *Vestnik drevnei istorii* 3, 152–160.

Williams, H. (1998) Monuments and the past in early Anglo-Saxon England. *World Archaeology* 30: 90–108.

Zinko, V. N. (2001) The five-year rescue excavations in the European Bosporus. In G. R. Tsetskhladze (ed.) *North Pontic Archaeology,* 295–317. Leiden, Brill.

Zinko, V. N. (2006) The *chora* of Nymphaion (6th century BC–6th century AD). In P. Guldager Bilde and V. F. Stolba (eds) *Surveying the Greek Chora: Black Sea Region in a Comparative Perspective*, 289–308. Aarhus, Aarhus University Press.

3

Foreigners in the burial ground:
The case of the Milesians in Athens

Celina L. Gray

Despite the unquestionably rich archaeological record of ancient Athens, there is an asymmetry in its funerary evidence. On the one hand, unprecedented numbers of preserved grave markers span more than a millennium, from the Geometric to the Roman periods. As objects of art-historical analysis and as archives of inscribed names, the works have been catalogued, collated and well-studied. But, on the other hand, for those interested in the archaeological intersection of burial marker and funerary practices, there is a frustrating reality. While thousands of well-preserved grave monuments are extant, there is often little corresponding data on the burials themselves, and those which are published tend to be limited both chronologically and geographically. In the end, for all the richness of data, only select groups of Athenian gravestones can be discussed in conjunction with full archaeological context. For the Roman period *necropoleis*, even less has been published; fortunately, recent work has added to our knowledge of these later Athenian cemeteries (Stroszeck 1999, 2000; Parlama and Stampolidis 2001). Although the lack of primary burial data may limit certain lines of questioning, extant funerary markers comprise an important inroad for analysing the region's inhabitants.

The usefulness of dislocated artefacts is apparent in a long-standing evidentiary problem, the disproportionate visibility of the Milesians, a foreign resident population in Athens. The Milesians, who through the use of an ethnic adjective identified themselves as 'natives' of Miletos in Asia Minor, appear primarily in two main types of documents: lists of participants in the late Hellenistic and Roman *ephebeia*, an institution which educated Athenian youths, and on grave markers of these same periods. The visibility of the Milesians in these documents is intriguing because it follows a period of tight control over the rights and status of Athens' foreign population. The epigraphical record suggests that, by the later Hellenistic era, changes in marriage laws and the relaxation in requirements for the ephebate provided mechanisms by which foreigners could gain entrance into the Athenian citizen body. While recent work (Vestergaard 2000) has looked more broadly at Milesian visibility in the epigraphical record, here a close examination of representative sculpted gravestones will allow us to consider how word and image combine together in the self-presentation of members of this population group.

For years, scholars have noted a curious trend in the Athenian epigraphical evidence. Among religious, civic and, in particular, funerary inscriptions, there existed surprisingly large numbers of individuals labelled with the ethnic adjective *Milesios* (Μιλήσιος, Μειλήσιος) or the feminine form, *Milesia* (Μιλησία, Μειλησία). This city ethnic appears sparingly in the Classical period, but becomes widespread in the funerary and ephebic inscriptions of the Hellenistic and Roman eras. The numbers are astonishing: among the names of self-identified foreigners known in Athens, there are 2011 Milesians; the second largest group, from Herakleia, numbers just 617 (Osborne and Byrne 1996, 72–98, 162–240). While the existence of large foreign communities is in keeping with the level of international trade and contacts which Athens enjoyed, the high proportion of these Milesians has long generated suspicion regarding the authenticity of the ethnic label: how could the Milesians so outnumber other foreign residents? The historical circumstances that led to the growth of this population in Athens remain uncertain, although they were likely economic in nature. Whatever the cause, the funerary monuments demonstrate that these transplanted individuals felt it important to claim roots in the city of Miletos.

Historians and epigraphists have mined Athenian gravestones as archives of names; the data available in a name's constituent parts (which can include the personal name, patronymic, demotic or ethnic, and other familial associations) allow for a range of prosopographical studies, as well as investigations of kinship and family ties, residential patterns, naturalization rates and citizenship laws. The use of the demotic in sepulchral inscriptions is a central issue for investigating the presentation of both citizens and non-citizens in the city's cemeteries. Citizens were divided after the Kleisthenic reforms of the late sixth century BC into 139 demes, the combined geographical-political units in which each man was registered as a citizen (Traill 1975, 81). Through the course of the Classical period, this demotic – in the form of an adjective or prepositional phrase – was increasingly added after the name and patronymic on both public and private documents (Aristotle, *Athenian Constitution* 21.4; Whitehead 1986, 71; Meyer 1993, 101, 110–112). The demotic remained constant within a citizen family, and was likely assigned on the basis of its residency in the late Archaic period: thus a man labelled as "from Koile" was so called because of his ancestor's residency in this deme, located within the city walls, southwest of the Acropolis (Traill 1975, Map 1). But in the ensuing centuries, this deme affiliation did not necessarily correspond to the family's place of residence or burial.

The increasing use of the demotic on gravestones and, by extension, the conspicuous display of citizen status, resulted to some degree from the growing exclusivity of citizenship in fifth-century BC Athens. After decades of growth in the citizen body through naturalization and intermarriage, these practices were brought under control by laws passed under Perikles in 451/0 BC. These laws limited citizenship to children borne of citizen males and women of citizen families (Aristotle, *Athenian Constitution* 26.4). The measures were irregularly enforced until the enactment of a second round of legislation at the end of the fifth century BC; by the fourth century BC, intermarriage carried severe penalties including fines for the Athenian partner, confiscation of the foreigner's property, and being sold into slavery ([Demosthenes] 59.16.124). Through the gradual limitation and then outright ban of intermarriage, a legitimate means of uniting citizen and non-citizen families was no longer available (Patterson 1988, 104–106).

Naturalization grants still occurred and, over time, adoption became more frequent, but the Periklean legislation, along with other measures, defined a citizen's exclusive rights and privileges. Not surprisingly, then, the definition of "foreigner" also became more codified. By the fourth century BC, foreigners who took up residence in Athens beyond a specified number of days – the exact number has not been preserved – were classified as metics (*metoikoi*), subject to special taxes, barred from owning land and excluded from most civic participation and priesthoods, although they could serve in certain military ranks (Whitehead 1977, 7–10, 82). Metics are often traceable within the epigraphic record because the "ethnic" adjective, designating their home city, stood in place of the citizen's demotic in the third position of the tripartite name (*e.g.* Eukarpos, son of Euporos, Milesian). The denial of certain rights, like land ownership, and the added burdens of taxes maintained the divisions between resident foreigners and the privileged citizen body in the legal and political realm, with ramifications for many individuals' lives. With the disappearance of intermarriage, the extent of intermingling among groups of differing legal statuses becomes even more difficult for scholars to determine from the extant sources.

The burial grounds, however, seem largely unaffected by such divisions. During the time of the more restrictive Classical citizenship laws, the Kerameikos excavations show no separation of non-citizens. The excavations cover a portion of the burial grounds which lined the roads leading out of the Dipylon and Sacred Gates on the northwest side of the city. The Sacred Way, which proceeds out the Sacred Gate towards Eleusis, has an offshoot, the so-called Street of the Tombs. At this split sits one of the most prominent Classical plots, belonging to the citizen family of Lysanias of Thorikos (Fig. 3.1, *no.* 18). The *peribolos* (grave precinct) and, indeed, this corner of the cemetery were dominated by the sculpted relief for Lysanias' son, the cavalryman Dexileos, killed in battle at Corinth in 394 BC (Knigge 1991, 111–113). The relief shows a triumphant horseman vanquishing an enemy, and it was prominently displayed at an angle to be most visible to those travelling along the road. Just west of Lysanias' precinct along the Street of the Tombs was located the precinct for a metic family from Herakleia, in which stood a tall rosette *stele* for Agathon and Sosikrates, the sons of Agathokles, a sculpted relief and several other markers (Fig. 3.1, *no.* 22; Knigge 1991, 121–122). Just around the corner from the Lysanias plot, on the south side, was another prominent burial spot for metics, in this case a family from Messene (Fig. 3.1, *no.* 21). The plot,

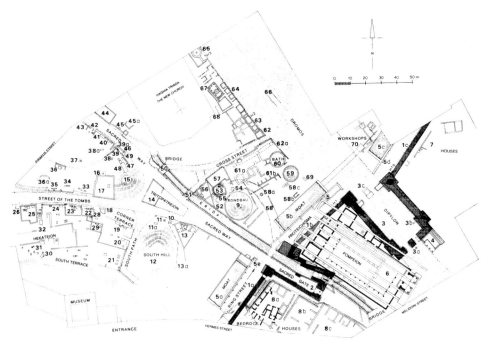

Figure 3.1 Plan of Kerameikos (after Knigge 1991, fig. 165).

in fact, contained over fifty burials, most of which seem not to have had associated grave markers, which suggests that perhaps other Messenians beyond the immediate family were buried here (Knigge 1991, 117–123; Closterman 2007, 638–640). While the situation outside of the Kerameikos is less well understood, the foreign population in the Classical era appears to have been concentrated in the urban demes and the area surrounding the ports, a pattern evident in later periods, as well. Indeed, the most ostentatious of Classical Athenian tombs – discovered outside the Long Walls, which extended from the city walls to Piraeus – was erected for Nikeratos and Polyxenos, a father and son from Istros, on the Black Sea. This podium tomb, erected in the latter half of the fourth century BC, is notable for its height (over eight meters), its elaborate sculpture (friezes and free-standing figures) and its polychromy; it has been reassembled in the Archaeological Museum of Piraeus (Allen 2003, 210–213).

There are sufficient examples, therefore, to show that no ban limited conspicuous displays by metics in the Classical Athenian burial grounds, even at a time when other privileges were restricted. In fact, many metic families buried their dead in highly conspicuous places and with elaborate tombs (Bergemann 1997, 146–148). For the fifth and fourth centuries BC, the Milesian evidence is slim, and the numbers of Milesian émigrés seem to have been small. Among the thousands of sculpted gravestones of the Classical period (see the index for Clairmont 1993, vol. V, 123), only four commemorate individuals with Milesian ethnics; in the fourth century BC, just a handful of other names are known from the non-sculpted works (Garland 2001, 64–65). One of the best preserved Milesian gravestones, for the family of Lamynthios, was found in Piraeus, the port area, where there was a concentration of foreign residents. The gravestone is a simple *stele* with a low, undecorated pediment and a shallow relief panel (Fig. 3.2; Athens, National Museum 906; Clairmont 1993, 525, *no.* 2.423; *IG* II² 9738). Two figures, both shown in profile, are carved within the panel: at left, a seated, bearded male shakes hands (the *dexiosis* gesture) with a smaller male figure at right. Although the break in the upper right corner of the gravestone has destroyed part of the inscription, the names have been easily restored. The layout and lettering indicate that the piece was first erected as a memorial for the Milesian Lamynthios and his son, Euboulides, whose names are carved above the sculpted scene. These names "label" the two figures shown in the relief panel. Later, the name of Lamynthios' wife, Ada, was added below the sculpted panel by a different letter-carver. On the monument, the ethnic label is prominently displayed in the second line of the inscription, but there seems to have been more concern to declare Lamynthios'

Figure 3.2 Classical funerary gravestone for the Milesian Lamynthios and family. Athens, National Museum 906 (National Archaeological Museum, Athens; copyright Hellenic Ministry of Culture/ Archaeological Receipts Fund).

role as patriarch of the family: he is named as the deceased, as the father and as the husband. Ada is identified only as a wife, without any patronymic.

The case of Aspasia, one of the most famous fifth-century BC personalities, shows that certain metics obtained special status or may have been able to bypass existing legislation. Born in Miletos to a prominent Milesian family, Aspasia moved to Athens and became the "de facto wife" of Perikles (Bicknell 1982, 243), the same man who sponsored the restrictive citizenship legislation. Aspasia bore a son, the younger Perikles, who

Figure 3.3 Roman period kioniskos of the Milesian Hermias. Athens, Agora Excavations I 5217 (American School of Classical Studies at Athens: Agora Excavations).

was ultimately granted citizenship despite his mother's foreign-born status (Bicknell 1982, 245). Moreover, Aspasia later married the citizen Lysikles, and bore another son. Although the tomb of Aspasia herself has never been found, a fourth-century BC gravestone from Piraeus seems to belong to her descendant, Aspasios, son of Aischines, of the deme Skambonidai (Athens, National Museum 1018; *IG* II² 7394; Bicknell 1982). In Aspasia's case, her personal connections allowed her children and their descendants entry into the citizen body.

With the implementation of sumptuary legislation under Demetrius of Phaleron (317–307 BC), the ostentatious displays of the late Classical cemeteries were checked. Cicero (*Laws* 2.26.66), our main source for the terms of the law, explains that it required the funeral take place before dawn, and specified that only a small column (*columella*, the Greek *kioniskos*) less than three cubits in height, a *mensa* (the Greek *trapeza*, a low table-like platform) or *labellum* (the form is uncertain) could be placed atop the mound of the grave. Of these three types of monuments, only the *kioniskoi* are preserved in large numbers. With the changing modes of commemoration, the burial grounds evolved, as the large, elaborate Classical monuments, including sculpted reliefs, rosette reliefs and *loutrophoroi* and *lekythoi* (stone water and oil vessels), all ceased to be produced. While older examples remained standing in some areas, new grave monuments were relatively plain. The simplicity of the columnar marker focused the viewer's attention on the inscription, since the carved letters of the name had become the primary means of decoration (Fig. 3.3). In select cases, sculptors were able to retain the idea of the Classical era markers by including relief carvings of small *loutrophoroi* and *lekythoi* on the *kioniskoi*. Just as the minimalism of the post-Demetrian markers highlighted the inscribed name, the legislation may have encouraged greater use by families of ephemeral tomb offerings such as flowers, wreaths, ribbons and vessels. A notable – and perhaps unexpected – result of the Demetrian legislation was that those families which had erected elaborate tomb markers before the legislation retained the primacy of their family's monuments within the sightlines of the cemetery; all subsequent additions to the cemeteries were smaller and less ornate (Small 1995, 161). Thus, the social or economic power of families from the later fourth century BC may have continued to shape the appearance of the cemetery for decades, if not longer.

Whether it is a by-product of the restriction on the most expensive monuments (and the growing availability of more affordable works), or a result of the area's changing demographics, the Hellenistic monuments became more uniform as the documented population grew increasingly diverse. At the same time, some of the burdens borne by the metic population began to ease, with the disappearance of the official metic status by the end of the third century BC (Niku 2007, 50–51). The inscriptions from the columnar markers, primarily gathered together in the *Inscriptiones Graecae* (*IG*), eloquently testify to the composition of the Athenian population, preserving the names of vast numbers of citizens and foreign residents from cities throughout mainland Greece, the islands and the Eastern Mediterranean. These inscriptions most clearly document the scale of the foreign communities in the Hellenistic era, and thus crystallize the "problem" of the Milesians, as they begin to appear in increasing numbers among the *kioniskoi*. But methodological difficulties remain, primarily because the *kioniskoi*, so prevalent in the Athenian cemeteries, have never been extensively studied. Often found in secondary use, they are dated almost exclusively on the form of the inscribed letters, a technique which is less reliable after the Classical period and outside official documents. Even with these methods, they are often difficult to date at all. For example, the columnar marker for the Milesian Hermias, son of Apollonios, was found in a modern context with no archaeological evidence to help with its dating (Fig. 3.3). With nothing diagnostic in the letter forms, the editors of the inscription simply assign the piece to the Roman period (Athens, Agora Excavations, I 5217; *IG* II² 9581; Bradeen 1974, 116, *no.* 572). Other pieces have been dated more narrowly to quarter- or to half-centuries.

While the *kioniskoi* continued to be manufactured through the Roman period, the sculpted funerary reliefs re-emerged in the first century BC after centuries of suppression. How, why and when the sculpted pieces started to be produced again is unclear; sporadic examples probably existed already by the late second century BC, with full-scale production restarting in the Augustan period (Moock 1998, 86). By 30 BC, Athens had been fully subsumed into the Roman Empire and it is perhaps no coincidence that, with this shift, the sculpted gravestone was deemed appropriate for funerary expression. Unfortunately, although we have Cicero's reference, in the first century BC, to the Demetrian legislation that halted production in the Classical period, there is no parallel source explaining when or how the laws ceased to be effective.

For scholars, the revived production of sculpted gravestones allows another dimension in analysing the population: with the use of both word and image, there can be a better understanding of Milesian self-presentation within the cemeteries of Athens and Attica. Nonetheless, even with the re-introduction of sculpted gravestones, *kioniskoi* continued to be popular. Their use may simply have been born out of familiarity, but the effective highlighting of the inscribed name and the column's evocation of archaic forms may also have contributed to their popularity (Houby-Nielsen 1998). What is striking is that from the first century BC until the slow demise of the genre in the early third century AD the Milesians were second only to Athenian citizens in their use of the sculpted gravestone. And while over one-hundred sculpted works preserve the names of Milesian dead, there is no corresponding representation from other foreign resident groups. For instance, the *Herakleiotai* from Herakleia Pontica, the second largest foreign group in Athens, can be found sporadically on the *kioniskoi* and plain *stelai* of the Roman period (*e.g.* Bradeen 1974, 103, *nos.* 476, 480; more generally, Mikalson 1998), but no sculpted gravestones commemorating their dead have yet to appear. Similarly, just a few examples of sculpted gravestones commemorate individuals from Antioch, Thrace and Rome, while a single example attests to residents from such locations as Thasos, Kythera, Rhodes and Byzantion (Moock 1998, 202).

The columnar markers, therefore, remained popular forms of commemoration for a cross-section of Athenian society, but the sculpted gravestones were less frequently used by foreign residents, at least those who recorded their city origins using the ethnic label. In the appearance of the sculpted gravestones, two trends are most conspicuous. First is the incorporation of many scenes popular on the Classical works, some of which certainly served as models for the sculptors in the late Hellenistic/Roman period workshops. Thus, the handshake motif seen on the Classical gravestone of Lamynthios (Fig. 3.2) is replicated on dozens of Roman period works, as was the "mistress and maid" scene in which a seated female is given a box by a standing servant figure. Such continuity in imagery created visible ties to Classical Athens and provided a visual lineage for the commemoration of these later individuals. The second trend, the use of frontal-facing standing figures, shows closer affiliations to developments elsewhere in the East; this frontality is also highly reminiscent of the funerary reliefs for Roman freedmen, which begin to be produced in Rome in the second quarter of the first century BC. Frontality appears infrequently on Classical Athenian gravestones, but in the Hellenistic period, the widespread usage of static standing figures was popularized in the Hellenistic Eastern gravestones. The types drew upon popular modes of representation for honorific statuary and by using these forms the deceased was endowed with many of the associated qualities (Zanker 1993; Moock 1998, 59). When these same figure types were re-imported into Attica for use on the Roman period gravestones, the associations with public statuary continued; this connection is expressed explicitly on a handful of *stelai* which show the deceased standing on a statue base (*e.g.*, Athens, Kerameikos P 1389, I 494; Moock 1998, 111, *no.* 147). Even without the base, the statue-like stance of many figures is evident, as on a second-century AD piece from Athens which commemorates a citizen male, Mousaios, and his sister, Amaryllis (Fig. 3.4; Athens, National Museum, 1233; *IG* II² 5568; Kaltsas 2002, 323–324, *no. 679*).

The gravestone of Mousaios and Amaryllis combines three of the most popular figure types in one scene: the man in the civic costume, the woman in the Isis costume, and the Large Herculaneum woman. These three types were part of a limited repertoire of popular images, along with the Small Herculaneum and the Pudicitia types for women, used in Attic funerary art of the Roman period. Each type was employed without any differentiation on the gravestones of all Athenian residents. Indeed, apart from the use of subsidiary servant figures shown in a smaller scale, there are no readily apparent attributes within the sculpted scenes to differentiate status among those commemorated,

Figure 3.4 Gravestone of Mousaios and Amaryllis, Flavian Period. Athens, National Museum 1233 (National Archaeological Museum, Athens; copyright Hellenic Ministry of Culture/Archaeological Receipts Fund).

which include citizens (with the demotic), foreign residents (with the ethnic) and the large number of dead commemorated with no identifying information beyond a single name and/or patronymic. Nor does there seem to have been a particular workshop or group of sculptors that was favoured by the Milesians; their sculpted gravestones range in size, style and in quality of carving. Given this lack of distinction, then, what was the purpose of the frequent use of the Milesian ethnic on the sculpted gravestone? Ought we to understand these monuments as completely separate or might they have created an aggregate effect of 'groupness' that *may* have been recognized by others in the community?

Certainly, there is tremendous variety among the sculpted gravestones of the Milesians despite the repetitive figure types and formulaic inscriptions. Their monuments date from the early period of production in the last decades of the first century BC to throughout the second century AD. Find-spots are clustered primarily in the urban areas,

Figure 3.5 Gravestone of the Milesian Nike, Augustan Period. Athens, National Museum 2558 (National Archaeological Museum, Athens; copyright Hellenic Ministry of Culture/ Archaeological Receipts Fund).

including many found re-used in the Agora excavations, clearly hailing from the cemeteries outside of the city walls; many more were found at Piraeus, while smaller groups can be found at Eleusis and at Rhamnous, near the northern border of Attica. In other words, the sculpted gravestones correlate with the other evidence which indicates that foreign communities tended to cluster in more densely populated areas. The extent to which this picture might change with increased archaeological exploration – mainly through rescue excavations – in the less populated areas of ancient Attica remains to be seen.

The corpus of Milesian gravestones also exhibits variations in size and quality, pointing towards a marked difference in the amount of money some families were able to expend on their grave monuments; presumably this expenditure suggests that there was a range of wealth within the community. One of the smallest of the Milesian tombstones is the half-meter high *stele* for Eukarpos and Philia, made of a thin slab of marble (just 4 cm thick) which carries relatively rough carvings and less precise lettering (Athens, National Museum 1195; *IG* II² 9836; Moock 1998, 122, *no.* 207). In contrast, an Augustan-period gravestone for a Milesian woman, Nike, stands more than one and a half meters in height and displays great wealth (Fig. 3.5; Athens, National Museum 2558; Moock 1998, 142–143, *no.* 302; Kaltsas 2002, 323, *no.* 678). Moreover, the *stele* highlights marriage patterns, a central issue in considering the relations between Milesians and other populations of Athens. The tall *stele* is topped by a pediment; the sculpted scene is placed within a niche framed by an arch. Two figures are depicted: a central standing female, shown in a frontal pose and, at left, a diminutive female servant in profile, who raises her arms up to the deceased. The main figure, commemorating Nike, is clothed in a long chiton topped by an intricately draped himation. This outer garment fully envelops the woman: it wraps tightly around her arms and torso and is drawn up over her head as a veil. Moreover, the crescent-shaped folds of her long mantle (the *himation*) descend from her breasts, and the *himation*'s diagonal line exposes her left hip in order to call attention to her mature female body (Zanker 1993, 224–225). Abundance and fertility were also emphasized through painted decoration in the pediment, where faint traces of an intricate vegetal pattern are still preserved. The inclusion of the small female servant places the deceased within a domestic context.

The sculpted relief commemorates Nike as an ideal wife: chaste, domestic and fertile. Above the scene, her name is carved in three lines on the flat plane of the *stele*: Νίκη Πολυκρίτου Μιλησία / Γναίου Ὀκταΐου Ἀλεξάνδρου / γυνή (*Nike, daughter of Polykritos, Milesian, wife of Gnaeus Octavius Alexandros; IG* II² 9803). The inscriptions are arranged so that the word wife (*gyne*) stands alone in the third line, centred directly above the head of the main figure. While the scene locates the woman strictly in a female space, the inscription positions Nike within the realm of her male relatives: her Milesian father and her Roman husband, Gnaeus Octavius Alexandros (Byrne 2003, 386). This use of the *gyne* label was not new and, in fact, was seen already on the Classical example for Ada, wife of the Milesian Lamynthios, above (Fig. 3.2). The usual pattern lists the woman's name, her patronymic and other information, followed by her husband's information in a grammatical construction with "wife" (*gyne* + genitive), which stands as the final word. This naming pattern on the columnar markers would have been especially useful, since the columns were almost always individual monuments commemorating a single deceased. Thus, such information was valuable in properly identifying the woman with her natal and marital families. But on the sculpted *stelai* of the Roman period, joint commemoration of husband and wife rendered this naming pattern unnecessary in many cases. Consequently on the sculpted pieces, the *gyne* with husband's name occurs in conjunction with female-oriented scenes, like Nike's.

A number of works, like that of Nike above, testify to the practice of intermarriage through the use of the *gyne* label. But many gravestones display marital ties in image alone, without any epigraphical specification; rather, the joint commemoration of an unrelated man and woman was sufficient to convey the institution of marriage, such as on the later first century AD gravestone of Sophia and Eukarpos (Fig. 3.6; Athens, National Museum, 1214; Moock 1998, 125, *no.* 221). The gravestone was crafted in the standard *naiskos* form, with a sculpted scene within architectural frame which supports a pediment. At left, a female figure stands in an Isis costume, holding the iconic attributes of the Isis cult: a *situla* (rattle) in her upraised right hand and a bucket for Nilotic water in her lowered left hand. At right, a male stands in a frontal pose, wearing the standard male costume of the period and carrying a scroll in his lowered left hand. Each figure is labelled with the tripartite name carved overhead: Σοφία Ἀγαπητοῦ ἐκ Κηραϊδῶν,

Figure 3.6 Gravestone of Sophia and the Milesian Eukarpos, second half of the first century AD. Athens, National Museum 1214 (National Archaeological Museum, Athens; copyright Hellenic Ministry of Culture/Archaeological Receipts Fund).

Εὔκαρπος Εὐπόρου Μειλήσιος (Sophia, daughter of Agapetos of the deme Keiriadai, and Eukarpos, son of Euporos, Milesian; *IG* II² 6311). The inscription shows clearly that this was an example of intermarriage, between a woman of a citizen family and a foreign resident. Such marriages begin to appear in the epigraphical record by the second century BC and possibly earlier. Only one inscription showing intermarriage is firmly dated to the third century BC, but the practice may have been legalized after the 220s BC (Niku 2007, 66–70). Intermarriage between Milesians and citizen families continues from the second century BC through the Roman period.

The Milesians seem to have been especially valued in these mixed marriages. As Vestergaard (2000, 102–103) points out, there is more evidence for Milesian participation in intermarriages between citizen and foreign residents than there is for any other of the foreign groups. While it is unlikely that Milesians as a community held a special legal status in Athens, many individuals or families may have been able to gain a social position and a level of wealth which rendered them more suitable for marriage with citizen families than other groups. It is nonetheless telling that among the marriages, Milesian women were far more frequently married to Athenian citizens than the reverse. With citizenship passed down through the male line, Athenian families may have been reluctant to contract a marriage, or simply to advertise one, that did not necessarily produce citizen children. Yet, economic or other considerations may, at times, have made it advantageous for an Athenian woman to marry a Milesian man, as on the *stele* of Eukarpos and Sophia above. But such cases are infrequent.

Just as the commemoration of women as wives allows us to consider the prestige of intermarriage for foreigners in late Hellenistic and Roman Athens, the portrayal of nude and athletic young men leads us to another shift in social interactions between the foreign and citizen populations. In the later second century BC, the doors of the ephebate (*ephebeia*) opened to foreign youths. The ephebate was a venerable Athenian institution, charged with the military preparedness of youths in their nineteenth-twentieth year (Aristotle, *Athenian Constitution* 42.3). For a time in the fourth century BC, all sons of Athenian citizen families participated in a two-year programme which included intensive training and garrison duty, subsidized by the state (Kennell 2006, ix–x). Soon, however, service was reduced to one year, and the financial burden increasingly fell to private citizens. By the late Hellenistic period, the strategic military need for the ephebate had diminished; philosophical and cultural pursuits took a greater role in the ephebe's education, but the military component remained strong, even through the Roman period. Even as the ephebate adapted to changing economic and political circumstances, the institution remained inextricably linked to the idea of the Athenian citizen. So it is a surprise when foreign names begin to appear in the lists of ephebes; the first well-dated inscription honours the ephebes of 123/2 BC (*IG* II² 1006 + 1031 + 2485; see *SEG* 38.114; Follet 1988, 29).

When the ephebate expanded its ranks, the Milesians quickly embraced the opportunity; likewise, youths from Rome and Cyprus also appear in measurable quantities in the first decades and the Cypriots continue to enrol their sons with regularity (Follet 1988, 28–29). Although some of the foreign youths may have been sent from the home cities to Athens for training, as argued by Vestergaard (2000, 100–102), it seems more likely that many foreign ephebes were the sons of families already living in Attica. Certainly, the correspondingly high visibility of Milesians in the funerary inscriptions suggests large numbers were residents in the region. The motivations behind the expansion of the ephebate are unknown, but by the later second century BC, circumstances in Athens were such that it was advantageous to non-citizens to enrol, and quite possibly, to gain citizenship through successful completion of the programme.

Even with the enrolment of non-citizen populations in the ephebate, ideals connected with the refinement of the mind and body of young Athenian citizen men continued to play a powerful role in the ideology of Roman Athens. The ephebe, a young, desirable man at the pinnacle of his physical beauty, was a rich subject for artistic expression as it had been for centuries. Extant sculpted reliefs which once stood in the Diogeneion, the main ephebic gymnasium, indicate that, as late as the third century AD, ephebes continued to be idealized as nude youths (Fig. 3.7; Athens, National Museum 1465; Kaltsas 2002, 335, *no.* 709). On this example, the ephebes honour the *kosmetes*, the magistrate in charge of the ephebate, with a sculpted relief inscribed with the names of the year's participating youths. At the top of work is a sculpted panel depicting two nude youths crowning the clothed man, who stands in a frontal position, wearing a civic costume. Each of the ephebes wears the *chlamys*, a short cloak, and holds a palm,

Figure 3.7 Ephebic relief, AD 212/213. Athens, National Museum 1465 (National Archaeological Museum, Athens; copyright Hellenic Ministry of Culture/Archaeological Receipts Fund).

the mark of victory. At the bottom of the relief, the ephebes are shown in boats, a reference to the mock naval battles and military training in which they engaged throughout their year (Newby 2005, 179–192).

The defining quality of the ephebe in sculpture was his nudity, off-set by a short cloak, a garment associated with the ephebe not only in sculpture, but also in literature and inscriptions (*e.g. Anthologia Palatina* 12.125). The nude youth, often shown with a cloak, can be found on over a dozen Roman-period gravestones. The nude male body provided a template onto which a variety of associations could be mapped (heroic, divine, athletic) and the nude youth appears in various forms on Classical gravestones, where the ephebe was often combined with the hunter – an association most eloquently articulated on the Ilissos Stele, dated to *c.* 330 BC (Athens, National Museum 869; Kaltsas 2002, 193, *no.* 382). By the Roman period, however, the connotations of the hunt have receded and the athletic and military associations of the ephebe are more prominently displayed. Even when hunters are shown on Roman-period gravestones, they tended to be clothed (*e.g.* Athens, National Museum 1192; Kaltsas 2002, 353, *no.* 747). The nude youths are frequently shown with weapons (*e.g.* Parlama and Stampolidis 2000, 205–206, *no.* 183), herms (*e.g.* Piraeus, Archaeological Museum 388; Moock 1998, 179, *no.* 499) or victory palms (*e.g.* Athens, National Museum 1662; Moock 1998, 138, *no.* 276).

Given the repetitive nature of the sculpted images, it is impossible to determine citizen or non-citizen status of the deceased on the basis of the costume or figure-type; as noted above, the scenes themselves provide no insight into the legal status of the deceased. Indeed, the Milesians adopt the nude youth imagery with the same enthusiasm as they employ other popular figure types. The nude youth figures used on both the Milesian and citizen gravestones are very close to those seen on the ephebic reliefs, with their combination of athletic and military attributes. Since the Milesians were certainly participating in the ephebate, it is not surprising to see this crossover, but the employment of the nude youth imagery need not have been restricted to actual ephebes.

Of the Milesian works employing the nude youth imagery, the most complex is the second century AD gravestone which commemorates Telesphoros (Fig. 3.8; Athens, National Museum 1775; *IG* II² 9898; Kaltsas 2002, 352–353, *no.* 745; Moock 1998, 138, *no.* 278). The small gravestone, which stands just over a half-meter tall, is rich with ornamentation. In the relief field, a nude youth wearing a cloak is shown leading his horse, as they walk to the right. The horse's raised foreleg and the three-quarter view of the male figure convey a sense of motion lacking on most Roman period gravestones. In the pediment, a dog chases a hare on the other side of a shield, moving towards the left. Thus both scenes work together to show a cycle of movement and pursuit, a

Figure 3.8 Gravestone of the Milesian Telesphoros, Hadrianic-Antonine periods. Athens, National Museum 1775 (National Archaeological Museum, Athens; copyright Hellenic Ministry of Culture/ Archaeological Receipts Fund).

striking motif given the stillness which typifies most funerary scenes. But the idea of motion is placed within a funerary context through the inscription, which runs from the horizontal cornice below the pediment onto the flat panel of the *stele*:

Τελεσφόρος Εὐκάρπου Μειλήσιος ἐτῶν κϛ΄.
Ἐξέφυγον πόλεμον δεινὸν καὶ ἦλθον ἄτρωτος,
μοῖραν δ᾽οὐκ εἴσχυσα φυγεῖν, ἀλλ᾽ ἐνθάδε κεῖμαι,
παῖδα λιπὼν μηνῶν δέκα ὀρφανόν, οἴμμοι

Telesphoros, son of Eukarpos, Milesian, twenty-six years old

> I escaped terrible war and set out unharmed;
> I was not strong enough to escape Fate, but here I lie
> Leaving a child of ten months an orphan. Woe is me.

Telesphoros' memorial incorporates nude youth imagery to highlight the poignancy of an untimely death.

Whether or not Telesphoros ever participated in the ephebate is unknown, but the employment of such an evocative figure necessarily refers back to the institution. In the visual culture of Athens, a young nude man *was* an ephebe and, here, through the slight disconnect between the age and status of the figure (young, heroic, ephebe) and the reality of the deceased's life (soldier, deceased, married with child), the artificiality of the image is underscored. Given the high numbers of Milesian participants in the institution known from the ephebic documents, it is not surprising to find the image of the nude youth used to commemorate the Milesian dead. In so doing, the families may have been able to lay claim to the prestige of this institution and its Athenian-ness and align themselves with the citizen population, into which, as we have already seen, they were also marrying.

Conclusion

There are multiple approaches which scholars have taken towards the funerary evidence of Athens. Even when, as is often the case, no burial data can enrich our understanding of extant monuments, the interplay between text and image on surviving works provides rich sources of data. While some of the laws and measures affecting the populations are preserved in written or epigraphical sources, in some cases, the funerary monuments themselves are key to understanding shifts in social policy. Here, for instance, two trends in the relations between citizens and non-citizens are played out within the funerary evidence: intermarriage and ephebic participation. In neither case do we have sufficient evidence from burials and tombs to apply to the question, but in each case, funerary art, despite its lack of context, nonetheless provides significant data in exploring the nature of the scholarly problem.

And yet, while we have looked at these two issues, what have we really learned about the people? Should we see them as individuals or can we see the roots of a larger community based on a shared "national" origin? To that end, the use of the ethnic continues to be the single most important clue. There was no legal requirement for Milesians to use the ethnic on their gravestones. Moreover, there may well have been individuals not from Miletos itself, but from other areas of surrounding Caria who claimed Miletos as a mother city because of its prestige and long-standing ties with Athens. Regardless of where people originated, what is important is how they sought to identify themselves in their new homeland. The use of the ethnic was a powerful means of gaining a sense of community, which was denied by the legislation of the Classical period. With the relaxation of the laws, there were still clearly limitations on what Milesians (and other foreigners) could and could not achieve. Some of their sons may have been able to gain citizenship through the ephebate, but given the number of names dating during the period following the ephebate's expansion, many members of the Milesian community could not or chose not to take this path, perhaps because of the involved expenses. Even for those who participated, there was a glass ceiling since foreign residents were still, by and large, disenfranchised within the Athenian state. And to that end, it is no surprise that, while intermarriage began to be practiced, such intermarriage more often than not involved Athenian men marrying foreign wives rather than the reverse.

Bibliography

Abbreviations
IG   *Inscriptiones Graecae.*
SEG   *Supplementum Epigraphicaum Graecum*

Ancient Sources
Aristotle. *Athenaion Politeia.* Ed. F. G. Kenyon, 1920. Oxford, Clarendon.
Cicero. *De Re Publica, De Legibus.* Trans. C. Walker Keyes, 1959. London, Heinemann and Cambridge, Mass., Harvard University Press.
Demosthenes. *Demosthenis Orationes.* Ed. W. Rennie, 1931. Oxford, Clarendon.

Allen, K. H. (2003) Becoming the Other. Attitudes and Practices at Attic Cemeteries. In C. Dougherty and L. Kurke (eds) *The Cultures within Ancient Greek Culture. Contact, Conflict, Collaboration*, 207–236. Cambridge, Cambridge University Press.
Bergemann, J. (1997) *Demos und Thanatos. Untersuchungen zum Wertsystem der Polis im Spiegel der attischen Grabreliefs des 4. Jahrhunderts v. Chr. und zur Funktion der gleichzeitigen Grabbauten.* Munich, Biering and Brinkmann.
Bicknell, P. (1982) Axiochos Alkibiadou, Aspasia and Aspasios. *L'Antiquité classique* 51, 240–250.
Bradeen, D. W. (1974) *Inscriptions. The Funerary Monuments. Athenian Agora*, 17. Princeton, American School of Classical Studies at Athens.
Byrne, S. G. (2003) *Roman Citizens of Athens. Studia Hellenistica*, 40. Leuven, Peeters.
Clairmont, C. (1993) *Classical Attic Tombstones.* Kilchberg, Switzerland, Akanthus.
Closterman, W. E. (2007) Family Ideology and Family History: The Function of Funerary Markers in Classical Attic Peribolos Tombs. *American Journal of Archaeology* 111, 633–652.
Follet, S. (1988) Éphèbes étrangers à Athènes: Romains, Milésiens, Chypriotes etc. *Cahiers du Centre d'Études Chypriotes* 9, 19–32.
Garland, R. (1982) A First Catalogue of Attic Peribolos Tombs. *The Annual of the British School at Athens* 77, 125–176.
Garland, R. (2001) *The Piraeus from the Fifth to the First Century BC.* 2nd edition. London, Duckworth.

Houby-Nielsen, S. (1998) Revival of Archaic Funerary Practices in the Hellenistic and Roman Kerameikos. *Proceedings of the Danish Institute at Athens* 2, 127–145.

Kaltsas, N. (2002) *Sculpture in the National Archaeological Museum, Athens*. Los Angeles, J. Paul Getty Museum.

Kennell, N. M. (2006) *Ephebeia. A Register of Greek Cities with Citizen Training Systems in the Hellenistic and Roman Periods*. *Nikephoros*, Beihefte 12. Hildesheim: Weidmann.

Knigge, U. (1991) *The Athenian Kerameikos. History- Monuments- Excavations*. Athens, Krene Editions.

Meyer, E. (1993) Epitaphs and Citizenship in Classical Athens. *Journal of Hellenic Studies* 113, 99–121.

Mikalson, J. D. (1998) The Heracleiotai of Athens. In G. Schmeling and J. D. Mikalson (eds) *Qui Miscuit Utile Dulci. Festschrift Essays for Paul Lachlan MacKendrick*, 253–263. Wauconda, Illinois, Bolchazy-Carducci Publishers.

Moock, D. von (1998) *Die figürlichen Grabstelen Attikas in der Kaiserzeit*. Mainz, von Zabern.

Newby, Z. (2005) *Greek Athletics in the Roman World*. Oxford, New York, Oxford University Press.

Niku, M. (2007) *The Official Status of the Foreign Residents in Athens, 322–120 B.C. Papers and Monographs of the Finnish Institute at Athens, 12*. Helsinki, Finnish Institute at Athens.

Osborne, M. J. and S. G. Byrne (1996) *The Foreign Residents of Athens. An Annex to the Lexicon of Greek Personal Names: Attica. Studia Hellenistica, 33*. Leuven, Peeters.

Parlama, L. and N. C. Stampolidis (2001) *Athens: The City Beneath the City. Antiquities from the Metropolitan Railway Excavations*. Athens, Goulandris Foundation and Museum of Cycladic Art.

Patterson, C. (1988) *Pericles' Citizenship Law of 451–50 BC*. (Reprint). Salem, New Hampshire, Ayer Company.

Small, D. B. (1995) Monuments, Laws, and Analysis: Combining Archaeology and Text in Ancient Athens. In D. B. Small (ed.) *Methods in the Mediterranean. Historical and Archaeological Views on Texts and Archaeology*, 143–174. Leiden, E.J. Brill.

Stroszeck, J. (1999) Kerameikosgrabung 1998. *Archäologischer Anzeiger*, 147–172.

Stroszeck, J. (2000) Kerameikosgrabung 1999. *Archäologischer Anzeiger*, 455–478

Traill, J. S. (1975) *The Political Organization of Attica: A Study of the Demes, Trittyes, and Phylai, and Their Representation in the Athenian Council*. *Hesperia Supplements*, 14. Princeton, American School of Classical Studies at Athens.

Vestergaard. T. (2000) Milesian Immigrants in Late Hellenistic and Roman Athens. In G. Oliver (ed.) *The Epigraphy of Death*, 81–109. Liverpool, Liverpool University Press.

Whitehead, D. (1977) *The Ideology of the Athenian Metic. Proceedings of the Cambridge Philological Society*, Supplementary volume 4. Cambridge, Cambridge Philosophical Society.

Whitehead, D. (1986) *The Demes of Attica 508/7- CA. 250 B.C. A Political and Social Study*. Princeton, Princeton University Press.

Zanker, P. (1993) The Hellenistic Grave Stelai from Smyrna: Identity and Self-image in the Polis. In A. Bulloch, *et al.* (eds) *Images and Ideologies. Self-definition in the Hellenistic World*, 212–230. Berkeley, University of California Press.

4

Memoria and *Damnatio Memoriae.* Preserving and erasing identities in Roman funerary commemoration

Maureen Carroll

Introduction

The Romans attached great importance to the preservation of memory. An investigation of the monuments they erected to ensure remembrance after death gives us profound insight into the ways in which texts and images were employed to convey information on peoples' lives. Funerary inscriptions, in particular, aided in defining a person's identity and in embedding that person in a well-defined social and cultural context. The naming of the deceased in an epitaph, as well as the dedicator of the memorial, commemorated both the dead and the relationship to family, friends, heirs and patrons that was publicly acknowledged in the inscription. Furthermore the text could be accompanied by a likeness of the deceased alone or with other individuals with whom bonds existed. It was considered important for the sake of memory to be able to contemplate portraits and statues of loved ones from time to time and to take consolation in sorrow from images of the departed. But what happened to the memory of the dead when their funerary monuments were neglected, vandalized, recycled or – much worse – if they were intentionally mutilated or had their texts and portraits erased and destroyed in order to condemn the dead to oblivion? These issues are explored in the following discussion.

Funerary monuments and the preservation of memory

The numerous tombs situated outside the walls of Romans settlements in many ways represented an extension of the public and private architecture inside the town. In an important sense the diversity present in the social life of the living community was reflected in the cemeteries filled over decades and centuries with monuments of various shapes and sizes that commemorated generations of the dead (Fig. 4.1). The physical appearance of funerary monuments and the texts written on them made it possible for

Figure 4.1 Some of the tombs lining the well-travelled road outside the Herculaneum Gate at Pompeii (photo, Author).

people to display and negotiate status, belonging, and social relations in the community. Ethnic and civic identities, education, public careers, professions, and complex family ties were expressed through these tombs and their commemorative inscriptions.

Whether located on the main roads in suburban and rural settings, or in the smaller, more intimate burial chambers on those thoroughfares, the tombs, their images, and their texts needed and addressed an audience (MacMullen 1982; Koortbojian 1996; Carroll 2006, 48–58). The funerary monument, according to Roman legal sources, was designed to preserve memory, and it was designed to reflect and be appropriate to the essence and standing (*substantia et dignitas*) of an individual or family (*Digest* 11.7.2.6; 35.1.27). The size and form of a monument, the building material, and the surrounding structures, gardens and other features of a burial plot were carefully chosen to convey a message and information about the person commemorated. Sextus Iulius Aquila from Gaul, for example, specified in his living will (*CIL* XIII.5708/*ILS* 8379) that "the finest imported marble" from Luna, modern Carrara, in Italy was to be employed in his tomb in Langres, and he also provided instructions for his statue and the landscaping around his tomb (Hatt 1951, 66–69; Lavagne 1987, 162–163). By leaving behind a lasting memorial, and especially by employing monumental writing to convey essential information on status and identity, one was thought to be able to "escape the grave" or "live on after death" (Horace, *Odes* 3.30.1–9; Petronius, *Satyricon* 71). The inscribed words on funerary monuments were clearly viewed as a mnemonic aid for future generations. It was *memoria*, a notion that encompassed fame and reputation in life and in death, that gave people the hope of some form of an afterlife (Varner 2001, 46).

Roman poets such as Naevius, Pacuvius (Aulus Gellius, *Attic Nights* 1.24.2–4), and Propertius (*Elegies* 2.1.71), and prolific authors such as Pliny the Younger (*Letters* 5.5), looked "forward to posterity" and trusted in their published works to "prolong their memories", but they were nevertheless greatly concerned about the survival of their name in a permanent medium such as inscribed stone. Pliny the Younger (*Letters* 9.19.3) knew that noble men would be famous for their deeds; nevertheless he held that "everyone who has done some great and memorable deed should…not only be excused but even praised if he wishes to ensure the immortality he has earned, and by the very words of his epitaph seeks to perpetuate the undying glory of his name." Recording something demonstrates a will to be remembered, and this attitude towards monumental writing and the perpetuation of memory persisted throughout the Roman period, even into the fifth century AD. In about AD 467, Sidonius Apollinaris learned of the desecration of his grandfather's funerary monument in Lyon, so he wrote to his nephew asking him to set things right (*Letters* 3.12.5). Most importantly, the nephew was to have the text Sidonius sent him carved in a new epitaph so that the memory of his grandfather would survive.

Inscriptions highlight the intimate connection between the written words and the spoken ones, and the epitaphs being read aloud enabled the words spoken at death and burial to survive for posterity (Carroll 2007/2008). A funerary inscription from Lyon (*CIL* XIII.2104) illustrates this point well: "Since the letters on the stone preserve my voice, it will live on through your voice when you read these lines" (Häusle 1980, 46–47). The dead, through their inscriptions, often asked the passer-by to call out his or her name. Perhaps the inscribed texts on funerary monuments replicated the calling out to the dead (*conclamatio*) in the primary ritual at death and burial, a phenomenon that in some ways was analogous to the written spells in Egyptian and Graeco-Roman texts that were considered an effective replication of the original, verbal rite (Frankfurter 1994, 195; Graf 1997, 131–133). *Vale* or *Salve* was called out three times to the deceased immediately after death and again when friends and family completed the funeral feast (*silicernium*) at the tomb and were taking their final leave of the dead nine days later. Anyone who passed a funerary monument and spoke the name of the deceased and the words *vale* or *salve* inscribed many epitaphs, therefore, repeated this ritual action and thereby conjured up the memory of an individual (*CIL* VI.32485/*ILS* 8123; *CIL* XIII.4280/*ILS* 8124). The permanent text on the stone also could preserve the words spoken at the funeral, the *laudatio funebris* (Crawford 1941/42; Flower 1996, 145–150). The inscribed *laudatio* on various funerary inscriptions (*CIL* VI.10230/ILS 8394; *CIL*

VI.37965) symbolically extended the funeral in time and allowed the eulogy to be recalled long after the spoken words had been forgotten.

The commemorative texts on tombs have in common that they all preserve the name of the deceased. The survival of one's name was of great importance in Roman society. For Pliny the Younger (*Letters* 5.8), at least, nothing affected him so strongly "as the desire of a lasting name." This sentiment is echoed in the epitaph (*CIL* VI.1343) of Marcus Antonius Antius Lupus, a military tribune put to death by the emperor Commodus. The inscription expressed the conviction that, despite his treatment by Commodus, his *name* would be a cause for perpetual celebration. Here we have the idea of *memoria* clearly meaning fame and posthumous reputation. Eloquent testimony to the importance of a name is found also in an epitaph (*CIL* XII.5276) of the early first century AD from Narbonne that reads: "…So that they have not died unknown with the loss of their name on foreign soil, the inscription on this little stone speaks of them."

The memory of the physical appearance of the deceased also could be secured by commissioning a permanent memorial bearing a likeness of one or more individuals. This might include images of illustrious family members who had died several years or even generations before, all of them part of an ancestor gallery. Particularly the leading noble families of Rome and the urban centres of the empire used portraiture to remind others of the great deeds of their ancestors, holding up these men as standards of behaviour for others. Funerary monuments with a portrait of the deceased or with multiple portraits of the family became fairly common amongst the middle and working classes as well as in the freedman sector of society in Italy and western Europe by the first century AD, the many variant combinations of portraits suggesting that the commissioner could specify what images should be carved. Some of these images may have been fashioned from death masks, although their actual survival is very rare (Pollini 2007). Approximately twenty death masks survive in various states of preservation. They have been found in Rome, Paris and Lyon, among other places, the masks having been taken from the faces of babies, children, youths and elderly men and women whose likeness in plaster, stone or bronze undoubtedly was to be fashioned from the casts of their faces (Fig. 4.2; Drerup 1980; Audin 1986, 85–86; Lasfargues 2000, 90–91; Coulon 2004, 164–165). Where we can identify the status of those individuals from whom facial casts were taken, we are not dealing with the aristocracy, suggesting that the custom of making portraits of members of the family using this technique had, by the first century AD at least, spread beyond the nobility.

Such portraits reminded the survivors of their loved ones, and they were a source of comfort in dealing with grief. Imagination and the act of reminiscence and recollection could keep a loved one alive in the heart and mind of the survivor. In the words of a foster-parent grieving for his child Asiatica in Careiae in northern Italy: "I often imagine your face to comfort myself" (*CIL* XI.3771). But fashioning an image in a permanent material could considerably extend the period of remembrance, as a text

commissioned by Cornelia
Galla from Ammaedara in
North Africa demonstrates.
The epitaph she had carved
for her dead husband tells
us that "she put up a marble
portrait of him…to keep the
memory of their earlier life
alive", adding that "his noble
face will comfort her eyes and
soul for a long time…." (*CIL*
VIII.434). One might even
engage in conversation with
the image (*simulacrum*) of a
loved one (Propertius, *Elegies*
4.11.83–84). Clearly there
was a very close relationship
between the image and the
person it depicted. It acted
as a focus of affection and
emotion, reminded the be-
holder of the character and
personality of that person,
and was an active prompt

Figure 4.2 Plaster death mask negative of an infant found in a Roman grave in Paris, Musée Carnavalet (photo, courtesy of SAEML Parisienne de Photographie).

in conjuring up memories that not only the immediate family might share in the present and the future. As we shall see below, because of its intimate connection with its prototype, the portrait could be an easy and effective target for anyone wishing to dishonour the person depicted and eradicate his memory by mutilating or removing his image.

Loss of memory and anonymity

Given the importance of the survival of one's name, burials without texts and without a record of the name of the departed raise questions about the preservation of memory. Many of the gravestones (*columellae*) in the approximate form of a stylised human torso and head from Pompeii and other Campanian towns bear no inscribed name at all (Kockel 1983; D'Ambrosio and De Caro 1983 and 1987; Magalhaes 1999; De' Spagnolis 2001). Nevertheless, each of these was positioned above an urn containing cremated human remains, and a lead or tile pipe for liquid offerings in memory of the deceased led directly to that cinerary urn buried in the ground (see Lepetz and

Figure 4.3 Group of columellae in the south-east cemetery of Pompeii in the Fondo Pacifico area (photo, Author).

van Andringa, this volume). If the *columellae* were anepigraphic, the individual burials within the plot remained anonymous, however many of these monuments were set up within the boundaries of a tomb or were connected with a built tomb marked by a titular inscription giving the owner's family name. But there are groups of *columellae* that stand on their own, sometimes arranged in a way to suggest that they are grouped to mark the burial places of a family or household (Fig. 4.3). These have no enclosure walls around them, and no inscription naming the owner of the plot of land on which they are clustered. Here probably only the immediate family and friends would know the identity of those buried in this constellation of stone markers.

There also were many who simply could not afford to have any permanent monument, and were therefore condemned to oblivion, either immediately or fairly quickly after interment. The evidence at a number of Roman sites suggests that burials often were completely anonymous, with no marker of any kind in any material. In the Isola Sacra cemetery between Rome's harbour towns of Ostia and Portus, several hundred burials of the second and third centuries have been found which consist of bodies interred in the soil, in terracotta sarcophagi or covered by terracotta tiles, or cremated and deposited in ceramic urns with the neck of a broken, uninscribed amphora visible above ground to mark the spot and to facilitate the pouring of libations to the dead (Calza 1940; Baldassare *et al.* 1996). This area was long thought to be the cemetery of the poor, although more recent research has shown that there was no particular area exclusively for poor burials at Isola Sacra or anywhere else in Italy (Graham 2006a and 2006b). The dead buried without a name suffered a loss of self and were forgotten. It was not the case that the poor were not interested in having their memory survive, rather unfortunate circumstance and the lack of even modest means resulted in anonymous burial and what Pliny the Younger (*Letters* 3.5.4) called "the injustice of oblivion."

Neglect was another factor affecting the preservation of memory. This could involve the oversight of the survivors to inscribe a text on a monument. Pliny the Younger (*Letters* 6.10.4–6) wrote about the neglected tomb of the consul Verginius Rufus in AD 106: "[The tomb] is still unfinished…I was filled with indignation and pity to think that nine years after Verginius' death his remaining ashes should still lie neglected without a name or inscription, although his glorious memory travels over the whole world. And yet he had made proper provision for recording in verse the immortal deed whereby his name lives forever…The dead [are] so easily forgotten that we ought to set up our own monuments and anticipate all the duties of our heirs." Here we should note that, although Pliny (*Letters* 2.1) was certain that Verginius would "continue to live forever" due to his glorious reputation, the lack of an inscription on his tomb was a serious hindrance to the perpetuation of that glory. The failure to complete a monument was another sign of neglect, and this pertains to sarcophagi in particular. Marble sarcophagi from the eastern Mediterranean and Italy often were manufactured with sections such as epitaph panels and portrait busts incomplete, so that the purchaser could have important personal details incorporated into the finished product. That this was not always carried out is apparent by the number of semi-finished and incomplete sarcophagi in the Roman world (Koch 1990, 64–65; Walker 1990, 83; Carroll 2006, 112–114). The memory of the person interred ultimately was lost.

The effects of rain, wind, fire and age on funerary monuments were only too apparent, and even the pyramids of ancient Egypt, according to Propertius (*Elegies* 3.2.19–26), were not considered "exempt from the ultimate decree of death", as they would eventually be destroyed or "collapse under the weight of the silent years." Martial (*Epigrams* 1.88) poked fun at elaborate marble tombs, writing that they were nothing more than "tottering masses of Parian stone, gifts of vain labour doomed to fall," and Ausonius (*Epitaphs* 32) lamented the fact that the decay of stone memorials and the disintegration of the letters carved on them meant that "death comes to the stones and the names on them." But until time and the elements took their toll, whenever that might be, even the poets knew that the best option people had in prolonging their lives in the memory of others was to erect a monument in permanent materials.

Intentional eradication of memory

Ultimately, no-one could stop the ravages of time, but something might at least be done about the violation and deliberate disturbance of the dead, the funerary monument, and the burial plot by vandals and usurpers. The fear of violation is clearly apparent in many epitaphs. Changes to the epitaph also were considered a punishable offence, as numerous surviving inscriptions reveal. Two epitaphs in Rome, for example, threaten legal and financial action against anyone who either effaced the names listed in the titular inscription or altered the epitaph in an attempt to introduce an unauthorised body into the tomb (*CIL* VI.22915; *CIL* VI.24799/*ILS* 8220).

The intentional, and perhaps vindictive, erasure of a name on a sepulchral inscription meant the eradication of the memory of that individual. *Damnatio memoriae*, the eradication after death of the name and image, and thus the memory, of an individual was a device occasionally used for hated emperors and deposed officials. Several instances of this public expression of disgrace are known. When Gnaeus Calpurnius Piso was accused of having poisoned Germanicus, adopted grandson of the emperor Augustus, and was condemned by the senate in AD 20 for treason, for example, his busts and statues were to be removed, his portrait mask was not to be displayed at any of the family's funerals or in the family's home, and his name was to be erased from all inscriptions. Both the *Annals* (3.17–18) of Tacitus and the surviving senatorial decree condemning Piso confirm this official and empire-wide condemnation of his memory (Flower 1996, 24–31; Griffin 1997; Potter 1998; Bodel 1999; Flower 2006, 132–138). In another case of *damnatio memoriae*, the images of the emperor Domitian, according to Suetonius (*Domitian* 23), were "torn down…and dashed upon the ground" after his death in AD 96, and the senators "passed a decree that his inscriptions should everywhere be erased, and all record of him obliterated." Many of Domitian's portraits may have been smashed, but some of them also were re-worked as likenesses of later emperors (Bergmann and Zanker 1981; Flower 2001).

The result of such systematically conducted condemnation in the public sphere furthermore can be seen on the arch of Septimius Severus and his family dedicated in AD 203 at the west end of the forum in Rome, although the driving force behind this *damnatio* is to be found within the imperial family itself (Brilliant 1967; Flower 2000, 65; Varner 2004, 156–199). After his father's death in AD 211, Caracalla and his brother Geta for a short time ruled the empire together, but in the same year Caracalla murdered his brother and officially damned his memory. Geta's name was erased on the monumental inscription of this arch in Rome (*CIL* VI.1033/*ILS* 425). Furthermore, on the arch dedicated in AD 204 to the Severan family by the moneychangers and merchants near the Forum Boarium in Rome we can see not only the erasure, possibly in AD 212, of the name and images of Geta, but also those of Caracalla's murdered wife Fulvia Plautilla and father-in-law Gaius Fulvius Plautianus (*CIL* VI.1035/*ILS* 426; Haynes and Hirst 1939, 17–27; Flower 2000, 65–66; Elsner 2003, 212–216; Elsner 2005, 94–95).

The destruction of the images of prominent and public individuals such as these was intended to render it impossible to remember the original after whom the likeness was fashioned (Gregory 1994, 97). On the other hand there are many inscriptions that were not so systematically deleted or re-inscribed, allowing the reader, with a bit of effort, to decipher the roughly erased name. In these cases, to quote Harriet Flower (2000, 59), "the erasure serves as a mark of shame rather than as a true attempt to remove the person from the record". Importantly there was a very close relationship between the image and the person depicted. In his study on mutilated images, Carl Nylander (1998, 238) suggested that, "image and prototype are to some extent 'identical', and what happens to the image somehow affects or reflects on the prototype". Thus, the frantic and vengeful destruction of the many golden statues of Domitian by the people of Rome, described by Pliny (*Panegyric* 52.4–5) was associated with the equivalent, if imagined, shedding of blood and the infliction of pain on the real Domitian.

From the middle of the first century AD and in many different regions within the empire, removing a name or an image to achieve the eradication of memory occasionally has its approximate equivalent in private funerary monuments, although disgrace, perhaps within the family or the community, is only one of the possible reasons for this measure. Even then, the shame and dishonour expressed did not have anything remotely like the political motivation and public impact that *damnatio memoriae* in official state contexts had, although in rare cases, as with the prominent and powerful family of the Licinii Crassi, the mutilation of private monuments could be politically motivated. Four members of this family had been executed since the reign of Claudius, primarily because of their threat to imperial power (Boschung 1986, 260–263, with a family tree; Rudich 1993, 202–203), and some kind of official revenge and memory eradication is apparent in the family's tomb chamber near the Porta Salaria in Rome (Kragelund *et al.* 2003; Van Keuren *et al.* 2003). Some of the funerary altars were smashed, and others, like that of Gaius Calpurnius Crassus Frugi Lucinianus, who was exiled under Nerva and executed by Hadrian, had their texts erased (Kragelund *et al.* 2003, Cat. 5, fig. 39; Van Keuren *et al.* 2003, fig. 17). Wiseman (2007, 423) suggests that this may have been done by decree of the Senate, the family then 'hiding' the monuments away in a modest underground chamber so that they could continue to pay their respects to their ancestors.

Usually, however, the erasure of texts and images on funerary monuments was not a political act, and there were many other reasons for erasing names in funerary inscriptions, such as changing personal circumstances, disinheritance, divorce, and legal conflicts. Often a reasonable case can be made for some of these as motivating factors, although we usually are ill informed as to the individual reasons for the disfigurement. Sometimes the erasure is so complete that we have no hope of reconstructing the original text and recognising a possible cause for the removal of a name (Fig. 4.4). In cases of official *damnatio memoriae* not only the name of the disgraced was erased or made illegible. As the ancient sources cited above make clear, images also were completely smashed or intentionally mutilated, particularly the face, an attempt symbolically to seek revenge on the dead body of the deposed person (Gregory 1994, 97). Studies thus far have tended to focus on the public and prominent cases of *damnatio memoriae*,

Figure 4.4 Funerary inscription of the Vennius family in Naples on which the last line of text with someone's name has been erased (photo, Author, courtesy of the Museo Archeologico Nazionale di Napoli).

particularly those in an imperial context. Harriet Flower, for example, was concerned in *The Art of Forgetting* with disgrace and oblivion in Roman political culture, as witnessed in officially imposed memory sanctions, but she rightly highlighted that the topic of private memory eradication warrants a study in its own right (Flower 2006, 11). In the following a selection of funerary monuments with erased text and mutilated images are discussed in the context of the intentional condemnation of memory on a private level.

On a funerary altar of the first century AD from Nîmes in southern Gaul are two registers of family portraits (Fig. 4.5; *CIL* XII.3564; Carroll 2006, 194). Such monuments often were commissioned on the occasion of the death of one member of the family, the other images having been fashioned at the same time to provide a memorial for the rest of the group when they eventually died. The top register commemorates the married couple Domitia Marituma(?) and Gnaeus Cornelius Tanais. On the lower panel a male relative is depicted, possibly the couple's son, Gnaeus Cornelius Urbanus, together with another person whose face and inscribed name have been almost completely chiselled away, leaving only a few traces visible upon close inspection. Since both rows of portraits are arranged in pairs, as images of married couples often were in contemporary relief sculpture in a funerary context, it is very possible that this erased portrait next to Gnaeus

Cornelius Urbanus was female and therefore depicted his wife. If this was the case, she must have fallen out of such favour with him (and his family) that the memory of her was intentionally destroyed by erasing her face and name. It is also possible, but less likely, that the two individuals on the bottom row were both children of Domitia Marituma and Gnaeus Cornelius Tanais, in which case the removed person was a brother or sister of Gnaeus Cornelius Urbanus. It is doubtful that the person whose memory was erased had already been buried in the tomb, for if he or she had been interred the place would have become sacrosanct – a *locus religiosus* – and mutilation of the memorial would have been condemned. In any case, the removal of a face and name from the monument is a clear indication of extreme conflict and tension within the family, and perhaps disgrace on some level, and we cannot rule out an element of revenge inherent in the eradication of the *memoria* of this individual. As in the destruction or mutilation of public portraits, the treatment of

Figure 4.5 Funerary altar of the Cornelii from Nîmes with one of originally four portraits (lower left) removed and the accompanying inscribed text erased (photo, Author, courtesy of the Musée Archéologique de Nîmes).

the image, to use Nylander's (1998, 238) words again, "reflects on the prototype". If imagery in a funerary context was charged with keeping the memory of the dead alive, destroying that imagery condemned the dead to oblivion.

It may appear a bit bold to claim that such bitterness could be the result of marital conflict and that it could manifest itself this way, but a large marble funerary altar with two inscriptions from the Via Flaminia in Rome should dispel all doubt that this kind of acrimony could result in the posthumous condemnation of memory. This altar was set up, as the epitaph on the front tells us, to Iunia Procula who died at the age of eight (*CIL* VI.20905; Kleiner 1987, Cat. No. 23, pl. 15.1–2; Evans Grubbs 2002; Ruffell 2003, 46–47). It was commissioned in the late first century AD by her father

M. Iunius Euphrosynus, for Iunia Procula, himself and the child's mother, the latter's name being completely erased some time later, apart from the final 'e' of her name. The woman's position in the family is nevertheless clear because she is named as wife and mother. Fortunately for us, the reasons for this *damnatio memoriae* are given in a second inscription added on the back of the monument at a later time by Euphrosynus. This tells us that the woman in question was Acte, his former slave whom he had freed in order to take her as his wife. He accuses her of poisoning, committing adultery and running off with the slaves, leaving him a broken, lonely man. Clearly in this case, the woman had not been buried on this site, so there was nothing prohibiting the defacement of the monument. Euphrosynus's hatred for Acte is so intense, that he curses her and wishes that she might be tortured, hanged by a rope, and her evil heart consumed by burning pitch. Curses such as this survive on tablets deposited in graves, subterranean contexts and in sanctuaries, the dead and the gods acting as powerful avengers invoked to mete out punishment (Gager 1992; Graf 1997; Johnston 1999). The original inscription recording the death of Iunia Procula and the familial relationship of those named in this text is entirely different in content and intent from the secondary and later inscription cursing Acte, indeed the original inscription suggests harmony in the marriage and common grief at the death of a beloved daughter. To disgrace her and condemn her to oblivion after her "crimes" against her husband, Acte's name had to be erased in the inscription that had been visible for some time on the front of the altar. This was the text that was seen and read by passers-by, and the conspicuous erasure of her name was the public aspect of her dishonour and her mark of shame. In accordance with Roman beliefs and superstitions, however, the eternal marks of infamy and shame (*stigmata aeterna*) were the words carved in stone in the other, later inscription. In order for Euphrosynus's curse to work, the condemned woman had to be named in this text designed specifically, like a curse tablet, to secure netherworldly and subterranean assistance in making her suffer. The potency of the curse was to be increased by the avenging spirit of Acte's dead daughter, an individual Graf (1997, 131) would refer to as an "infernal postman". For that reason the relationship between the deceased girl and her cursed mother is much closer than that between the cursed woman and the general viewer of the tomb. We could hardly wish for better and clearer testimony to the motivation in the private sphere for disgrace and revenge within the family, leading to the condemnation of the guilty party's memory.

A significant change in marital status and a serious rift in personal relations are clearly apparent from the epitaph of Lucius Fabius Faustus in Narbonne in southern Gaul. Faustus had a gravestone inscribed during his lifetime for himself and his wife, but the name of the wife subsequently was erased, leaving only the word 'wife' (*coniugi*) intact (Fig. 4.6; *CIL* XII.4795; Carroll 2006, 122–123). Perhaps the removal of her name was the result of a divorce. Whatever the reason, he clearly no longer wanted to be buried with her or have her name on his tomb, yet the spousal relationship with this dishonoured woman is clear, as is the marital and spousal relationship recorded on the funerary altar of

Iunia Procula cited above. These are particularly interesting cases, as they share salient features with cases of official *damnatio memoriae.* We can compare these private funerary inscriptions with an official dedication by the prefect of Egypt to the emperor Claudius and his family in AD 47/48 in Rome (*CIL* VI.918/*ILS* 210; Flower 2002, 61–62; Flower 2006, 185). This inscription was put up in hope "for the health of Tiberius Claudius Caesar Augustus Germanicus…. and of [Valeria Messalina Augusta] and of [their] children…." The text referring to Claudius and his children is intact, however the name of Valeria Messalina has been removed completely, as has the word 'their' in conjunction with the couple's children. It is, therefore, apparent to anyone reading the inscription that the

Figure 4.6 Funerary stele of a couple from Narbonne with the erasure of the wife's name (photo, courtesy of Musées de Narbonne, Jean Lepage).

person who has been shamed here is the wife of Claudius and the mother of his children. The relationship of the two is still recognizable, and perhaps it is this that highlighted her public disgrace as a result of her marital infidelity and alleged plans to stage a coup against her husband, both actions being described in detail by Suetonius (*Claudius* 26) and Tacitus (*Annals* 11.12, 26–38). As only the second woman ever at that time to have been the focus of senatorial memory sanctions (Flower 2006, 182–189), it was decreed that "her name and image should be removed from private and public places" (Tacitus, *Annals* 11.38). Although the erasure of a personal name was intended to negate that person's existence, in both this official and public erasure of a name and in the private cases of *damnatio memoriae* discussed earlier, the removal of text, but not all the text, meant that the condemned or shamed were eliminated in a highly visible way, but the chisel marks and scars left on the stone had the effect of removing these individuals without them being completely forgotten.

Damnatio memoriae in the funerary sphere could involve completely erasing the name of an individual, as it did in these cases, but it could also entail the replacement of the original name with a new one. This is illustrated by a stone commissioned in

Figure 4.7 Funerary monument of a couple from Narbonne with the name of the man's second wife re-carved over the erased name of his first wife (photo, courtesy of Musées de Narbonne, Jean Lepage).

the mid-first century AD by Gaius Livanius Auctus in Narbonne with an inscription and an image of a married couple (Fig. 4.7; *CIL* XII.3564; Carroll 2006, 193–194). This man may have divorced or spurned his wife during his lifetime, but he clearly remarried and wanted his second wife's name and his relationship with him remembered for posterity. To do this, he had the stonemason cut the stone slightly deeper where his first wife's name had been and write over the erasure with the name of his new spouse, Cornelia Maxima, daughter of Sextus. As a result, the memory of his first wife was banned from his monument and from public knowledge. Her elimination from the stone, however, is far less conspicuous than the other epitaphs leaving the scars of erasure, because a new name became the focus of attention.

Some decisive event in the private life of a Spanish family is also evident on a marble plaque from Emerita Augusta originally naming five owners of a tomb (*AE* 1983, 494). The head of the family, whose name was later erased, set up this tomb for himself and his family, the latter consisting of his wife Varia Avita, his father-in-law Publius Varius Ligur, his mother-in-law Licinia Thelis, and his brother-in-law Publius Varius Severus (Edmondson 2000, 323–324). Not only was the man's name conspicuously erased from the inscription, but also the clause that he erected the tomb for himself. Another name was later added to the inscription by a different letter-cutter, indicating that someone named Iulia Severa was admitted into this burial community. We do not know what this man did to distance himself from the others, but his wife and her family joined ranks to see him excluded from the tomb and his memory eradicated.

What lay behind the vindictive removal or severe mutilation of portraits on some funerary monuments probably will never be clear, but there are several examples of this kind of memory eradication. A marble altar of the early second century AD in Rome commemorating a family of six, four sons and their parents, has all the portrait heads chiselled away (Kleiner 1987, No. 77, pl. 43.1–4). The inscription naming them, however, survives, although it has been wilfully damaged and some letters are erased. Several *stelae* from Capua have been given similar treatment. One of them set up to commemorate a woman named Avillia has had the two portrait busts below the inscription so thoroughly carved down that only rough patches of chisel marks are left (Eckert 1988, Cat. No. 75, fig. 75; see also Cat. No. 56, fig. 56, Cat. No. 80, fig. 80, Cat. No. 86, fig. 86). Of course, this kind of damage could be interpreted as simple vandalism of a later period, but it is striking that a certain amount of work went into removing the portraits. One would expect the stones to be smashed and broken to pieces if there were other forces, such as Christian religious fervour, at work here.

There is much evidence for co-occupancy and co-ownership of tombs, particularly of the late Republican and early imperial house-tombs (*columbaria*), built partially or totally above ground to accommodate multiple cremation burials on the roads leading into Rome and its port towns (Toynbee 1971, 113–116, 130–143; von Hesberg 1992, 40–41, 76–80; Hope 1997; Caldelli and Ricci 1999; Heinzelmann 2000, 63–69). These *columbaria* often reached vast proportions, especially if they were built by the imperial family to house hundreds of urns containing the ashes of their numerous slaves and freedmen, many of them having served together in the same household when they were alive. Other *columbaria* contained numerous burial niches that were sold, given away, or traded freely (Nielsen 1996). Each niche generally accommodated two cinerary urns, and the epitaph panel below normally was divided into two sections, one per occupant of the niche. There are numerous examples, especially in the *columbarium* on the Via Appia belonging to the empress Livia, of epitaph panels with an erased text on them (Gregori and Mattei 1999, Nos. 1304, 1321, 1351, 1401). Sometimes the name is simply erased, other times one name is substituted for another. There is no certainty about the reason for these changes. Individual or multiple cinerary niches, however, were often purchased in advance of death and the inscriptions marking them cut with

Figure 4.8 Marble funerary inscription from a columbarium in Rome on which the name of the woman who commissioned it has been crudely erased (photo, courtesy of New York University).

the owner's name; if the niche was later sold to someone else perhaps the purchaser had the inscription panel altered to suit him. Equally, conflicts, friction and changes in marital status cannot be ruled out. Lucius Gellius Felix, for example, was commemorated by his wife in the second century AD with a marble panel in a *columbarium* outside Rome (Fig. 4.8; *CIL* VI.38417a). She commissioned the panel during her lifetime for Felix, herself and their offspring, but for some reason her name was erased in a very crude fashion, and lost for posterity, leaving only the words "to her husband…" and "for their children" intact. According to Flower (2006, 10–11), enough survives of the erased letters to reconstruct her name as Valeria Onomaste. It might be that Valeria Onomaste remarried and was buried elsewhere with a new husband, but it is also possible that the relationship between her and her children had deteriorated in some way. By leaving the text passage referring to the personal relationship between the couple untouched the erasure of her name perhaps drew more attention to tension between family members than would otherwise be the case if the reference to the woman's existence as a wife and mother had also been removed. And given that such crude scars on the stone actually drew attention to the erased name, as we have seen above, we might well wonder whether it was intentional that even her name should still be recognisable upon close scrutiny.

The Roman household consisted of the nuclear family, members of the extended family, and various dependents, both servile and freed. These individuals had close ties

Figure 4.9 Funerary inscription of an ivory merchant and his family and dependents in Rome showing the erasure and replacement of a name on the lower left (photo, Author).

with each other not only during their lives, but also in death. Numerous epitaphs make provision for the burial of dependents, without necessarily naming them individually, but others specify precisely who was allowed to be buried in the family tomb (*CIL* VI.16664/*ILS* 8262; *CIL* VI.16068; *CIL* VI.16286). By the same token, some epitaphs name those who were barred from the tomb; often this was a freedman or freedwoman of the family (*CIL* VI.11027; *CIL* VI.13732/*ILS* 8115; Thylander 1942, A168). Usually disloyalty, non-fulfillment of obligations or unspecified offences against the patron were given as grounds for this drastic action. Some alteration to the provision of a tomb for dependents of the family is evident on a titular inscription in Rome belonging to the ivory carver Publius Clodius Bromius, freedman of Aulus and Clodia, and his concubine Curiatia Ammia (Fig. 4.9). The inscription names five other household members: the couple's "pet" (a term usually referring to a slave child or adopted orphan), two of their joint freedmen and one of her freedwomen. Originally another person, certainly a freedman or freedwoman, had been named as an entitled occupant of the family tomb, but this name was erased to accommodate another freedman of Bromius. Whilst it is possible that the originally named individual simply sold his share in the tomb and was replaced by another buyer, it is equally possible that one of the family's dependents was ejected or barred from the burial community, and his memory, as a result of his name being deleted, was eradicated. On another inscription from the same city, the names of some members of the household of Aulus Vitellius Chryseros and his freedwoman wife Vitellia Prima were erased, ensuring that they were forgotten (*CIL* VI.29080). Two other individuals – Julia Rufina and Julius Helpidephoros – were taken into this burial group in their stead. Their names were inscribed over the erasure, thereby replacing one identity with another.

Slaves and freed slaves frequently were co-owners of a tomb or they were responsible for setting up a monument to each other, the master's household within which they had lived having become a family substitute of sorts. Illustrative of such emotional ties and family bonds is an epitaph in Rome set up by Aulus Memmius Urbanus to commemorate his fellow freedman Aulus Memmius Clarus: "…we were sold into slavery together, we were freed together from the same household, and no day could have separated us, apart from this fateful one" (*CIL* VI.22355a/*ILS* 8432). As one would expect, not all such co-operatives of freedmen were so harmonious, and conflicts within such groups might lead to permanent changes in existing epitaphs. A large inscription from Rome, for example, commemorated eight freedmen and freedwomen who had had a common master, Aulus Orcius, but four of those names were erased, indicating that something had happened for them to lose co-ownership of and be denied access to the tomb (Gregori 2003, No. 3272). The crudely erased sections of the inscription were not re-carved with new names, indicating that these four were not replaced by newcomers in the burial community. The situation is slightly different with an epitaph commemorating three individuals in Portus, none of them related by blood (Thylander 1942, A259). Their names were inscribed on a marble panel, but the name of one of them was later chiselled out, leaving only Marcus Ulpius Filetus and Titus Flavius Onesimus cited as designated owners. This third individual may have moved away and purchased a place in another tomb, or a dispute could have led to his expulsion. What is certain is that at some point another person named Marcus Vipsanius Felix was allowed burial in the tomb, and his name was added in smaller letters by a different hand at the bottom of the marble panel.

That legal disputes and conflicting issues of ownership could lead to corrections and erasures on funerary inscriptions is made clear by an inscription from the Puteoli region. In this text, we read of a quarrel over the ownership of a large plot of land with buildings that was settled by the sub-prefect of the Roman fleet at Misenum in the late second century (*CIL* X.3334). Publius Aelius Abascantus, a freedman of a certain Patulcius Diocles had bought the land from the latter's heirs, but then died, at which point the heirs of Patulcius Diocles attempted to take the land back from P. Aelius Rufinus, the son of the dead man, claiming that it should never have been sold to Rufinus in the first place because there were tombs of the Patulcii on it and it was therefore a *locus religiosus* and inalienable by law. On personal inspection of the land, the fleet sub-prefect, however, could not find the numerous and dispersed graves claimed by the heirs of Patulcius Diocles, and therefore ruled that the boundary stones marking the limits of the plot should have the names of the Patulcii on them

Figure 4.10 Funerary altar of the Rabirii on the Via Appia outside Rome. The third figure on the right and the inscription below have been re-cut from an earlier figure and text (photo, Author).

erased. One of these boundary stones containing a list of names has survived, and it demonstrates clearly that the family name Patulcius was indeed deleted following this ruling (*CIL* X.2826; Schrumpf 2006, 152–157). Without the second text explaining the situation, we would be left wondering why the names of so many individuals had been deleted from the boundary stone.

In official 'state' *damnatio memoriae* imperial portraits of those fallen from grace could be re-cut and re-used by their successors, as several studies of Roman portraiture have revealed (Bergmann and Zanker 1981; Pollini 1984). This alteration of a portrait was not uncommon in private sculpture too (Matheson 2000). The tomb of the Rabirii, a family of freedmen, offers a good opportunity to see the changes made to private portraiture in funerary commemoration even during the lifetime of the monument. This tomb of late first-century BC date on the Via Appia outside Rome was adorned with three portrait busts (*CIL* VI.2246; Kleiner 1977, No. 63; Eisner 1986, 47–48; Carroll 2006, 124–125). The inscription below the middle and left figure identifies Gaius Rabirius Hermodorus and Rabiria Demaris, both former slaves; the original identity of the man on the right will forever remain unknown, however, because the portrait later was re-worked and the accompanying inscription re-cut (Fig. 4.10). The head of the man was changed to depict a female one, although the male torso was left unaltered. The re-cut inscription below names this woman as Usia Prima, a priestess of Isis. There is no indication whatever of the circumstances leading to this complete replacement of identity.

Substituting old memories and creating new ones

The intentional removal of someone's identity from a funerary monument within a few years of its erection, possibly by someone else named in the inscription, is admittedly different from the alteration of texts decades later by completely unrelated individuals for the purpose of re-use. But whether decades or even centuries had expired, alterations to and erasures of texts for secondary use or recycling nonetheless negated the identity of the original monument owner, replacing the salient characteristics of that person with those of another. Even though it was forbidden by Roman law to let tombs deteriorate, funerary monuments were bound to fall into disrepair if there was no-one left to see to their upkeep. A legal ruling cited by Roman jurists on the permissibility of rebuilding a collapsed monument indicates that tombs were not always maintained in best shape (*Digest* 47.12.7). Pliny the Younger (*Letters* 10.68–69), as the governor of Bithynia, agreed to write a letter to the emperor Trajan as chief priest to ask permission on behalf of the province's citizens to relocate family graves and monuments that had fallen into disrepair. Epitaphs themselves mention the need for repairs to the tombs to which they were attached (*CIL* VI.13188; *CIL* VI.18079; *CIL* VI.18080).

Damaged or abandoned funerary monuments, however, often were not rebuilt, but were recycled for their material. Several recycled gravestones have been excavated, for example, in Areas A, B, D, E, F and G in the cemetery outside the Porta Nocera at Pompeii where *columellae* were made from reworked marble slabs, columns, cornices and other pieces of architectural material (D'Ambrosio and De Caro 1987, 216–219, 222–223, 225). Likewise marble inscriptions that had once adorned earlier tombs were simply turned over and reused in the last years of Pompeii, for example in Tomb 5OS and Tomb 17bOS, before the city was destroyed by Vesuvius in AD 79, with the old text partially intact but out of sight (D'Ambrosio and De Caro 1983). Tombs that had collapsed or been badly damaged in the devastating earthquake of AD 62 were probably quarried for these later tombs. By turning over and re-inscribing the once existing texts on such monuments, the ancient viewer had no insight into the identity of the person whose memory had been snuffed out. It is likely that those responsible for making secondary use of older material had no relationship whatever with the original proprietors; nothing vindictive is apparent, nor is there any hint of an attempt to shame or disgrace the individuals originally named.

Occasionally containers for the ashes and bones of the dead were re-used, presumably for the remains of someone else. This, at least, is what the erasure of an inscribed name on a marble cinerary urn of the first century AD in Rome suggests (Andreae 1995, Cat. No. 242a/XLI 2, pl. 412). The first two lines of this inscription have been erased, leaving only the third and last line of the inscription *suis et sibi*, for himself and his (family/dependents) intact. In those first lines was once the name of the person for whom the container was made, but by removing the name (and the ashes!) the altar was recycled and could be re-used by someone else. The new identity of the second owner was not inscribed.

The secondary use of funerary monuments even centuries later is well illustrated by a monument of a family from Ulcisia Castra, modern Szentendre, in Hungary. This grave stele adorned with portraits of the family was reused in the third century AD by Publius Aelius Crispinus, an officer of the second legion, by using the opposite face of the stone and turning it upside down (Maróti 2003, No. 36). The original inscription, naming the family and first owners of the stone, may have been cut off (the stone is broken here), thereby effectively removing any trace of the identity of these people. Perhaps the family originally commemorated here had died out, and their now neglected gravestone was acquired by Crispinus as convenient raw material for his own memorial. The same may have been the case with a gravestone of the first century AD from Walsheim in Germany (Fig. 4.11; Cüppers 1990, 659–660). Here the original inscription below the depiction of the deceased dining in the company of servants was erased two centuries later to commemorate Barbatius Silvester, a magistrate from Speyer on the Rhine who was mourned by his sons and grandson.

Figure 4.11 Grave stele of a soldier of the first century AD in Walsheim, re-used by another man with a new inscription in the third century (after Cüppers 1990, fig. 601, drawing, J. Willmott).

Although his name and personal details have not survived, it was almost certainly a soldier or veteran who was the owner of the original stone, as the funerary banquet was a motif commonly chosen by this sector of society on the Rhine frontier at that time (Carroll 2005). This man probably had no descendents or surviving family to care for and protect his tomb. The same is certainly the case for a soldier depicted in uniform on his gravestone of the first half of the first century AD from Cologne. His monument, recently recovered during work on the sewers of Cologne, originally stood in one of the cemeteries flanking the main extramural roads, but it was secondarily used in the second half of the fourth century as a paving stone to repair the main north-south street inside the city (Trier 2006, 63). Although the inscription on this stone does not survive, the soldier is recognizable as a legionary soldier and, therefore, he will have belonged to either the first or twentieth legions who in the 30s of the first century were redeployed to Bonn and Neuss (then Britain), taking whatever civilian dependents they had with them (Carroll and Fischer 2000; Carroll 2003, 24–26). None of these cases in Hungary or Germany is singular, and it is fairly common in the late Roman period to see funerary monuments recycled and the memories they originally helped to preserve lost forever (Kinney 1997; Coates-Stephens 2002; Carroll-Spillecke 1993, 382–384).

Conclusions

The texts and images on Roman funerary monuments demonstrate the will to be remembered and they give us insight into the routes taken to ensure the survival of memory. Commemorative rituals such as the offering of food and drink to the dead and the banquet at the tomb held by surviving friends and family were certainly a way of honouring and remembering the dead (Dunbabin 2003, 125–132; Graham 2005; Carroll 2006, 71–74). But the provision of an inscribed text on the tomb recording the names of the dead and details of their former lives, sometimes in combination with a visual image, contributed more permanently and more publicly towards the perception of keeping memory alive. They were, in fact, vehicles for remembrance. An inscription (*CIL* VI.37965) of the second century AD in Rome illustrates this point admirably. This inscription was set up for Allia Potestas, apparently by Allia's patron, whose common-law wife or concubine she was, and it reveals that this man attempted to preserve her memory in several ways (Gordon 1983, 145–149; Friggeri 2001, 168–169). He wore a bracelet inscribed with her name, and he specified that Allia's portrait was to be placed in his tomb. Here we have two of the essential prompts for triggering memory – the name and the physical image – but surprisingly he says that neither gave him much comfort. It was the funerary inscription itself that he regarded as the best vehicle to perpetuate her memory and tell the story of his grief. It is important here to note that the epitaph was designed to tell a story, not just about Allia but also about the man who loved her and was bereft at losing her. The epitaph declared that as long as the verses on the stone survived she would live on. In other words, a memorial afterlife was assured by the inscription that could be seen by anyone who cared to read it and reflect on it.

As Pliny the Elder (*Natural History* 2.154) said, the use of monumental writing meant that a longer life was given "to men's name and memory"; likewise images of individuals ensured that "the memory of men was immortalised." Clearly, in Roman thought, the recording of a name in a funerary inscription served as a transmitter of memory and a device by which the deceased could live on, at least symbolically. The provision of a visual image of the deceased served the same purpose. By neglecting, mutilating or erasing inscribed personal names and portraits on funerary monuments, the individual was symbolically dislodged and removed from his social and personal context and his memory obliterated. A person's hopes of continuing to live on after death by being remembered were intentionally and cruelly dashed.

Bibliography

Abbreviations
AE   *L'Année Epigraphique*
CIL   *Corpus Inscriptionum Latinarum.* Berlin, Berlin-Brandenburg Academy of Sciences and Humanities, 1863–
ILS   H. Dessau, *Inscriptiones Latinae Selectae.* Berlin, Weidmann, 1892–1916

Andreae, B. (ed.) (1995) *Bildkatalog der Skulpturen des Vatikanischen Museums. Museo Chiaramonti*. Berlin, Walter de Gruyter.
Audin, M. (1986) *Gens de Lugdunum*. Brussells, Collection Latomus.
Baldassare, I., Braqantini, I., Morselli, C. and Taglietti, F. (1996) *Necropoli di Porto. Isola Sacra*. Rome, Libreria dello Stato.
Bergmann, M. and Zanker, P. (1981) "*Damnatio Memoriae*". Umgearbeitete Nero- und Domitiansporträts. Zur Ikonographie der flavischen Kaiser und des Nerva. *Jahrbuch des Deutschen Archäologischen Instituts* 96, 317–412.
Bodel, J. (1999) Punishing Piso. *American Journal of Philology* 20, 43–63.
Boschung, D. (1986) Überlegungen zum Liciniergrab. *Jahrbuch des Deutschen Archaologischen Instituts* 101, 257–287.
Brilliant, R. (1967) *The Arch of Septimius Severus in the Roman Forum*. Rome, American Academy at Rome.
Caldelli, M. L. and Ricci, C. (1999) *Monumentum familiae Statiliorum. Un riesame* (*Libitina* 1). Rome, Edizioni Quasar.
Calza, G. (1940) *La necropoli del Porto di Roma nell'Isola Sacra*. Rome, Libreria dello Stato.
Carroll, M. (2003) The Genesis of Roman Towns on the lower Rhine. In P. Wilson (ed.) *The Archaeology of Roman Towns: Studies in Honour of Professor John S. Wacher*, 22–30. Oxford, Oxbow.
Carroll, M. (2005) Portraying opulence at the table in Roman Gaul and Germany, in M. Carroll, D. Hadley and H. Willmott (eds) *Consuming Passions. Dining from Antiquity to the Eighteenth Century*, 23–38. Stroud, Tempus.
Carroll, M. (2006) *Spirits of the Dead. Roman funerary commemoration in Western Europe*. Oxford, Oxford University Press.
Carroll, M. (2007/2008) '*Vox tua nempe mea est*'. Dialogues with the dead in Roman funerary commemoration. London, Accordia Research Papers 11, 2007/2008, 37–80.
Carroll, M. and Fischer, T. (2000) Archäologische Ausgrabungen 1995/96 im Standlager der römischen Flotte (*Classis Germanica*) in Köln-Marienburg. *Kölner Jahrbuch* 33, 519–568.
Carroll-Spillecke, M. (1993) Das römische Militärlager *Divitia*-Deutz in Köln-Deutz. *Kölner Jahrbuch* 26, 321–444.
Coates-Stephens, R. (2002) Epigraphy as *spolia*. The reuse of inscriptions in early Medieval buildings. *Papers of the British School at Rome* 70, 275–296.

Coulon, G. (2004) *L'enfant en Gaule romaine*. Paris, Éditions Errance.

Crawford, O. C. (1941/42) Laudatio Funebris. *Classical Journal* 37, 17–29.

Cüppers, H. (ed.) (1990) *Die Römer in Rheinland-Pfalz*. Stuttgart, Theiss Verlag.

D'Ambrosio, A. and De Caro, S. (1983) *Un Impegno per Pompei. Fotopiano e Documentazione della Necropoli di Porta Nocera*. Milan, Touring Club Italy.

D'Ambrosio, A. and De Caro, S. (1987) La necropoli di Porta Nocera. Campagna di scavo 1983. In H. von Hesberg and P. Zanker (eds) *Römische Gräberstraßen. Selbstdarstellung-Status-Standard*, 199–228. Munich, Verlag der Bayerischen Akademie der Wissenschaften.

De' Spagnolis, M. (2001) Costumi funerari romani nella necropoli monumentale romana di Pizzone a Nocera Superiore. In M. Heinzelmann, J. Ortalli, P. Fasold and M. Witteyer (eds) *Römischer Bestattungsbrauch und Beigabensitten in Rom, Norditalien und den Nordwestprovinzen von der späten Republik bis in die Kaiserzeit* (Culto dei morti e costumi funerari romani. Roma, Italia settentrionale e province nord-occidentali dalla tarda Repubblica all'età imperiale), 169–178. Wiesbaden, Dr. Ludwig Reichert Verlag.

Drerup, H. 1980. Totenmaske und Ahnenbild bei den Römern. *Römische Mitteilungen* 87, 81–129.

Dunbabin, K. M. D. (2003) *The Roman Banquet. Images of Conviviality*. Cambridge, Cambridge University Press.

Edmondson, J. (2000) Conmemoración funeraria y relaciones familiares en Augusta Emerita. In J.-G. Gorges and T. Nogales Basarrate (eds) *Sociedad y cultura en Lusitania romana. IV Mesa Redonda Internacional*, 299–327. Mérida, Junta de Extremadura.

Eisner, M. (1986) *Zur Typologie der Grabbauten im Suburbium Roms*. Mainz, Philipp von Zabern.

Elsner, J. (2003) Iconoclasm and the preservation of memory. In R. Nelson and M. Olin (eds) *Monuments and memory, made and unmade*, 209–232. Chicago, University of Chicago Press.

Elsner, J. (2005) Sacrifice and narrative on the Arch of the Argentarii at Rome. *Journal of Roman Archaeology* 18, 83–98.

Evans Grubbs, J. (2002) *Stigmata Aeterna*: A Husband's Curse. In J. F. Miller, C. Damon and K. S. Myers (eds) *Vertis in usum. Studies in honor of Edward Courtney*, 230–242. Munich, K. G. Saur.

Flower, H. I. (1996) *Ancestor Masks and Aristocratic Power in Roman Culture*. Oxford, Oxford University Press.

Flower, H. I. (2000) *Damnatio memoriae* and epigraphy. In E. R. Varner (ed.), *From Caligula to Constantine. Tyranny and transformation in Roman portraiture*, 58–69. Atlanta, Michael C. Carlos Museum.

Flower, H. I. (2001) A tale of two monuments: Domitian, Trajan and Some Praetorians at Puteoli (*AE* 1973, 137). *American Journal of Archaeology* 105, 625–648.

Flower, H. I. (2006) *The Art of Forgetting. Disgrace and Oblivion in Roman Political Culture*. Chapel Hill, University of North Carolina Press.

Frankfurter, D. (1994) The magic of writing and the writing of magic. The power of the word in Egyptian and Greek traditions. *Helios* 21, 189–221.

Friggeri, R. (2001) *The Epigraphic Collection of the Museo Nazionale Romano at the Baths of Diocletian*. Rome, Electa.

Gager, J. G. (1992) *Curse Tablets and Binding Spells from the Ancient World*. Oxford, Oxford University Press.

Gordon, A. E. (1983) *Illustrated Introduction to Latin Epigraphy*. Berkeley, University of California Press.

Graf, F. (1997) *Magic in the ancient world.* Cambridge (Mass.), Harvard University Press.

Graham, E.-J. (2005) Dining al fresco with the living and the dead in Roman Italy. In M. Carroll, D. Hadley and H. Willmott (eds) *Consuming Passions. Dining from Antiquity to the Eighteenth Century*, 49–65. Stroud, Tempus.

Graham, E.-J. (2006a) Discarding the destitute: Ancient and modern attitudes towards burial practices and memory preservation amongst the lower classes of Rome. In B. Croxford, H. Goodchild, J. Lucas and N. Ray (eds) *TRAC 2005. Proceedings of the Fifteenth Annual Theoretical Roman Archaeology Conference, Birmingham 2005*, 57–72. Oxford, Oxbow.

Graham, E.-J. (2006b) *Death, disposal and the destitute. The burial of the urban poor in Italy in the late Republic and early Empire*, BAR International Series 1565. Oxford, Archaeopress.

Gregori, G. L. (2003) *Supplementa Italica Imagines. Suppplementi fotografici ai volumi italiani del CIL Roma (CIL VI.) 2. Antiquarium comunale del Celio.* Rome, Edizioni Quasar.

Gregori, G. L. and Mattei, M. (1999) *Roma (CIL VI) 1: Musei Capitolini. Supplementa Italica-Imagines.* Rome, Edizioni Quasar.

Gregory, A. (1994) 'Powerful images': responses to portraits and the political uses of images in Rome. *Journal of Roman Archaeology* 7, 80–99.

Griffin, M. (1997) The Senate's Story. *Journal of Roman Studies* 87, 249–263.

Häusle, H. (1980) *Das Denkmal als Garant des Nachruhms. Beiträge zur Geschichte und Thematik eines Motivs in lateinischen Inschriften.* Munich, C.H. Beck'sche Verlagsbuchhandlung.

Hatt, J. J. (1951) *La Tombe Gallo-Romaine.* Paris, Presses Universitaires de France.

Haynes, D. and Hirst, P. (1939) *Porta Argentariorum.* London, MacMillan.

Heinzelmann, M. (2000) *Die Nekropolen von Ostia. Untersuchungen zu den Gräberstraßen vor der Porta Romana und an der Via Laurentina.* Munich, Verlag Dr. Friedrich Pfeil.

Hope, V. M. (1997) A roof over the dead: Communal tombs and family structure. In R. Laurence and A. Wallace-Hadrill (eds) *Domestic Space in the Roman World. Pompeii and Beyond,* 69–88. Portsmouth, Journal of Roman Archaeology.

Johnston, S. I. (1999) Songs for the ghosts. Magical solutions to deadly problems. In D. R. Jordan, H. Montgomery and E. Thomassen (eds) *The World of ancient Magic. Papers from the First International Samson Eitrem Seminar at the Norwegian Institute at Athens, 4–8 May, 1997,* 83–102. Bergen, Paul Åströms Förlag.

Kinney, D. (1997) *Spolia.* Damnatio and *Renovatio Memoriae. Memoirs of the American Academy in Rome* 42, 117–148.

Kleiner, D. E. E. (1977) *Roman Group Portraiture: The Funerary Reliefs of the Late Republic and Early Empire.* New York, Garland.

Kleiner, D. E. E. (1987) *Roman Imperial Funerary Altars with Portraits.* Rome, Giorgio Bretschneider Editore.

Koch, G. (1990) Ein dekorativer Sarkophag mit Scherengitter in der Henry E. Huntington Library and Art Gallery, San Marino. In M. True and G. Koch (eds) *Roman Funerary Monuments in the J. Paul Getty Museum*, Vol. 1, 59–70. Malibu, J. Paul Getty Museum.

Kockel, V. (1983) *Die Grabbauten vor dem Herkulaner Tor in Pompeji.* Mainz, Verlag Philipp von Zabern.

Koortbojian, M. (1996) *In commemorationem mortuorum*: Text and image along the "streets of the tombs". In J. Elsner (ed.) *Art and Text in Roman Culture*, 210–233. Cambridge, Cambridge University Press.

Kragelund, P., Moltesen, M. and Stubbe Østergard, J. (2003) *The Licinian Tomb. Fact or Fiction?* Copenhagen, Ny Carlsberg Glyptothek.

Lasfargues, J. (2000) *Objects that recount World History. Lugdunum.* Lyon, Conseil General du Rhône.

Lavagne, H. (1987) Le tombeau, mémoire du mort. In F. Hinard (ed.) *La mort, les morts et l'au-delà dans le monde romain. Actes du Colloque de Caen 1985*, 159–166. Caen, Université de Caen.

MacMullen, R. (1982) The epigraphic habit in the Roman Empire. *American Journal of Philology* 103, 233–246.

Magalhaes, M. M. (1999) Le inscrizioni e l'area funeraria dei *Q. e C. Poppaei* a *Stabiae* (loc. Calcarella di Privati). *Rivista di Studi Pompeiani* 10, 224–235.

Maróti, E. (2003) *Die römischen Steindenkmäler von Szentendre, Ulcisia Castra*. Szentendre, Museen des Komitats Pest.

Matheson, S. B. (2000) The private sector: Reworked portraits outside the Imperial circle. In E. R. Varner (ed.) *From Caligula to Constantine. Tyranny and transformation in Roman portraiture*, 70–80. Atlanta, Michael C. Carlos Museum.

Nielsen, H. S. (1996) The physical context of Roman epitaphs and the structure of "the Roman family". *Analecta Romana Instituti Danici* 23, 35–60.

Nylander, C. (1998) The mutilated image: "We" and "They" in History – and Prehistory? In L. Larsson and B. Stjernquist (eds) *The World-View of Prehistoric Man*, 235–252. Lund, Coronet Books.

Pollini, J. (1984) *Damnatio memoriae* in stone: two portraits of Nero recut to Vespasian in American museums. *American Journal of Archaeology* 88, 547–555.

Pollini, J. (2007) Ritualizing Death in Republican Rome: Memory, Religion, Class Struggle, and the Wax Ancestral Mask Tradition's Origin and Influence on Veristic Portraiture. In N. Laneri (ed.) *Performing Death. Social Analyses of Funerary Traditions in the Ancient Near East and Mediterranean*, 237–285.Chicago, The Oriental Institute.

Potter, D. S. (1998) Senatus consultum de Cn. Pisone. *Journal of Roman Archaeology* 11, 437–457.

Rudich, V. (1993) *Political Dissidence under Nero. The Price of Dissimulation*. London, Routledge.

Ruffell, I. A. (2003) Beyond Satire: Horace, Popular Invective, and the Segregation of Literature. *Journal of Roman Studies* 93, 35–65

Schrumpf, S. (2006) *Bestattung und Bestattungwswesen im Römischen Reich*. Bonn, V & R Unipress.

Thylander, H. (1952) *Inscriptions du Port d'Ostie*. Lund, C.W.K. Gleerup.

Toynbee, J. M. C. (1971) *Death and Burial in the Roman World*. Baltimore, Johns Hopkins University Press.

Trier, M. (2006) Spurensuche in der Kölner Unterwelt. *Archäologie in Deutschland* 4, 62–63.

Van Keuren, F. *et al.* (2003) Unpublished Documents Shed New Light on the Licinian Tomb, Discovered in 1884–1885, Rome. *Memoirs of the American Academy in Rome* 48, 53–140.

Varner, E. R. (2001) Punishment after death: mutilation of images and corpse abuse in ancient Rome. *Mortality* 6, 45–64.

Varner, E. R. (2004) *Mutilation and Transformation, Damnatio Memoriae and Roman Imperial Portraiture*. Leiden, Brill.

Von Hesberg, H. (1992) *Römische Grabbauten*. Darmstadt, Wissenschaftliche Buchgesellschaft.

Walker, S. (1990) The sarcophagus of Maconiana Severiana, in M. True and G. Koch (eds) *Roman Funerary Monuments in the J. Paul Getty Museum*, Vol. 1, 83–94. Malibu, J. Paul Getty Museum.

Wiseman, T. P. (2007). Names Remembered, Names Suppressed. *Journal of Roman Archaeology* 20, 421–428.

From fragments to ancestors: Re-defining the role of *os resectum* in rituals of purification and commemoration in Republican Rome

Emma-Jayne Graham

Roman ways of remembering

Recent studies of commemorative practice have highlighted the ways in which such activity was harnessed by all members of the ancient urban community for a variety of ends. Funerary monuments, in particular, have formed the focus of many discussions of the way in which the remembrance of the deceased provided an opportunity for both the living and the dead to assert, (re)negotiate and create a desirable social persona (see for example, Carroll 2006; D'Ambra 2002; George 2005; and Hope 1998, 2000b, 2001 and 2003). It is important to remember, however, that these monuments were not only about public displays of identity or the assertion of individual status; they were also closely linked to strong emotional and religious forces which influenced the desire of the ancients to be *remembered* by the living. Ancient legal texts define a monument as "something which exists to preserve a memory" (*Digest* 11.7.2.6), and Varro (*On the Latin Language* 6.49) informs us that the word 'monument' derives from the Latin verb *monere* – "to remind". This desire not to be consigned to oblivion was as influential as the wish to use the commemorative process to promote one's status and identity, and commemoration was intimately entwined with religious fears about the existence of the afterlife – if nothing awaited the soul it was necessary to ensure that the deceased maintained some form of existence in the world of the living. The funerary monument itself was essential to this process. Placed in a highly public location, designed to be eye-catching and to communicate biographical information about the identity and beliefs of the deceased, the funerary monument served to bring the dead to life in the consciousness of the living. Creating a 'memory', real or artificial, in the minds of relatives and strangers allowed the deceased to achieve a degree of immortality and to prolong their existence amongst the living, at the same time as making public statements about their personal relationships and sense of identity.

Nevertheless, as Williams (2003, 7) has pointed out, "monumentality is certainly not a pre-requisite for remembrance," and the creation of a funerary monument was not the only way in which this process could occur. In order to fully comprehend the commemorative activities of the ancient community it is essential to investigate other ways in which the dead could be remembered and their existence celebrated. This has been explored more generally by Connerton (1989), whose model of 'inscribing' and 'incorporating' practices of remembrance is particularly relevant to this discussion. Connerton posits two different methods by which the dead might be recalled, remembered and celebrated. On one hand, 'inscribing practices', involves the creation of a 'permanent' device (in this case a funerary monument or tomb) that "traps and holds information long after the human organism has stopped informing" (Connerton 1989, 72–73). Hence a monument bearing either an epitaph containing biographical information, a portrait bust, or occupational relief depicting that individual at work or the tools of their trade, which was capable of continuously communicating this information to the living, can be defined as an 'inscribing' form of remembrance. On the other hand, Connerton (1989, 72–73) defines the active participation of surviving mourners in commemorative activities, ceremonies and bodily practices as 'incorporating practices'. He suggests that repeated ritual activity allowed the living to recall the dead and to celebrate their memory, without the need for a 'permanent' memorial. In a Roman context such ritual activities can be seen to include those which immediately surrounded the death of an individual – the *conclamatio* in which the dead was called repeatedly by name provides a good example, as does the funeral itself, which included a procession through the streets accompanied by the loud wailing of mourners and music. At the pyre or grave other rituals were also performed, including the consuming of a funerary feast; an activity that was repeated nine days later on the *novemdialis* and at other specific times during the year. During all of these activities the dead were actively recalled through the actions of the living, something that was repeated when they performed the same rites for other deceased individuals.

Although 'incorporating practices' of remembrance probably held particular significance for the poorer members of the urban community who lacked the necessary economic resources to create a lasting, or personalised, funerary monument (Graham 2006a and 2006b), they played an equally significant role in the remembrance processes of other social groups. In fact, close scrutiny reveals that the list of Roman funerary rituals that can be considered to involve 'incorporating' practices of remembrance is long and complex, although often these mnemonically charged activities have not been considered as such. An example of one such mortuary ritual is the rather obscure rite of *os resectum* (cut bone). Its place within funerary activities has rarely been questioned since archaeological evidence for it was recovered during the early eighteenth century, but a reassessment of this rite as an incorporating act of remembrance suggests that it may have played a far more significant role in ancient rituals of purification and commemoration than has been previously thought. This paper will highlight some of the problems with existing understandings of *os resectum* and offer a re-interpretation of the ritual and its place within the funerary process that allows us to appreciate its significant role in both purification rituals and the remembrance process.

Exploring os resectum

The custom of *os resectum* is mentioned briefly in ancient literature by three well-known authors: Cicero, Festus and Varro. They fail, however, to provide a consensus of opinion regarding the precise meaning and nature of the rite, and do not provide clear details about how it may have been performed. Despite this, it is largely around these descriptions that our current understanding of *os resectum* has been shaped and it is therefore essential that any discussion of the process begin with them. Festus (*On the Meaning of Words* 62) provides the briefest but most specific reference to *os resectum* and states simply that a corpse may only be legitimately burned once a finger has been cut off and set aside. Cicero (*Laws* 2.22.55) unfortunately elaborates little on this statement in his discussion of burial laws and practices, including it amongst a list of other activities that he feels he has no need to describe:

> It is unnecessary for me to explain when the period of family mourning is ended, what sort of sacrifice of wethers is offered to the Lar, in what manner the severed bone (*os resectum*) is buried in the earth, what are the rules in regard to the obligation to sacrifice a sow, or when the grave first takes on the character of a grave and comes under the protection of religion.

Varro (*On the Latin Language*, 5.23), however, provides a few more tantalising details about the practice, when he tells us that:

> … if on the burial mound of a Roman who has been burned on the pyre clods are not thrown, or if a bone of the dead man has been kept out for the ceremony of purifying the household, the household remains in mourning; in the latter case, until in the purification the bone is covered with soil …

The rather imprecise accounts provided by Cicero, Festus and Varro have led to several interpretations of this custom, the most popular of which centres on the importance that was attached to proper religious burial. Roman beliefs about the afterlife and the fate of the soul were notoriously nebulous and because beliefs largely came down to a matter of personal conviction people often tended to hedge their bets. Even Epicurus, who strongly denied the existence of the afterlife and taught that the soul was destroyed at the moment of death, provided in his will for offerings in perpetuity to his father, mother, and brother (Nock 1972, 286). Such uncertainty naturally led to fears about what the living and the dead might expect if the soul did continue some form of existence subsequent to death and this was reflected in a widespread belief that they were capable of affecting one another's existence (Toynbee 1971, 34). In particular it was feared that the souls of the dead would terrorise the living unless they received proper funerary rites and a religious burial that provided their remains with a covering of earth. Horace alludes directly to this practice of proper burial in one of his *Odes* (1. 28) during which the corpse of a sailor pleads with a passer-by to help his soul to find rest:

> What! Shrink you not from crime whose punishment falls on your innocent children? It
> may hap imperious Fate will make yourself repent. My prayers shall reach the avengers
> of all wrong; no expiations shall the curse unbind. Great though your haste, I would not
> task you long; thrice sprinkle dust, then scud before the wind.

Horace's words make it quite clear that the restless dead could pose a serious threat
to the well-being of the living, even after they themselves had died. Furthermore, he
appears to suggest that a token covering of earth, literally a few handfuls, was believed
to be sufficient to allow the shade to rest peacefully. If the corpse did not receive these
rites then the shade was condemned to a fearful state of existence – unable to enter
the afterlife or rejoin the living world, it was compelled to remain trapped between
them (Hope 2000a, 120). The fact that denial of burial was, from time to time, used
as a form of extreme punishment demonstrates the force of these beliefs (Kyle 1998,
131); denial of burial, real or symbolic, thus entailed eternal punishment and allowed
the authorities to extend their powers beyond the grave. Proper burial was evidently
considered to be a vital part of the funeral, but how did the most common method of
disposal at the time, cremation, align with these needs? How could the body receive
proper burial after incineration? *Os resectum* has been interpreted as the primary
solution to this problem (see Becker 1988; Hope 2000a, 105–106; Lindsay 2000, 168;
Pellegrino 1999, 11; Toynbee 1971, 49). Removing an element of the corpse prior to
burning, in order to provide it with a separate burial in earth, allowed the deceased
to receive a proper religious interment and ensured that both the living and the dead
remained peaceful and content in their respective worlds. De Visscher (1963, 23) and
Simon-Hiernard (1987, 93) have suggested that *os resectum* thereby legitimised the
interment and allowed the grave to receive the legal status of *locus religiosus*, which
ensured that the dead possessed an inviolable place of rest. Such status was bestowed
on the site of burial only through the proper inhumation of the corpse; something
that the words of Cicero (*Laws* 2.22.57) appear to confirm when he claims that "…
until turf is cast upon the bones, the place where the body is cremated does not have
a sacred character…."

   Gaetano Messineo (1995, 263; 1999, 111–112) has suggested that the rite may
also have been referred to by Plutarch (*Matters relating to customs and mores* IV.79),
who asks,

> Why was it permitted to take up a bone of a man who had enjoyed a triumph, and had
> later died and been cremated, and carry it into the city and deposit it there, as Pyrrhon
> of Lipara has recorded? Was it to show honour to the dead?

Messineo's interpretation rests on the suggestion that *os resectum* was restricted to the
elite, in particular to triumphors who were granted the rare privilege of burial within
the city. This theory may offer an explanation for the uncertainty of Cicero, Varro and
Festus, who may have been describing an infrequent event, but as we shall see, the
archaeological evidence for *os resectum* does not support this interpretation. Furthermore,

Plutarch specifically refers to the *collection* of bone after cremation, whereas the term *os resectum* (cut bone) points towards the deliberate removal of bone from the corpse. Moreover, the ancient laws of Rome, the Twelve Tables (10. 5), state unequivocally that "He is not to collect the bones of a dead man, in order to hold a funeral afterwards." Alternatively, Messineo (1995, 1999, and 2001) proposed that *os resectum* was used as a means by which to ensure proper burial in situations where it was impossible for the mourners to perform the traditional ceremonies citing, for example, instances of the death of soldiers or travellers in war or foreign lands. There are indeed documented examples of remains being returned to their homeland for burial, and Cicero (*Laws* 2. 24. 60) observed that although it was forbidden to collect the bones of the deceased, "here an exception is made in case of death in war or on foreign soil" (see Carroll 2009). Other examples include the account of Tacitus (*Annals* 3.4) concerning the death of Germanicus in Syria and the subsequent return of his remains to Rome, and a similar, although perhaps less ostentatious instance, recounted by Martial (*Epigrams* 9.30),

> Antistius Rusticus has died on Cappadocia's cruel shores: O land guilty of a dolorous crime! Nigrina brought back in her bosom her dear husband's bones, and sighed that the way was all too short; and when to the tomb she envies she was giving that sacred urn, she deemed herself twice widowed of her ravished spouse.

The most commonly cited explanations of *os resectum* therefore stress its role as a guarantee of legitimate burial on each occasion of death. However, there are problems associated with all of these interpretations that render each of them unconvincing. This fact becomes clearer still when the primary archaeological evidence for the rite is re-assessed.

Bones, pots and vineyards: the evidence from San Cesareo

When, in 1732, a large number of small, single-handled ceramic vessels containing pieces of burnt bone were discovered near the church of San Cesareo on the Via Appia at Rome, it appeared that convincing evidence for *os resectum* had been uncovered. It is almost solely on the basis of a comparison of the ancient sources discussed above with this evidence that *os resectum* is understood today.

The excavations at San Cesareo which recovered the vessels and their unique contents took place amid frenzied archaeological investigations of the area of the Via Appia immediately outside the Porta Capena (Fig. 5.1). This area had long been home to vineyards and agricultural lands belonging to some of the major religious houses of the city, but at the beginning of the eighteenth century it became increasingly evident that the soil concealed a vast wealth of ancient treasures. Antiquarians such as de Vettori, Strozzi, Contucci, Bevilacqua, Frasconi, Baldini and the famous Francesco de'Ficoroni, descended on the area in order to extract as many spectacular finds as possible (Fig. 5.2).

Figure 5.1 The church of San Cesareo on the Via Appia during the 1700s, drawn by Giuseppe Vasi.

Figure 5.2 Francesco de'Ficoroni as caricatured by Pier Leone Ghezzi during the 1700s (Congresso di archeologi di Roma, Biblioteca Apostolica Vaticana, Ott. Lat. 3116 fol. 191).

It would not be until the following century that the famous *columbaria* of both the *Vigna Codini* and *Pomponius Hylas* would be found in this area, and the nearby tomb of the Scipios would not be fully explored until 1780, but the fertile ground yielded a great many other funerary structures, sarcophagi, sculpture, metalwork, frescoes (many of which were subsequently destroyed) and other ancient riches. The majority of these structures were destroyed as treasure hunters sought more portable items to add to their collections or to sell on the thriving antiquities market. The same appears to have been true of San Cesareo, an example which demonstrates particularly well the early desire for objects rather than archaeological data and the difficulties that later scholars face when trying to reconstruct the context in which these items were discovered. It is from Ficoroni that we first hear of the San Cesareo discoveries when he tells us that, in 1732, Giuseppe Mittelli

Figure 5.3 The vessels recovered from San Cesareo (photo, Author, courtesy of the Museo Nazionale Romano, Rome).

excavated 'burial chambers' in the vineyard belonging to the church of San Cesareo that were filled with burnt bone (Montalto Trentori 1937–38, 297). The material recovered by Mittelli was catalogued in the following years by Giovanni Baldini (1738, cited in *CIL* VI² 1103), who provides a more comprehensive account of the discovery:

> In the vineyard of San Cesario, situated on the right side of the Via Appia on the way out of Rome, of the order of the Collegio Clementino, the year 1732 in the month of July as the walls of the ancient tombs were falling into ruin, … is found in a tomb chamber an extraordinary quantity of little earthenware vessels all heaped up together. These little vessels were all of approximately the same size, capacity and appearance. Small bases, wide around the body, slim necked with a wider opening, with a handle … a few of them thinly varnished, some in black, some in a reddish colour, most of them unvarnished, beautifully pristine, almost as if they had just been taken from the kiln (see Fig. 5.3).

Baldini (1738, cited in *CIL* VI² 1103) was particularly interested in two aspects of these vessels. He explains how each small pitcher was found to contain "a splinter and [a] fragment of a larger human bone burned and calcified and evidently inserted so that when the vase was shaken they fell into the opening, but did not come out." Despite

using tweezers to remove a few of these fragments for closer examination, Baldini provides no further details about them, although the pieces of burnt bone appear to have been relatively quickly associated with the rite of *os resectum*. The second aspect of the San Cesareo vessels to attract attention was the presence of short texts incised on their exterior (see Figs 5.4 and 5.5). With a few exceptions each of these recorded the name of an individual accompanied by a specific date. For example, one reads: *Q(uintus) Afran(ius) a(nte) d(iem) / IV n(onas) Nov(embris)* (Quintus Afranius, November 2; *CIL* VI² 8218); and another: *Baebia Q(uinti) l(iberta) a(nte) d(iem) / IX k(alendas) Octobris* (Baebia, freedwoman of Quintus, September 22; *CIL* VI² 8227).

Figure 5.4 One of the San Cesareo vessels as depicted in 1734 by Pier Leone Ghezzi (Congresso di archeologi di Roma, Biblioteca Apostolica Vaticana, Ott. Lat. 3116 fol. 191).

The texts include references to men and women, slaves, former slaves, and freeborn citizens and, on the basis of a general absence of *cognomina*, the use of the pre-Caesarean calendar, and the style and fabric of the pots, the vessels and their contents were assigned to the first or second century BC. Unfortunately the "more than three hundred" vessels originally recovered in 1732 had been reduced to 125 by the time Baldini finished cataloguing them, the missing vessels perhaps sold on the antiquities market by the workmen assigned to their care. The remaining vessels eventually found their way into private collections and today the whereabouts of approximately fifty are known. The majority are housed in the Museo Nazionale Romano, but thanks to Baldini, and Antonio Lupi, we have a record of 186 of the original inscriptions.

It is easy to see why these vessels and their skeletal contents were associated with the rite of *os resectum*. They appear to confirm that a piece of bone was removed from

Figure 5.5 Two of the San Cesareo vessels today (photo, Author, courtesy of the Museo Nazionale Romano, Rome).

the body of the deceased (most probably an easily removable finger bone) for separate burial after the cremation of the other remains. Messineo (1995, 1999 and 2000) has used the names and dates on the small vessels to support his theory concerning the return of a token element of an individual who had died on foreign soil and has argued that the texts served to identify that person and the date on which they died. The texts, he argues, allowed the mourning family to calculate the age at which they died and to mark this occasion with the appropriate annual ceremonies. However, the vessels themselves provide evidence that can be used to counter this argument: the presence of women within the texts throws doubt on his "death in war" hypothesis; the vessels are local Tiber Valley Wares and are not from foreign lands; and the mixture of social levels represented within the texts does not seem consistent with individuals who would have travelled long distances from home. It seems unlikely that the remains of slaves would have been returned to Rome for burial, especially if they were of non-Roman origin. Equally, although family or household groupings can be identified amongst the San Cesareo assemblage, it is evident that not all of the individuals shared a direct or formal relationship and there seems little reason to assume that all token remains returned from abroad were interred at the same site.

There are clearly several problems with existing theories, but perhaps the most significant is the fact that Baldini described the bones he saw as "burned and calcified."

All of the theories that have been proposed to explain the role of *os resectum* within Roman burial customs assert that the bone was removed prior to cremation in order to act as a representative part of the *unburned* corpse. If we are to understand *os resectum* is time to look at the evidence for it from a new perspective.

Purifying the living and the dead

Varro's words (*On the Latin Language* 5.23), when describing the rite of *os resectum,* provide the key to expanding our understanding of this complex rite. In this passage Varro places more emphasis on the living than the dead and states specifically that bone was "kept out for the purifying of the household," making little reference to how the soul of the deceased benefited from the subsequent burial of the bone. Furthermore, he actually makes a distinction between *os resectum* (or, as he refers to it, *exceptum*) and the act of throwing earth on the corpse, a fact that suggests the former needs to be placed in a different context.

In ancient Rome, the moment of death rendered the family of the deceased, and anyone who came into contact with the corpse, spiritually impure. Lindsay (2000) has examined concepts and ideas of death pollution in the ancient city and provides extensive evidence that spiritual pollution was taken very seriously by members of the community at Rome. There existed many rituals, ceremonies and traditions designed to limit the extent of death pollution given its immense impact on the lives of mourners. The status that ensued from death pollution forbade partaking in certain public activities, including public bathing, and was particularly damaging for priests, magistrates and other office holders. It was removed only once the mourners had undergone a cleansing ritual known as the *suffitio.* Varro's statement implies that *os resectum* may have been involved in the process of rendering the mourners clean once more. Moreover, the *suffitio* ceremony may have served to mark the final separation of the dead from the living and the creation of new states of existence. It was from this point that the dead were transformed into ancestors.

Various lustrations were performed by members of the mourning household once the initial funeral activities had been completed. These included the *exfir*, which involved the sweeping of the house with a special broom (Lindsay 2000, 166, citing Festus 68L); failure to perform this act would result in a further death. The *suffitio* was another of these important cleansing ceremonies and, although evidence for how it was performed remains rather poor, it is known that it occurred some time after the deposition of the cremated remains of the dead and that it required mourners to step over fire and be sprinkled with water from a laurel branch. These acts would not have been out of place within wider Roman religious practice since the purification of polluted objects, peoples and places with fire and water was a well-established element of religious activity. The *Parilia* festival, for example, celebrated on the 21st April, involved a series of public purification rituals that involved both fire and water in much the same way as the *suffitio*. Ovid (*Fasti*, 4.735ff) describes his own participation in the festival: "truly I have leapt over the fires, placed three in a row, and the moist laurel has sprinkled water over me." Equally, during the *Portunalia* festival (August 17), keys that were to be offered to the god *Portunus* were first purified in the hearth (Scullard 1981, 176). The *suffitio* was probably associated with the *novemdialis*, the last day of the nine-day long unclean period of mourning, when the mourners gathered once more for a funerary feast and to offer prayers and gifts to the departed soul whilst continuing to celebrate their memory. The bone that had been removed from the corpse may have been used within these rituals of purification and remembrance, being cleansed in the fire, along with the mourners, and then finally laid to rest. These ceremonies marked the beginning of the ritual commemorative acts that would continue to be performed annually on the deceased's birthday, the anniversary of their death and during the various festivals of the dead.

The proposal that bone removed from the corpse was retained for use in these ritual activities of purification and remembrance can be supported by the observations of Baldini (1738, cited in *CIL* VI² 1103) concerning the original bone fragments discovered at San Cesareo. He describes these as "a splinter and [a] fragment of a larger human bone, burned and calcified;" a description that does not seem to align with the fact that the ancient literary sources speak of bone being removed *prior* to cremation. If this was the case we would expect the bones to show no evidence of burning. However, if this information is assessed in light of Varro's comments on the purification of the household, as well as what is known about the cleansing properties of fire and its use within the *suffitio* process, it can be proposed that the bone fragments were subjected to burning and purification during this later ceremony, before they were then deposited accordingly. Cleansing the bone, the final remaining piece of the dead, may therefore have been essential for the lustration of the entire mourning household.

Initially it is difficult to imagine why it was important to include a token element of the corpse in the cleansing ritual and exactly how this act allowed the family to find a release from their polluted state of existence when they themselves were not being subjected directly to the cleansing properties of the flames. However, when these activities are viewed in the context of Van Gennep's (1960) theories concerning rites of passage and the separation of the living and the dead, which align particularly well with Roman beliefs and practices, the significance of *os resectum* can be appreciated more fully. The period of mourning known as the *funesta* began at the exact moment of death and plunged both the corpse and the bereaved family into a state of spiritual un-cleanliness. During this time they occupied a liminal zone that existed outside of the worlds to which both properly belonged. The living existed outside of normal society; considered 'socially dead' they were unable to participate in everyday activities until they were released from this state of existence. The dead were equally unable to move on and be welcomed amongst the community of ancestors awaiting them in the

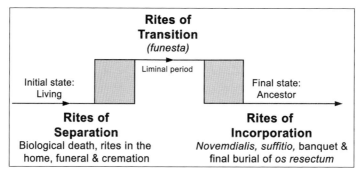

Figure 5.6 Schematic diagram depicting the rites of passage surrounding Roman death (after Leach 1976, 78).

afterlife until the appropriate rituals, prayers, offerings and ceremonies had been enacted. They were, perhaps, 'socially un-dead'. In terms of Van Gennep's tripartite structure of rites of passage (depicted pictorially by Leach 1976, 78; see Fig. 5.6), this period of mourning can be described as involving *rites of transition*, with both parties occupying a marginal zone outside of a defined community. Only once the *rites of incorporation* had been performed, in this case the *suffitio*, could they return to their proper states of existence and begin the process of (re)negotiating their relationships with the other members of that community, whether they were ancestors or the living.

In the context of this discussion it is important to observe that both the living and the dead who occupied this liminal, polluted zone required purification before they could leave it. For the deceased to begin their new existence in the next world their physical remains had to be cleansed in order to release the bonds that tied them to the society of the living. Perhaps more importantly, both the living and the dead had to move into their respective new roles and leave the liminal zone at the same time, since the existence of the zone was defined only by their co-presence within it. It was therefore essential that an unclean element of the dead was retained for this cleansing ritual, and the *os resectum* provided a token element of the polluted persona of the deceased that could be purified in the final stages of the funeral. Only once the *suffitio* had been performed, and the living and the dead released from their impure state, could the bone be laid to rest and covered with earth – a symbol of both parties being assimilated into the appropriate community and establishing new relationships with other members of that community.

Identifying os resectum

This hypothesis has immense implications for the way in which the San Cesareo vessels are interpreted. It is most probable that, once the *suffitio* ceremonies were complete and the bone purified, the family reunited the bone with the other incinerated remains of that individual in the cremation urn itself, perhaps with a token handful of earth to ensure that it constituted a legitimate interment. If this was the case, and the *os resectum* did not normally receive a separate receptacle, then it implies that the bone-filled pots from San Cesareo do *not* represent the norm. This perhaps is not surprising given that, despite an estimated 80 people dying each day at Rome (Bodel 2000, 128–129), only approximately 300 such examples of *os resectum* have been recovered, and all from a single site. Perhaps the wrong questions have been posed; instead of looking for other graffitied pots containing bone we must ask why they were employed for the separate burial of *os resectum* here and not elsewhere? What was it about this group of people or the context in which they were acting that led them to perform the ritual in this way? It is not possible to answer these questions here but this new approach offers an opportunity to move forward with our understanding of *os resectum* and San Cesareo and makes it possible to examine the pots and their inscriptions as a distinct group of artefacts connected with a *variation* of a common ritual practice, rather than the primary evidence for that practice. We must look for *os resectum* elsewhere too.

Although it is largely impossible to identify bones that were burnt at different times, scientific studies have shown that it *is* possible to differentiate between bones subjected to different temperatures (Fig. 5.7). Experiments have shown that bone subjected to heat undergoes changes in colour, as well as at the microstructural level, that can help to identify the maximum temperature that the specimen was exposed to (Buikstra and Swegle 1989; Holden *et al.* 1995; Shipman *et al.* 1984). Although these colour changes are deemed insufficient to identify temperature precisely, they can indicate a range within which the temperature falls (Shipman *et al.* 1984, 312–314). Importantly, in the context of this re-assessment of *os resectum*, it has been observed that when heated for a relatively short duration "bones are likely to survive intact or mostly intact and cannot be expected to have reached the maximum temperature of the heating device" (Shipman *et al.* 1984, 322–323). This may explain the good preservation of the bones recovered from San Cesareo, for if the *os resectum* was burned during the *suffitio*, and was not subjected to the very high temperatures (approximately 900°C) of the funerary pyre, it must be assumed that it was placed in a smaller fire for a shorter period of time. Campfires ordinarily reach temperatures of around 400°C which is a temperature, and a type of fire, that is conceivable for that used within the *suffitio*. If the mourners were required to leap over the flames it is unlikely that a larger, or hotter, fire was built for this purpose, and any blaze would certainly not have been required to burn for as long as the pyre, probably only for the duration of the ritual and perhaps also the accompanying feast. Unfortunately, the bones from San Cesareo have been lost since Baldini's initial observations and it is therefore not possible to assess the degree of burning to which they were subjected. However, if this data was applied to other cremated remains recovered from Rome, and indeed elsewhere, it may be possible to identify other instances of *os resectum* that may have been overlooked (Graham, Sulosky and Chamberlain, in preparation).

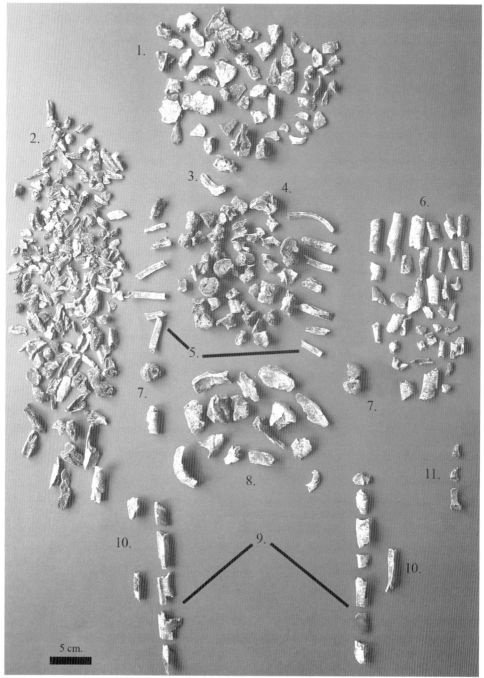

Figure 5.7 A cremation burial from Lincoln, England with a possible example of os resectum in the form of differentially burnt finger bones (number 11) (photo, Andrew Chamberlain, with permission).

Os resectum *as a 'technology of remembrance'*

So far we have focused on re-defining *os resectum* as a complex purificatory rite, but it is also essential to acknowledge its significant mnemonic role within mortuary activities. Successful commemoration does not depend solely on the creation of a lasting monument, and we have seen how Connerton (1989) has demonstrated the effectiveness of 'incorporating' practices of remembrance. The practice of *os resectum* and its relationship with the *suffitio* can also be understood in this context. The *suffitio* was one of many activities that took place between the time of death and the end of the official period of mourning which involved the perpetuation of the memory of the deceased through ritual or bodily performances. As a result, it should perhaps be considered a mnemonic process as much as a purificatory one. As the mourners placed the *os resectum* in the fire and performed the required ceremonial activities, including stepping over the fire and being immersed in its cleansing smoke, they would have brought a memory of the deceased to life in their minds. In the process, the experience would have recalled all of the other times, and individuals, for whom they had performed the same rituals, thus continuing the remembrance process for each of these people. This process is something that Williams (2004, 282) has observed for Anglo-Saxon cremations where "each new cremation rite would recall events at previous funerals." Such observations need not apply only to the cremation of the corpse itself but can be extended to encompass the other funerary activities in which the mourners participated. Placing the *os resectum* into the fire, with its evident parallels with the primary cremation, will have reminded the participants of the earlier incineration of the corpse and evoked the emotional responses they had experienced at the time. By this stage the *os resectum* was only a part of the corpse but it continued to be a powerfully emotive embodiment of the deceased; the last physical part of it to remain amongst the living. The main purpose of the rite may have been to release the participants from their spiritually polluted state, but at the same time the activities allowed the living to gather together in order to recall and celebrate the memory of the deceased, and to create new memories of that process.

Furthermore, the rites of the *suffitio* represented, and indeed facilitated, the final separation of the dead from the world of the living. Once both parties had been cleansed and the *os resectum* had been burnt and buried, or reunited with the other cremated remains of the deceased, the liminal zone ceased to exist. The living subsequently returned to 'real life' and the dead finally became ancestors. It was from this point onwards that the process of lasting and ongoing commemoration began. Until this point the corpse itself had formed the focus of commemorative activity but after the *suffitio* this role was adopted by the grave or funerary monument. It was to here that the family returned on special occasions to offer libations and prayers and, most importantly, to bring the memory of their dead relative alive once more through these activities. The *suffitio* thus signified the end of the relatively short-lived corpse-centred processes in which the deceased was honoured, celebrated and finally separated from the living, and the beginning of the all important long-term remembrance process that was to continue, ideally for eternity, although in reality only for as long as the grave held meaning for the living. This transition built on the memories that were created during the funerary activities – each time a funerary feast was consumed, certain prayers muttered or other funerary rites performed, the living would recall the experiences and emotions of this earlier event and thus collectively continued to memorialise their ancestors.

The retained bone fragments were not forgotten within these continuing ritual commemorations and this can be seen in the early Imperial *columbarium* of Pomponius Hylas, also near the Via Appia at Rome. A marble slab, equipped with a terracotta libation tube, was inserted into the floor of the subterranean burial chamber. When the original excavators lifted the slab in 1831 they discovered in the space below a large quantity of small bone fragments that belonged to many individuals (Pavia 1996). It is very probable that the assemblage represents another way in which the *os resectum* could be deposited once it had served its purpose and further indicates that the San Cesareo vessels do not necessarily reflect normal practice. Significantly, the presence of a libation pipe also signals that some form of post-depositional ritual activity occurred in relation to these retained bone fragments and that mourners returned to the place of deposition in order to perform acts that were designed to appease the souls of the departed, but that were also a vital element of the ongoing ritual commemorative process.

Conclusion

The evidence presented here sheds important new light on the rite of *os resectum* and its role in the funerary ritual. It is clear that *os resectum* can only be truly understood within the context of ritual purification ceremonies, and that current interpretations of the process are too reliant on uncritical readings of ambiguous ancient literature and archaeology. San Cesareo has been viewed as the *os resectum* 'type-site' since its discovery in 1732, but when the evidence for the rite is re-assessed it becomes evident that deposition within a small inscribed ceramic jug was probably not a required element of the ritual. It is also apparent that *os resectum* played an essential role within a complex ritual that was considered particularly important for purifying the household and its members after a death; without it the dead remained trapped outside the realms of the living and the dead where they could find no peace. What is more, the rite was closely bound up with recurring rituals of commemoration, and it was these 'incorporating' technologies of remembrance which marked the transformation of the deceased into an ancestor.

Acknowledgements

Much of the work for this chapter was funded by a Fellowship at the British School at Rome. I particularly wish to thank Maria Pia Malvezzi at the BSR for her assistance in obtaining permission to study the San Cesareo material and the Museo Nazionale Romano at the Baths of Diocletian for allowing me to do so, in particular Mariella Panatta. Thanks also to Andrew Chamberlain for permission to use the photographs of the Lincoln cremation.

Bibliography

Abbreviation
CIL   *Corpus Inscriptionum Latinarum*

Ancient Sources
Cicero. *De Re Publica, De Legibus*. Trans. C. Walker Keyes, 1959. London, Heinemann and Cambridge, Mass., Harvard University Press.
Festus. *On the meaning of words Sexti Pompei Festi, De verborum signifiatu quae supersunt cum Pauli Epitome*. Trans. W. M. Lindsay, 1913. Lipsiae, B. G. Teubrieri.
Horace. *The Odes and Epodes*. Trans. C. E. Bennett, 1927. London, William Heinemann.
Justinian. *The Digest of Justinian, 4 Volumes*. Trans. A. Watson, 1985. Philadelphia, University of Pennsylvania Press.
Martial. *Epigrams*. Trans. D. R. Shackleton Bailey, 1993. London, William Heinemann.
Ovid. *Ovid in Six Volumes*, vol. 5: *Fasti*. Trans. J. G. Frazer, 1989). London, William Heinemann.
Plutarch. *Matters relating to customs and mores, Plutarch's Moralia*, vol. 4: *Roman Questions*. Trans. F. C. Babbitt, 1936. London, William Heinemann.
Tacitus. *Tacitus in Five Volumes*, vol. 5: *The Annals*, books 13–16. Trans. J. Jackson, 1937. London, William Heinemann.
Varro. *On the Latin language*. Trans. R. G. Kent, 1938. London, William Heinemann.

Becker, M. J. (1988) The contents of funerary vessels as clues to mortuary customs: identifying the *os exceptum*. In J. Christiansen and T. Melander (eds) *Ancient Greek and Related Pottery. Proceedings of the 3rd Symposium*, 25–32. Copenhagen, NY Carlsberg Glyptolek and Thorvaldsens Museum.
Bodel, J. (2000) Dealing with the dead: undertakers, executioners and potter's fields in ancient Rome. In V. M. Hope and E. Marshall (eds) *Death and Disease in the Ancient City*, 128–151. London, Routledge.
Buikstra, J. E. and Swegle, M. (1989) Bone Modification Due to Burning: Experimental Evidence. In R. Bonnischen and M. H. Sorg (eds) *Bone Modification*, 247–258. Orono, University of Maine.
Carroll, M. (2006) *Spirits of the Dead: Roman Funerary Commemoration in Western Europe*. Oxford, Oxford University Press.
Carroll, M. (2009) Dead soldiers on the move. Transporting bodies and commemorating men at home and abroad. In A. Morillo, N. Hanel and E. Martín (eds.). *Limes XX. Actas del*

XX Congreso Internacional de Estudios sobre la Frontera Romana (Anejos de Gladius 13), 19–28. Madrid, Ediciones Polifemo.

Connerton, P. (1989) *How societies Remember*. Cambridge, Cambridge University Press.

D'Ambra, E. (2002) Acquiring an Ancestor: the Importance of Funerary Statuary among the Non-Elite Orders of Rome. In J. M. Højte (ed.) *Images of Ancestors*, 223–246. Denmark, Aarhus University Press.

George, M. (2005) Family Imagery and Family Values in Roman Italy. In M. George (ed.). *The Roman Family in the Empire. Rome, Italy, and Beyond*, 37–66. Oxford, Oxford University Press.

Graham, E.-J. (2006a) *Death, disposal and the destitute: The burial of the urban poor in Italy in the late Roman Republic and early Empire*. British Archaeological Reports International Series 1565. Oxford, Archaeopress.

Graham, E.-J. (2006b) Discarding the destitute: Ancient and modern attitudes towards burial practices and memory preservation amongst the lower classes of Rome. In B. Croxford *et al.* (eds) *TRAC 2005. Proceedings of the Fifteenth Annual Theoretical Roman Archaeology Conference. Birmingham 2005,* 57–71. Oxford, Oxbow Books.

Graham, E.-J., Sulosky, C. and Chamberlain, A. (in preparation) A probable case of *os resectum* in a Romano-British cremation burial from Lincoln.

Holden, J. L., Phakey, P. P., and Clement, J. G. (1995) Scanning electron microscope observations of heat-treated human bone. *Forensic Science International* 74, 29–45.

Hope, V. M. (1998) Negotiating Identity and Status: the Gladiators of Roman Nîmes. In J. Berry and R. Laurence (eds) *Cultural Identity in the Roman Empire*, 179–195. London, Routledge.

Hope, V. M. (2000a) Contempt and respect: the treatment of the corpse in ancient Rome. In V. M. Hope and E. Marshall (eds) *Death and Disease in the Ancient City*, 104–127. London, Routledge.

Hope, V. M. (2000b) Inscription and Sculpture: the Construction of Identity in the Military Tombstones of Roman Mainz. In G. Oliver (ed.) *Funerary Inscriptions: Problems and Prospects*, 155–186. Liverpool, Liverpool Classical Press.

Hope, V. M. (2001) *Constructing Identity: The Roman Funerary Monuments of Aquileia, Mainz and Nîmes*. British Archaeological Report. International Series 960. Oxford, Archaeopress.

Hope, V. M. (2003) Remembering Rome: memory, funerary monuments and the Roman soldier. In H. Williams (ed.) *Archaeologies of Remembrance. Death and Memory in Past Societies,* 113–140. New York, Kluwer Academic/Plenum Publishers.

Kyle, D. G. (1998) *Spectacles of Death in Ancient Rome*. London, Routledge.

Leach, E. (1976) *Culture and Communication*. Cambridge, Cambridge University Press.

Lindsay, H. (2000) Death-pollution and funerals in the city of Rome. In V. M. Hope and E. Marshall (eds) *Death and Disease in the Ancient City*, 152–173. London, Routledge.

Messineo, G. (1995) Nuovi dati dalla necropoli tra Via Salaria e Via Pinciana. *Archeologia Laziale* XII, 1, 257–266.

Messineo, G. (1999) Dalle necropoli del suburbio settentrionale di Roma. In A. Pellegrino (ed.) *Dalle Necropoli di Ostia. Riti ed Usi Funerari*, 110–127. Rome, Soprintendenza Archeologica di Ostia.

Messineo, G. (2001) Dalle necropolis del suburbia settentrionale di Roma. In M. Heinzelmann, J. Ortalli, P. Fasold and M. Witteyer (eds) *Römischer Bestattungsbrauch und Beigabensitten in Rom, Norditalien und den Nordwestprovinzen von der späten Republik bis in die Kaiserzeit* (Culto dei morti e costumi funerari romani. Roma, Italia settentrionale e province nord-occidentali dalla tarda Repubblica all'età imperiale), 35–45. Rome, Deutches Archäologisches Institut Rom.

Montalto Trentori, L. (1937–38) Scoperte archeologiche del secolo XVIII nella vigna di San Cesareo. *Rivista dell'Istituto Nazionale d'Archeologia e Storia dell'Arte* 6, 289–308.

Nock, A. D. (1972) Cremation and burial in the Roman Empire. In Z. Stewart (ed.) *A. D. Nock, Essays on Religion and the Ancient World,* 277–307. Oxford, Clarendon Press.

Pavia, C. (1996) *Il Colombario di Pomponius Hylas.* Collana archeologica supplemento di Forma Urbis 6. Rome, Sydaco Editrice.

Pellegrino, A. (1999) I riti funerari ed il culto dei morti. In A. Pellegrino (ed.) *Dalle Necropoli di Ostia. Riti e Usi Funerari, 7*–25. Rome, Soprintendenza Archeologica di Ostia.

Scullard, H. H. (1981) *Festivals and Ceremonies of the Roman Republic.* London, Thames and Hudson.

Shipman, P., Foster, G. and Schoeninger, M. (1984) Burnt Bones and Teeth: an Experimental Study of Color, Morphology, Crystal Structure and Shrinkage. *Journal of Archaeological Science* 11, 307–325.

Simon-Hiernard, D. (1987) Remarques sur le rite de l'*os resectum.* In *Nécropoles à incineration du Haut-Empire.* Table ronde de Lyon 1986. Rapports archéologiques préliminaires de la région Rhone-Alpes, 93–95.

Toynbee, J. M. C. (1971) *Death and Burial in the Roman World.* London, Thames and Hudson.

Van Gennep, A. (1960) *The Rites of Passage.* London, Routledge.

de Visscher, F. (1963) *Le Droit des Tombeaux Romains.* Milan, Giuffrè Editore.

Williams, H. (2003) Introduction: The Archaeology of Death, Memory and Material Culture. In H. Williams (ed.) *Archaeologies of Remembrance. Death and Memory in Past Societies,* 1–24. New York, Kluwer/Plenum.

Williams, H. (2004) Death Warmed Up: The Agency of Bodies and Bones in Early Anglo-Saxon Cremation Rites. *Journal of Material Culture* 9(3), 263–291.

Publius Vesonius Phileros vivos monumentum fecit: Investigations in a sector of the Porta Nocera cemetery in Roman Pompeii

Sébastien Lepetz and William Van Andringa
with the collaboration of Henri Duday, Dominique Joly,
Claude Malagoli, Véronique Matterne, Marie Tuffreau-Libre

Whilst, in the past, our knowledge of Roman burial was limited largely to the information gained from the study of funerary inscriptions, tomb architecture and the evidence for the treatment of the corpse (inhumation or cremation), today many other aspects of death and burial, including funerary rites and the commemorative activities that took place at the grave and in the tomb, have become the focus of archaeological exploration on cemetery sites.

This important broadening of our perspectives is related, among other things, to an appreciation of Roman literary and legal texts on death and burial. A Roman tomb had the social significance of preserving an individual's memory and expressing his status in the community, but it was, above all, a place of worship dedicated to the *Manes*, a collective of infernal deities who represented the dead once their mortal remains had been laid to rest. Legal texts present the burial place as a *locus religiosus*, a sacred place, which explains why some rituals were seen as a necessity; the texts mention, in particular, the sacrifice of a sow (Gaius, *Institutes* 2.4 and 2.6; Cicero, *Laws* 2.22). Ritual activities were not restricted to the actual construction of the tomb; they played a role throughout the funeral ceremonies. Their role was to ensure a proper separation between the living and the dead, an important point for a community coping with death and striving to return to the natural order of things. These rituals celebrated a series of events aimed at freeing the living survivors of the pollution of death and modifying the status of the deceased in order for him/her to become the recipient of a funerary cult. Once the dead were settled in their new abode, these symbolic actions were repeated during subsequent festivals in their honour.

What, exactly, do we mean when we talk about funerary rituals? In the Roman texts, the central focus is not how the corpse was treated and disposed of, *i.e.* burning or burying, but rather the sacrifice followed by the banquet in which the living and the dead participated (Scheid 1984 and 2005). This funerary banquet was repeated on the ninth day after death to mark the end of the period of mourning, as well as at other times when people would visit the tombs during the festivals of the dead. These meals took place at the tomb, within the enclosure of the cemetery plot, to mark the transition in status of the deceased. From a Roman point of view, the family was thereby purified and the *iusta*, the laws that regulated their obligations to the dead or to the gods that represented them, were respected. The objects placed on the funeral pyre were not intended to feed the dead, nor did they represent provisions for the individual's journey into the other world, rather they were *munera*: gifts and sacrificial offerings presented to the dead and the infernal gods (Lepetz and Van Andringa 2004b).

Ritual practices were performed at the consecration of the tomb and during the period in which the status of the deceased was in flux, but there were also other rituals that were performed with the purpose of achieving a strict separation between the living and the dead using the subtle symbolism of 'reversal'. John Scheid (1984) has argued that the sometimes extravagant use of perfume and sweet-smelling incense was designed as a strategic counterfoil to the smell of death and the stench of rotting corpses. In the same vein, oil lamps and torches simulated a nocturnal context and situated the funeral in contrasting temporality to the daytime activities of the living. Furthermore, the coin, the token given to the ferryman Charon, according to Juvenal (*Satires* 3. 267), appears to have been consciously burned on the funeral pyre before being mixed with the cremated human bones in the cinerary urn. Here again we have this sense of 'reversal': unburnt coins for exchanges amongst the living, burnt coins for transactions with the dead.

Thus, although the treatment of the corpse – cremation or inhumation – is undoubtedly linked with Roman society's ideas about death, it is, properly speaking, not on the same level as the religious rituals (the sacrifice, the banquet, offerings of food, wine or perfumed oils) which defined the symbolic boundary between death and life.

As we can see, these practices as a whole are of significance for the ceremony surrounding death. In a way, these rituals constitute a behavioural and symbolic definition of death in Roman times, since they very precisely ordered and regulated the relationship between the living and the dead. They enabled the living to have a certain amount of control over death and the contamination that came with it. The central role of rituals in the representation of death underscores the importance of these acts as a focus of archaeological research in Roman cemeteries.

This study focuses on the Roman necropolis outside a city gate of Pompeii known as the Porta Nocera (Lepetz and Van Andringa 2006 and 2008). Whilst our work is centred on the evidence for ritual activities, the excellent state of preservation of the archaeological remains offers us the perfect opportunity to approach the topic more broadly and to examine all the information available about the history of the cemetery and its occupants (some of whom are well known through epigraphy), the arrangement

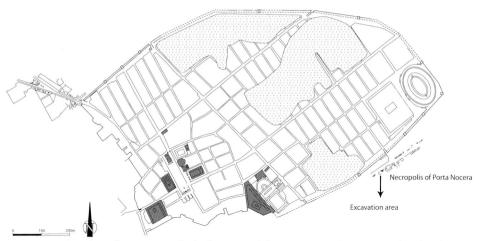

Figure 6.1 Plan of Pompeii with the location of the excavation (DAO: Carole Chevalier).

of the tombs, and the organisation of sepulchral space (*e.g.* architecture, inscriptions, funerary artefacts), as well as the various funerary activities that can be reconstructed on the basis of the material (human and animal bone, ceramics, plant remains, charcoal, *etc.*) retrieved both on the surface levels and in the fill of the graves.

The aim of this project is, therefore, to utilise a whole range of evidence in order to define, as precisely as possible, what exactly a burial in the first century AD entailed and what attitudes towards death prevailed in a Roman community. A distinct advantage is that the context in which we work is that of a Roman colony, and it is, therefore, possible to make use of written sources in interpreting the archaeological phenomena.

The history of the Porta Nocera necropolis

In Pompeii, as in all Roman cities, cemeteries were situated on the edges of urban space (Fig. 6.1), a principle based on the notion that the dead brought pollution to the living, and that the world of the dead needed to be separate from that of the living (Kockel 1983; D'Ambrosio and De Caro 1984). Our fieldwork focuses on the particularly well-preserved occupation levels around the tombs. The study area consists of a series of tomb enclosures and graves that belonged to freedmen (Tombs 21, 23, 25, 25a OS). These monuments are aligned along the road from Nocera, Pompeii's eastern neighbour, which ran parallel to the city wall and joined the Stabiae Gate and the harbour at the mouth of the Sarno river (Fig. 6.2).

A deep sondage opened in front of Enclosure 23 OS shows that this road was built through a substrate of volcanic tuff. All the various road levels appear to date to the Roman period. The organisation of the cemetery with its monumental tombs flanking

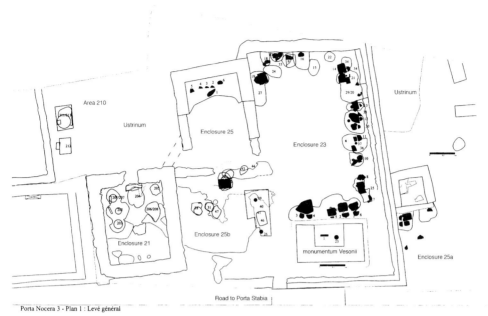

Figure 6.2 Plan of funerary Enclosures 17, 19, 21, 23, 25 and 25a OS and the position of the excavated tombs (original plan by the topographers of ESTP School (Paris), synthesised by Vincent Lallet).

the road is, therefore, Roman in date, and, consequently, it post-dates the foundation of the Roman colony in 80 BC. The other purpose of the trench was to obtain material from various levels of use and occupation in order to be able to evaluate the intensity of funerary activity in adjoining plots. The presence of funerary artefacts in varying quantities and their consistency with the material found within the tomb plot itself acts as a measure of the extent of funerary activity over a longer period of time in this part of the necropolis.

The organisation of sepulchral space: Enclosures 23/25 and 25a OS

The best represented period in this part of the cemetery is the imperial period, in particular the era of the Julio-Claudian emperors, a time in which the allotment of space in this sector of the necropolis took place (Fig. 6.2). Publius Vesonius Phileros had his funerary monument built here within an existing plot around AD 50–60. The monument is of a particular type seen in Pompeii and other places in the Roman empire, and is designed as an *aedicula* or columned porch containing portrait statues of the tomb's inhabitants on a podium (Fig. 6.3).

Figure 6.3 Frontal view of the funerary monument of Publius Vesonius Phileros, Enclosure 23 OS (photo, W. Van Andringa, MFP/FPN).

There is also an epitaph inscribed in three sections on a large panel of white marble (D'Ambrosio and De Caro 1984, 23 OS, see Fig. 6.4):

> P(ublius) Vesonius, G(aiae) l(ibertus), / Phileros augustalis / vivos monument(um) / fecit sibi et suis; / Vesoniae, P(ublii) f(iliae), / patronae et / M(arco) Orfellio, M(arci) l(iberto), / Fausto, amico.

The epitaph indicates that the monument was built for P. Vesonius Phileros during his lifetime, and that he was a freedman of a Roman matron, as indicated by the reversed letter 'C', the abbreviation of G(aia), an equivalent of *mulier* or 'woman' (this usage is attested by Quintilius, *Institutes* 1.7.28). The inscription also reveals that Phileros had this monument built not only for himself, but also for two other people: his patroness and former owner, Vesonia, a Roman citizen, and Marcus Orfellius Faustus, a freedman, whose status as Phileros's friend (*amicus*) gained him a place within the burial community.

In the *aedicula* at the top of the monument, a statue group depicts Vesonia, the patroness (*patrona*) and citizen, flanked by the two freedmen in togas, the costume of Roman citizen men; these are the three occupants officially admitted into the new tomb (Fig. 6.4). The inclusion of Vesonia in the tomb of her former slave is not surprising, as this gesture was a visible expression of the sense of duty (*pietas*) a freedman felt towards

Figure 6.4 *The epitaph in white marble indicates that the monument was built for P. Vesonius Phileros during his lifetime. A second inscription (tabella defixionis) was fixed to the facade of the monument below the original one (photo, W. Van Andringa, MFP/FPN).*

his former owner. Honouring the patroness and providing her with a place of burial were some of the obligations and responsibilities a respectable freedman had towards the person who had granted him freedom (Fabre 1981).

Additional words later inscribed in the epitaph reveal that the tomb owner had become an *Augustalis* some time after the monument was erected, the college of the *Augustales,* or priests of the imperial cult, being the main focus of public activity and patronage of the city's wealthier freedmen. The subsequent engraving of *et suis* (and his dependents) in the inscription demonstrates that the use of the funerary plot was now extended to the family and dependents of the deceased. There are, thus, two groups of individuals included in the tomb: the relatives of the deceased (the *sibi et suis* of the inscription), and the others whose relationship with Phileros is specified, the *patrona* and the *amicus*. Such a situation is consistent with Roman funerary law which allowed for the inclusion of third parties, whether friends, business partners or patrons, in the tomb, provided that an agreement of sale or donation was confirmed in writing. In this case, it is the qualities of *patrona* and *amicus* that favoured the admission of Vesonia and Faustus into the burial community. But the history of the monument is rather more complex, as we can see from a second inscription that was fixed to the facade of the monument below the original one (Fig. 6.4). It is a curse tablet (*tabella defixionis*) that appeals to the *Penates*, the household gods, and gods of the underworld for justice, following a court case in which Phileros was pitted against "the one that pretended to be (his) friend." Numerous clues point towards M. Orfellius Faustus, the other official resident of the tomb, being the friend referred to in the inscription (Elefante 1985):

> Hospes paullisper morare / si non est molestum et quid euites / cognosce amicum hunc quem / speraveram mi esse ab eo mihi accusato / res subiecti et iudicia instaurata; deis / gratias ago et meae innocentiae omni / molestia liberatus sum; qui nostrum mentitur / eum nec di Penates nec Inferi recipiant.

> Stranger, stay a little, if it is not too much trouble and learn what to avoid. This man, whom I had hoped was my friend, I am forsaking: a case was maliciously brought against me; I was charged and legal proceedings were instituted; I gave thanks to the gods and to my innocence, I was freed from all distress. May neither the household gods nor the gods below receive the one who misrepresented our affairs.

The epigraphy of the monument thus reveals that in the Neronian period (AD 54–68) a slave of the Vesonii had been freed by (possibly) the last living member of the family. Having inherited a share of the Vesonii family wealth, Phileros had become very rich and was one of the most affluent freedmen in the city. The establishment of this funerary plot was, in part, a confirmation of his new social status, which may explain the dimensions of the tomb as well as its location near the city gates and its proximity to the tombs of some of Pompeii's most prominent families, such as the *Eumachii, Clodii,* and *Tilii,* among others.

In view of the epigraphic evidence, one of the main aims of the excavations inside the tomb enclosure was to explore the allocation of spaces for individual burials, and

Figure 6.5 Arrangement of the graves behind the funerary monument. The two freedmen's graves are placed side by side in the niche underneath the monument. The patroness's burial is placed in front of the monument, on the left side (photo, A. Gailliot, MFP/FPN).

in particular those for two families. The arrangement of the three people named in the main inscription is not reflected in the space within the enclosure. In the inscription and in the *aedicula* facing the road, the two freedmen appear on either side of their patroness, thus respecting the official social hierarchy with her as the central figure. But inside the enclosure and behind the tomb, the two freedmen's graves are placed side by side in the recess situated underneath the monument, in other words they are subordinate to the *monumentum*. The patroness's grave, on the other hand, stands free of the monument (Fig. 6.5). This arrangement demonstrates the many layers of meaning in a Roman tomb: the exterior of the monument presents the social rank and status of the deceased and his place within the local society; away from the most visible part of the tomb, however, other parameters could very well take precedence, such as available space (tombs were protected by funerary law) or personal preferences (which undoubtedly played a role in the case of Phileros and Faustus).

The family members of Phileros were buried at the base of the funerary monument, the graves being positioned parallel to the podium (graves 3, 4, 5, 6, see Figs 6.2 and 6.5). The restricted space available also explains why other individuals were placed in front of the oldest tombs at the back of the enclosure (grave 15). Some relatives of Phileros have been identified, such as P. Vesonius Proculus, his son, who, according to his epitaph, died at the age of thirteen (Fig. 6.5).

Figure 6.6 The grave and the broken stele of Phileros under the niche. The paving which covers the ground in front of the broken stele was added later. The destruction of the paving in front of Phileros's stele is modern (photo, A. Gailliot, MFP/FPN).

The status of the tomb as sacred and inalienable brings into focus the crucial issue of the re-organisation of sepulchral space. In Pompeii, one can observe that older tombs sometimes were respected and still visited long after they had changed owners: graves 17 and 19, which belonged to an older arrangement, for example, were covered with gravel after Phileros had staked a new claim to the plot. The location and boundaries of the older burials needed to be marked out so that survivors could continue to perform rites and obsequies. It is also apparent, however, that some tombs were disturbed by the subsequent re-organisation of the enclosure, and this raises the question of how sepulchral space was re-allocated. The excavation of burial 28 showed that the urn in it was accidentally broken before being re-buried. Another, very specific, type of re-organisation of funerary space is alluded to in the secondary inscription mentioning the betrayal to passers-by of "the one he had hoped would be a friend." The excavation of the monument confirmed that the above mentioned friend was M. Orfellius Faustus, in other words, one of the original trio of people to whom space in the tomb had been allocated. The fate of Faustus's grave is of particular interest in this context: this man, who was officially recognised as an *amicus* and had been granted hospitality by Phileros in his tomb, was then accused of having betrayed his host and became the object of a curse. Although Vesonius Phileros did not erase Faustus's name in the epitaph or remove the statue of him, there was nothing to prevent Phileros from summoning the gods through the magical practices of *defixio* and beseeching them to let Faustus roam the earth forever unburied. It was not forbidden for Phileros to block off the grave pit that had been prepared for Faustus, as long as the latter was still alive. As a matter of fact, Roman legal texts confirm that a tomb was not considered a sacred site until a body was buried in it, and only the spot where a body was interred was protected by law against profanation (Thomas 1999). Since Faustus was still alive, Phileros was able to bar his former friend once and for all from the burial place he had originally provided for him in anticipation of death. And this is what he did, destroying the slab that sealed the cavity for two adjoining and still empty graves. He then erased his former friend's *stele* before backfilling the cinerary urn designated for Faustus and the ceramic pipe into which libations would have been poured on his remains. Finally, the now obsolete grave was covered with a new sealing surface into which pieces of black stone marked Phileros's name and defined the parameters of a now extended grave available solely for Phileros (Fig. 6.6).

The Organisation of Tombs: pyres and graves

In Pompeii, traces of funeral pyres survive as small mounds of charcoal and ash where the pyre or *ustrinum* had been (D'Ambrosio and De Caro 1987). A pyre area has been located at Tomb 25a, behind the niche accommodating a family of freedmen (Fig. 6.7). This area, clearly dating to the period following the earthquake of AD 62, is made up of a series of shallow depressions with heat-reddened walls. Various conclusions can be drawn. The limited quantity of charred material (serving dishes, cooking vessels, oil lamps, cuts of meat) mixed with the ashes shows that offerings placed on the pyre were rather modest, even if we consider differences in the social status of the deceased. We observed that new pyres were usually lit in the same place as the older ones, the latter having been cleared away, but not completely. Occasionally a pyre was sealed by a layer of silt. Finally, the presence of unburnt remains, such as oil lamps and *balsamaria*, on the ground where those cremations occurred suggests that some grave goods were not thrown into the fire, but were used by the participants during the funerals. Here we have another reflection of the separation between the living and the dead.

During the second phase of the cremation process, the burnt human bones were collected and placed in an urn. The wood ash from the pyre and small residual bone fragments might be gathered up from the centre of the pyre and swept into an ash pit, several of which have been discovered (see Fig. 6.7), or deposited in the grave around the cinerary urn. In burial 21, for instance, the residue collected after cremation was deposited at the same time as an amphora containing the cremated remains of two of the three individuals in the grave (Fig. 6.8). Henri Duday's study of this material indicates that this secondary collection of burnt material from the pyre allowed for a

Figure 6.7 Pyre area under excavation localised behind the niche 25a (photo, A. Gailliot, MFP/ FPN).

Figure 6.8 Burial 21, the residue collected after cremation was deposited around the cinerary urn (an amphora containing the cremated remains of three individuals) (photo, A. Gailliot, MFP/FPN).

Figure 6.9 Excavation of burial 2 (Vesonia, patroness of Phileros, in the centre) (photo, A. Gailliot, MFP/FPN).

more complete deposition of the calcined bones of the corpse. The scrutiny of pyre debris in the burial pit also allows us to retrieve and identify a variety of burnt offerings and it facilitates a reconstruction of the funeral ceremony. The carbonised bones of fish and goat, for example, were recognised in a deposit in burial 21. Are these, therefore, the remains of meals shared between the living and the dead during the funeral? As the evidence indicates, gathering up, clearing, and transferring the remains of the pyre played a part in the sequence of the funeral and interment, and these events should be included in the definition of a burial.

As for the arrangement of graves within the enclosure, the most significant data come from Enclosure 23 OS. About thirty burials deposited between the time of Augustus (31 BC–AD 14) and Vespasian (AD 69–79) have been identified here. With the exception of the burials of very young children, the graves are marked by a *stele* and sealed with a slab. The adult burials are all cremation burials, as this was the customary method of disposing of the dead during this period in Pompeii. Such cremation burials can be divided into two subgroups: single occupancy graves and multiple occupancy graves.

A single occupancy burial, the more common type of the two, is exemplified by grave 2 in which the remains of the *patrona* Vesonia were interred. The burial pit is more than a metre deep, with a cooking vessel used as a container for the cremated remains of Vesonia on the bottom (Fig. 6.9). The grave was then closed and a ceramic libation pipe installed. The arrangement was completed with an inscribed limestone *stele* and a basalt sealing slab. Two observations can be made: firstly, this arrangement is rather simple and unassuming (there is one pit, one urn, one libation pipe); and, secondly, the end of the libation pipe is not in contact with the urn, but simply with the bottom of the grave pit. In other cases (burials 5, 15, 19, 21) the libation pipe pierces the top of the cinerary urn and is connected directly with the ashes of the deceased, but there are also graves with no opening for libations at all (burials 16, 17, 18). The fragmentary *balsamarium* found on the ground indicates that perfumed oil was poured into the grave or on the sealing slab in front of the *stele*.

Burial 14/21/29 is a multiple occupancy grave of the period between AD 50–70, and it has been studied by Dominique Joly and Henri Duday (see Fig. 6.8). The methodical excavation of its contents provided us with a good assessment of the complex history of this grave. The first burial is a double one with a two-year-old child interred in a tile cist associated with an upright amphora containing the cremated remains of a child of perinatal age (approximately nine months old at death). Why was the two-year-old child inhumed and not cremated? Clearly a choice was made by the family, but what is certain is that the child had a proper funeral, demonstrated by the *balsamaria* placed around its head. The grave was then closed. After a period of time, the duration of which is difficult to estimate, it was re-opened for the deposition of an amphora containing the cremated remains of a second, adolescent individual and the collected remains of the funeral pyre. The tomb was closed again and a *stele* was erected above (although this may have happened already at the time of the first burial). After another lapse of time, long enough for toads to have fallen into the libation pipe and been trapped in the amphora, the grave was re-opened yet again for the burial of a third person, another adolescent. Fragments of a single oil lamp in the urn and in the small mound of pyre debris clearly demonstrate the association between this third individual and the pyre. The tomb was then closed once and for all by a complex libation device consisting of two distinct elements: a fragment of the original, but broken, libation pipe and a wine funnel turned upside down. The ground-level arrangements were then modified by erecting a *stele*, laying down a basalt sealing slab south of the grave and placing three re-used marble plaques around the opening for libations. The layout of these graves intended for more than one individual was planned in advance, as was evidently the selection of a receptacle for the ashes, in this case an amphora, rather than an urn.

Inhumation appears to have been the preferred method of disposal for very young children in the Porta Nocera necropolis, but Roman written sources suggest that this was a more general phenomenon for infants under six months of age (Juvenal, *Satires* 15.139–140; Pliny, *Natural History* 7.16.68, 72). So far there are three such inhumations, none of which has a grave marker, associated with tomb 23 and the grave of an adult. They are always located at least in the proximity of an adult's grave, as is the case with burial 27, situated next to burial 19 (Fig. 6.2). Anthropological analysis carried out by Henri Duday has allowed greater precision in recognising the age of individuals, and they demonstrate that ancient rules governing the treatment of the body according to age at death were not always adhered to strictly; there are cases of inhumed children older than two or three years, and there is also one case of a cremation burial (burial 21) of a baby under the age of six months. Obviously, other factors, besides age, affected the method of disposal.

Funerary activities and evidence for rituals

Evidence for ritual practices in the funerary enclosure of Publius Vesonius Phileros is diverse in nature. As the foregoing discussion has shown, a variety of materials and sources are available for study: inscribed *stelae*, sculpture, ceramics, human and animal bone, and carbonised fruits. These remains appear in different contexts. They can be found in the graves themselves, in the burial pits where cremated human remains are deposited, or on ground surfaces. Sometimes in primary positions, sometimes in secondary ones, sometimes intact, and sometimes fragmentary, they are reflections of distinct actions and particular moments in the ceremonies of burial and commemoration. Whilst the study of architecture, topography and stratigraphy is an elementary part of the funerary archaeology of Classical antiquity, the systematic analysis of traces attesting to funerary ritual is less so. Ceramics and a study of their forms certainly provide interesting chronological information, but the role of ceramics in ritual is poorly understood. Organic remains, because they are inconspicuous, fragile and ephemeral, also have received little archaeological attention. The method our team followed to retrieve information on ritual practices was one of careful excavation of the various occupation layers, grave pits, urns and remains of human bone, and three-dimensional recording of artefacts, followed by wet-sieving most of the excavated soil samples. It was all about choosing an excavation strategy that was appropriate for the exceptional state of archaeological preservation the site offered.

The preliminary results of the pottery analysis conducted by Marie Tuffreau-Libre and Claude Malagoli indicate the use of a significant quantity of glass and ceramic unguent flasks (*balsamaria*) in the occupation levels. These *balsamaria* were sometimes found broken on the spot, right next to grave *stelae*, or they were retrieved intact from the graves themselves. In the upper levels on the site, the ceramics are characterised by a great number of thin-walled, fine-ware cups and goblets produced locally or regionally. This abundance of tableware is linked to the presence, consumption and use of liquids in the tomb enclosure. More common in the lower levels are the coarse wares. Further analysis will be required to explain the links between this material and the activities in the enclosure during the individual stages of funerary rituals. The presence of *balsamaria* that have been distorted from exposure to heat and of burnt pottery already gives us some idea about the kind of objects that were put on the pyre with the body.

This rather traditional approach to material analysis involves the study of ceramics that survive in a good state of preservation and in large quantities; the retrieval of such assemblages in excavations is relatively straightforward. In contrast, the investigation of smaller or more fragile fragments of material, such as charcoal, grains or carbonised fruits, requires very careful excavation of soils and sediments. The retrieval of this material has to be as thorough as possible; hand excavation of plant macro-remains, however meticulous, is not enough. Soil sieving is essential. Several hundreds of kilograms of soil have been wet-sieved and examined under the binocular magnifying glass (during the first year, almost all of the soils were sampled in this way). This technique allows us to collect thousands of organic remains (grains, carbonised fruits, fragments of bread or cake) which represent approximately 98% of the plant macro-remains.

The research carried out by Veronique Matterne and Marie Derreumaux enables us to recognise the plant species present in occupation layers and to begin to understand their significance in funerary practices. Around fifteen species have been identified. The material is carbonised, allowing it to survive, but, because the offerings were exposed to fire, some of the constituent parts of bread, cereal cakes and fruits cannot be identified. There may be more than one reason why fruits were burned. They may have been placed on the funeral pyre and burned with the corpse, or they may have been sacrificed in commemorative banquets and burned on tables or on the slab sealing the grave pit. In either case, it is the activity within the tomb enclosure (successive digging of grave pits, movement of people) that explains the dispersion of these elements on the ground.

In the enclosure belonging to Phileros, figs and grapes are by far the most common vegetal finds, followed by nuts (hazelnuts, walnuts) and legumes (peas, chickpeas). Olives, chestnuts and pomegranates also appear, but less frequently. Along with these edible species, there are also non-edible ones, such as weeds. They probably ended up here accidentally, although the presence of some non-edible species, such as the cypress tree, may reflect a particular use. It is possible that the aromatic qualities of cypress wood made it a desirable object for the funeral pyre, although charcoal analysis has yet to confirm the presence of this wood. The data are not yet fully analysed, but the presence of cypress cones on the pyre warrants further investigation.

Some of the edible fruits and grains were eaten before being exposed to the flames; these include chestnuts and olives, of which only shells and pits have been found. But most of the vegetal remains had not been consumed. This distinction between eaten and not-eaten is particularly important, and it may enable us to differentiate between the food offered to the deceased, or perhaps the gods, and that consumed and shared by the living.

This differentiation, however, is not possible with the faunal remains, because the bones from cuts of meat that were placed in the fire cannot be distinguished from the bones of meat that was eaten before being tossed on the pyre. On the other hand, the bones, unlike vegetal remains, provide us with the opportunity to study food that clearly *was* placed on the pyre. Bones can be found either in the tombs or on the ground, although if they are retrieved from the latter context, it remains to be seen how they are related to the food rituals conducted during the funeral or commemorative feasts.

Cut marks can be observed on some bone fragments, but that, in itself, is not enough to establish a link with the rituals. An assemblage of thousands of unburnt bones has been collected from surface levels. Of these, somewhat less than four-hundred have been identified, most of them belonging to domesticated animals. Nearly three-quarters are pig, sheep or goat bones. Pig seems slightly more common than the other two species (32% as opposed to 23%), but it is also worth mentioning than twenty per-cent of the animal bones could not be linked to a specific species. Cattle bones are the next most common (10% of all the ruminants), with other species, such as poultry and fish, considerably less frequently represented.

The bones are quite fragmented and the surfaces often distorted, eroded or weathered. It is likely that some of these bones come from the levels modified and disturbed through the repeated digging of graves. They remain, nonetheless, closely linked to the history of religious activity centred on the tomb. Another group of faunal remains – dog and horse bones – probably has a different history and does not represent the remains of meals. The presence of these bones can perhaps be explained by the kind of activities characteristic of a life on the outskirts of town, such as the disposal of waste and rubbish. The bones in question here may have been extracted from refuse dumps or torn by dogs from discarded carcasses. Some bones show signs of having been digested and broken down by gastric juices. This evidence, and the presence of dog faeces on the site, suggest that some of the pig and sheep bones are exogenous and were not part of any ritual at the grave.

Animal bones that clearly can be associated with rituals, however, are those that are calcined. In most cases, these are found in the burials, mixed with cremated human bone. They occasionally can also be found scattered on the ground, as a result of the reorganisation of burials within the tomb enclosure and of the activities that took place there. Seven burials have provided us thus far with burnt animal bone (burials 2, 5, 6, 15B, 21A, 21B and 26). The distortion and fragmentation of bone often prevents us from recognising the species concerned, and sometimes it is even difficult to separate animal from human bone. Of the thirty mammal bones, only one-third has been identified to date. Pig is undoubtedly present in two burials, and sheep or goat in two others. Fish is present in two burials, whereas the bones of cattle and a cockerel occur only in one. The situation is rather similar for the bone retrieved from the occupation levels; only a quarter of this material is identifiable. Pig is better represented here than sheep/goat. Whether or not animal is mixed with human bone, these artefacts represent the remains of cuts of meat that were placed on the funeral pyre. The degree of burning is similar to that of the human bone, with animal bone also being cracked and light grey or white in colour as a result of being exposed to the high temperature of the pyre. They do not resemble, and should not be confused with, the bones of dark grey or black colour that are sometimes retrieved from domestic hearths or that represent the remains of meat cooked over a fire.

From cremation to the commemorative ceremonies: reconstructing the ritual events

The current state of our research in the Porta Nocera cemetery enables us to reconstruct some of the sequences of ritual events associated with death and burial. It is possible to associate some features encountered in our excavations with certain actions performed at the grave-side or following the funeral ceremony. Regarding the disposal of the body, information on the activities associated with cremation is provided by the analysis of human bone and the treatment of the corpse. Wood charcoal retrieved on site has been analysed to determine the ecological, technical and symbolic aspects of cremation rituals. Preliminary research conducted by Sylvie Coubray suggests that funeral pyres consisted of a wide range of woods; a strict selection of species does not seem to have been practiced, although walnut is the type of wood most widely used. Concerning the practices relative to the cremation process, textual sources tell us that rituals marked the separation between the living and the dead. Perfumes and incense were poured over the corpse, the funeral couch and the pyre (Ovid, *Fasti* 3.561; *Tristia* 3.69). Aromatic oils helped to combat the stench of exposed corpses and the smell of burnt flesh, but they played their main part in the symbolism of 'reversal' in affirming the new status of the deceased: the contrast between perfume and putrefaction, night and day, black and white, and deathly silence and the noise of life (Scheid 1984, 137). Offerings, such as incense and oil, as well as the crockery used during the funerary banquet, were thrown into the flames of the funeral pyre. Other objects, some of which may have been offerings or possessions of the deceased, were also placed on the pyre. The pyre objects found in our investigations were sometimes burnt and mixed with cremated human remains; these include joints of meat, fragmentary oil lamps, carved bone inlay from the funeral couch and items of wooden furniture such as small chests. However we usually find the artefacts not in the pyre debris, but in secondary positions on the ground. *Balsamaria*, melted and deformed by intense heat, pottery sherds, fruits, grains and animal bones belong to this group of finds (Fig. 6.10). Ancient texts do not provide us with much detail on the nature of the food that was placed on the pyre, but the excavated evidence helps us to fill some of the gaps in our knowledge, and we now know that meat, such as mutton, pork, and poultry, as well as fruits and vegetables ended up there. Remains of the funerary meals consumed by the living seem to also have been thrown on the pyre, as is suggested, for example, by the broken and empty shells of hazelnuts and walnuts.

The excavations also shed light on other rituals relevant to the question of what burial entails. The discovery in some burial pits (burials 5, 15, 16, 19) of intact *balsamaria*, some turned upside down as in burial 27, for example, are of significance in this context. The position of this flask, in particular, suggests that its contents were emptied when the grave pit was backfilled. It was not an offering, but the receptacle for a liquid that was used in some way during the interment of the body. It is also possible that the positioning of the flask again reflects the symbolism of 'reversal' that is characteristic

Figure 6.10 Remains of a pyre (area 210 behind Enclosure 21 OS) with burnt and unburnt material in situ (balsamaria, oil lamps, pottery sherds, nails) (photo, W. Van Andringa, MFP/FPN).

of funerary rites. The unguent flasks we excavated were placed in different positions: sometimes they were in contact with the body, whether inhumed (burial 29A, Fig. 6.11) or cremated (burial 211, area 210, Fig. 6.12), and at other times they are found outside the urn (burials 5 and 15). This distinction prompts us to ask what the purpose of the libations might have been. To what extent were the libations the final anointing of the mortal remains before they were covered with earth?

The choice of the receptacle used to contain the remains of the dead appears to have been a technical consideration. In most cases, particularly in single occupancy graves, the container used was a cooking pot (see Fig. 6.9). In the case of burial 25, however, belonging to "Publius Vesonius Procolus, who died at XIII years of age," as the inscribed *stele* tells us, the mortal remains were collected and placed in a tile cist (Fig. 6.5). When more than one individual was involved (burials 15 and 21), amphorae were used as cinerary urns (Fig. 6.8). A coin was left on top of the cremated remains (coins are absent in inhumation burials).

While awaiting the results of the on-going pollen analysis, which might provide us with rare evidence for flower or plant offerings associated with the burial, the absence

Figure 6.11 Balsamarium in contact with the body in burial 29A (photo, A. Gailliot, MFP/ FPN).

Figure 6.12 Unguent flasks and a burnt pine cone in contact with the cremated body (burial 211, area 210) (photo, A. Gailliot, MFP/FPN).

of any unburnt offerings in the graves is striking. It does not appear that it was common practice to deposit plates filled with fruit, meat or any other food with the human remains. The only possible exception, thus far, is burial 29A (Fig. 6.11). In this grave containing the remains of a child aged 18 to 33 months, the proximal extremity of a pig's femur was found next to the child about half-way up its body. The bone has butchery marks and it represents that part of the pig that produced the best meat for hams. But a thin layer of soil separates the human bones from the pig bone, suggesting that soil might have filtered into the burial pit in some way after the meat was deposited or that the soil was there before the meat was. In either case, the two elements are not in direct contact with each other, and, therefore, the relevance of the pig bone to the buried child remains uncertain.

Figure 6.13 Enclosure 23 OS, graves along the western wall under excavation. Notice the libation pipes and the sealing slabs (photo, A. Gailliot, MFP/FPN).

Funerary rituals were performed not only during the funeral; they also played an important part in the way the dead were commemorated during the festivals of the dead, such as the *Parentalia*, or on the birthdays of the deceased. On these occasions the tomb was honoured and the memory of the dead celebrated. A sacrifice was performed, destined now for the *Manes*. Offerings of wreaths, flowers, wine and food were brought to the tomb, and perfumed oils were poured on it (Ovid, *Fasti* 2.533 *ff.*). This latter action is particularly well documented in Pompeii, where most graves were fitted with libation pipes, usually of terracotta, placed upright with the top end protruding from the ground in front of the *stele* and the bottom end in close proximity to the buried human remains (Fig. 6.13). The neck of a ceramic vessel inserted into a cut in the sealing slab above the grave pit acted as a libation device in grave 19, liquids being poured into it

Figure 6.14 Broken balsamaria at ground level around burial 16 (photo, W. Van Andringa, MFP/ FPN).

running down into the buried urn. Sometimes, as we have seen in the case of graves 2 and 6, there was no direct contact between the urn and the libation pipe, the pipe ending instead at the bottom of the grave pit. Once the libations were finished, the flasks used to pour them were left behind or sometimes broken on the *stele*. Deposits on the ground furnish us with an important quantity of fragmentary *balsamaria* (Fig. 6.14). This fragmentation probably can be explained by pedestrian traffic within the enclosure, but it is probable that some of the breakage was intentional. The careful methods of excavation of the ground surfaces in the tomb enclosure have shown that the graves were visited for many years. The oldest *balsamaria* found around burials 17 and 18 are of terracotta and are typical of the first decades of the first century AD. Broken *balsamaria* were retrieved also from the upper and later levels, but these are of glass and belong to the third quarter of that century.

During the commemorative ceremonies, meals were consumed at the tomb. Some tombs, such as that of Cneius Vibrius Saturninus in the cemetery outside the Herculaneum Gate or Tomb 7ES in the Porta Nocera cemetery, even have a masonry dining couch, a *triclinium*. No structure of this sort has been found in the excavated area under discussion, but the ground was scattered with pottery sherds from vessels associated with food preparation as well as animal bones, suggesting that food-related rituals took place here. If this is indeed the case, these rituals involved the consumption of meat and probably bread, fruit and vegetables, although no traces of the latter survive. Finally, at different times celebrating the cult of the dead, funerary rites were accompanied by the burning of sometimes large quantities of incense. Interestingly, a terracotta tile found near the *stele* of grave 18 may be a remnant of such a rite: residues of charcoal mixed with a substance, possibly resin, were embedded in the fabric of the tile.

Conclusion

Every season of excavation at this site has demonstrated that funerary spaces are extremely complex and archeologically rich. They are compact spaces in which frequent and varied activities took place, linked to the duties of the living towards the dead in the Roman world. At the death of a member of the *familia,* funerals were celebrated beside the tomb. While the torches were lit, the pyre was erected in the enclosure. The dead received offerings of oil, perfume, and a bit of fish and fruit; the living participated in a funerary feast. The cremated remains of the deceased were then scrupulously gathered up and placed in an urn with a coin for the ferryman Charon. If no pre-existing grave was available (there are cases of multiple occupancy graves), a deep pit was dug at a place chosen in advance, with the soil put to one side. The urn was then placed in the pit, sometimes with the pyre debris, and oil and perfume was poured over the bones or on the bottom of the pit as the final rite before the formal closure of the grave. This act was a crucial step, as it marked the consecration of the grave and its transformation into a *locus religiosus.* The area surrounding the libation pipe was then back-filled and the surface marker put in place. The apparent lack of care in the arrangement of grave markers, and the use of recycled materials for them, suggest that the family, by then, had left the tomb. Once the bones of the deceased had been covered with soil, the tomb was considered completed and from then on it was under the protection of the *Manes.* The tomb was now ready for all subsequent visits of family or friends in conjunction with festivals like the *Parentalia*, birthdays, and other anniversaries, and it was easily accessible, being located close to the city gates and probably no more than ten minutes away from the homes of those who came to honour the dead. People repeatedly returned to the tomb with flowers and fruit as offerings to be burned and they poured perfumed oils into the libation pipe. The trampled soil and traces of trodden paths in the enclosures indicate that the tombs attracted frequent visitors.

Other funerals would later follow, and the digging of each new grave would see more excavated soil displaced. The level of the ground in the tomb precinct rose, and eventually traces of the earlier graves and rituals were covered. Sometimes, for whatever reason, people stopped visiting the tomb and it was abandoned. Since space was scarce, especially in areas near the city gates, the entire plot, or a section of it, could be sold, and a new monument built, as ostentatiously as possible, as a sign of social status. The whole procedure began again, the new occupants respecting older, existing graves as much as they could, but repeatedly shifting enough soil to bury all traces of them.

This sequence of events and actions associated with death, burial and commemoration is corroborated by our ongoing excavations in the necropolis of Porta Nocera. They confirm the density of occupancy of a funerary enclosure, they demonstrate the complexity and wealth of the surviving archaeological evidence, and they also justify the method of excavation we have chosen: precise documentation of the contents of the graves and surrounding occupation levels, three-dimensional recording of all artefacts distributed on the ground surfaces, and an interdisciplinary approach to all evidence retrieved for analysis, be it human bone, animal bone, ceramics, plant macro-remains, charcoal, or pollen. Despite the modest size of the funerary precinct examined, this site was one of intensive activity: it was visited, walked in, used in numerous ways, and it was constantly modified and re-organised. More than thirty graves were dug on a 32 m² plot in Enclosure 23OS within a period of less than a century. As a place of separation between the living and the dead, where the dead were laid to rest, and where the *Manes* who protected them resided, this world of the dead, from an archaeological point of view, is as rich and varied as the world of the living.

Acknowledgements

This programme of the École française de Rome has benefited from the support of the Université de Picardie Jules Verne, the Centre National de la Recherche Scientifique (CNRS) (UMR 5197, 5809, 6566) and the Soprintendenza Archeologica di Pompei, represented by its Soprintendente, Professor P. G. Guzzo, and the Director of Excavations at Pompeii, Dr. A. D'Ambrosio. We are also grateful to M. Gras, Director of the École française de Rome and Y. Rivière, Directeur d'Etude pour l'Antiquité, for their support of this project. The results presented here are the fruits of collaborative and interdisciplinary work. In addition to the authors of this paper, the team includes Marie-Josée Ancel, Carole Chevalier, Sylvie Coubray, Thomas Creissen, Marie Derreumaux, Antoine Gailliot, Solenn de Larminat, Tuija Lind, Anne-Laure Brives, Bui Thi Mai, Vincent Drost, Souen Fontaine, Vincent Lallet, and Philippe Prévot. For more information, see our website : http://www.mourirapompei.net

Bibliography

D'Ambrosio, A. and De Caro, S. (1984) *La necropoli di Porta Nocera. Un impegno per Pompei.* Milan, Total.

D'Ambrosio, A. and De Caro, S. (1987) La necropoli di Porta Nocera. Campagna di scavo 1983. In H. Von Hesberg and P. Zanker (eds), *Römische Gräberstrassen. Kolloquium München 28–30 Oktober 1985,* 199–228. Munich, Bayerischen Akademie der Wissenschaften.

Elefante, M. (1985) Un caso di defixio nella necropoli pompeiana di Porta Nocera? *Parola del Passato* 225, 431–443.

Fabre, G. ed. (1981) *Libertus: recherches sur les rapports patron-affranchi à la fin de la République romaine.* Rome, École française de Rome.

Guzzo, P. G. (1998) *Pompei oltre la vita. Nuove testimonianze dalle necropoli.* Pompeii, Soprintendenza Archeologica di Pompei.

Kockel, V. (1983) *Die Grabbauten vor dem Herkulaner Tor in Pompeji.* Mainz, von Zabern.

Lepetz, S. and Van Andringa, W. (2004a) Archéologie du rituel: fouille de la nécropole romaine de Porta Nocera à Pompéi. Chronique des Activités archéologiques de l'École française de Rome. *Mélanges de l'École Française a Rome. Antiquité* 116–1, 626–630.

Lepetz, S. and Van Andringa, W. (2004b) Caractériser les rituels alimentaires dans les nécropoles gallo-romaines: l'apport conjoint des os et des texts. In L. Baray (ed.) *Archéologie des pratiques funéraires. Approches critiques. Actes de la table ronde des 7 et 9 juin 2001, Glux-en-Glenne,* 161–170. Bibracte 7. Glux-en-Glenne, Bibracte.

Lepetz, S. and Van Andringa, W. (2005) Archéologie du rituel: fouille de la nécropole romaine de Porta Nocera à Pompéi. Chronique des Activités archéologiques de l'École française de Rome. *Mélanges de l'École Française a Rome. Antiquité* 117–1, 339–346.

Lepetz, S. and Van Andringa, W. (2006) Archéologie du rituel: fouille de la nécropole romaine de Porta Nocera à Pompéi. Chronique des Activités archéologiques de l'École française de Rome. *Mélanges de l'École Française a Rome. Antiquité* 118–1, 376–379.

Lepetz, S. and Van Andringa, W. *et al.* (2006) Pour une archéologie de la mort à l'époque romaine: fouille de la nécropole de Porta Nocera à Pompéi. *Académie des Inscriptions et Belles-Lettres: Comptes-Rendus,* avril–juin, 1131–1161.

Lepetz, S. and Van Andringa, W. *et al.* (2008) I riti e la morte a Pompei: nuove ricerche archeologiche nella necropoli di Porta Nocera. In M.-P. Guidobaldi and P. G. Guzzo (eds), *Nuove ricerche archeologiche nell'area vesuviana (scavi 2003–2006), Convegno Internazionale organizzato dalla Soprintendenza archeologica di Pompei, Rome, 2007,* 377–388. Rome, "L'Erma" di Bretschneider.

Matterne, V. and Derreumaux, M. (2008) A Franco-Italian investigation of funerary rituals in the Roman World: "les rites et la mort à Pompéi", the plant part, a preliminary report. *Vegetation History and Archaeobotany* 17, 105–112.

Scheid, J. (1984) *Contraria facere*: renversements et déplacememnts dans les rites funéraire. *Annali dell'Istituto Universitario Orientale di Napoli. Dipartimento di Studi del Mondo Classico e del Mediterraneo Antico. Sezione filologico-letteraria* VI, 117–139.

Scheid, J. (2005) *Quand faire, c'est croire. Les rites sacrificiels des Romains.* Paris, Aubier.

Thomas, Y. (1999) *Corpus aut ossa aut cineres.* La chose religieuse et le commerce. *Micrologus* VII, 73–112.

7

Marking the Dead:
Tombs and Topography in the Roman Provinces

John Pearce

Introduction

The extrovert property of tombs, their projection of identities through text, image and structure, is a well-known characteristic of Roman funerary culture. Monuments that sought to perpetuate memory through dialogue with an audience are distributed across the empire (Carroll 2006), but the placing of tombs in the provinces has received limited investigation, despite an abundance of information on setting which is paralleled in few other archaeological contexts. Scholarly effort has instead been directed at classifying and identifying cultural affiliation, 'indigenous', 'Roman' or 'provincial Roman' of various shades, through formal characteristics. The spatial setting, the street of tombs outside the town or the monument on the villa estate, has perhaps been considered an aspect so banal as to not require further investigation. Yet study of Italian urban cemeteries, primarily those of Rome, Ostia and the Campanian cities has shown that monumentalised *Gräberstraßen*, or 'streets of tombs', are key components of the 'townscape', the cumulative and ideologically-loaded impression of an urban society to be derived from their buildings (von Hesberg and Zanker 1987; Zanker 2000). Taking its cue from these studies, this paper seeks to demonstrate that the spatial setting of tombs can provide significant evidence for understanding funerary culture and societies beyond central Italy. The study of burial practice has not in general been well integrated into the broader study of provincial Roman societies (Morris 1992; Pearce 2000) and this paper argues that consideration of spatial relationships provides one vehicle for that integration. Its focus lies, therefore, not on the funerary ceremony itself, but on the possibilities for subsequent encounters between the dead and the living. In particular it contends that the distribution of monuments and the frequency of association with different site types, town, 'agglomération secondaire'/'small town' or villa, allied to consideration of the form taken by tombs, gives insights into the socio-political structure of provincial communities. Attention to the setting of individual monuments amplifies and nuances interpretation of this broader distribution. The paper advocates this approach using a sample of data from Roman Britain, a province with a limited memorial culture, as judged by quantity or sophistication, but nevertheless where monuments and their placing give insights into the histories and characters of communities. It is hoped that the broad-brush approach will be forgiven if the paper helps to give new impetus to this neglected but potentially rich area of study.

Death and space in the Roman world

Tombs have been a fundamental source for interpreting the organisation of space in the Roman world. Their mapping is a key procedure in urban topography. Since the division of the living and the dead specified in urban charters (*e.g. Lex Ursonensis*, 73–74) is, until late Antiquity, almost universally observed around Roman towns, the location of burials over time may indicate the (changing) limits of the occupied area and thus urban size. The development of Amiens and Gloucester are classic illustrations of the potential of such evidence for urban topography (Bayard and Massy 1983; Hurst 1985; see also Esmonde Cleary 1987). In a rural setting, funerary monuments were sometimes built at property boundaries (or later served as a reference marker of them) and may therefore also be exploited as a guide to landholding (*e.g.* Burnand 1975; Meffre 1993).

The analysis of Roman burial culture, in general, and tombs, in particular, has, from the 1970s onwards, given productive insights into the self-representation of different groups in Roman society, especially freedmen, tombs being more accessible than other civic spaces to draw the achievement and transformed status of the socially mobile to wider attention (Woolf 1996). The fundamental volume edited by von Hesberg and Zanker (1987), in particular the editors' introduction, demonstrated how study of self-representation could be enhanced by attention to spatial setting, using Rome and other cities in central Italy to demonstrate significant change in funerary culture from the late Republic to late Antiquity. They identified an increasing tendency on the part of aristocrats and wealthy freedmen in the second and first centuries BC to build tombs oriented towards an audience of passers-by, striving to surpass one another in scale, materials and innovation in form, with text and decoration on the exterior of the monument and directed at the road frontage. This culminated in the massive tombs of Republican aristocratic families and freedmen (*e.g.* the tombs of Caecilia Metella and Eurysaces), and in the mausoleum of Augustus. By the end of the first century AD, however, the interior of the tomb became the primary locus of funerary display, with painted and stuccoed walls and ceilings and the dead placed in marble sarcophagi. The exteriors became more homogeneous in scale and form, as seen for example in the cemetery beneath the Vatican. Later, the establishment of martyrial shrines prompted a further reconfiguration of prestigious cemetery space, providing a focus for burial *ad sanctos*, alongside the occasional spectacular integration of monumental tombs within imperial palace complexes, for example at the palaces of Maxentius in Rome or Diocletian in Split.

Other contributors to the same volume (*e.g.* Philippe Leveau 1987), as well as reviewers (*e.g.* Roth-Congès 1990), argued that the relationship between tomb and setting may have differed elsewhere in the empire. Hope's (2001) comparison of Mainz, Aquileia and Nîmes makes clear that the chronology of tomb building certainly varies between cities and can be related to their particular social dynamics. Von Hesberg (1992, 45–52) too has outlined differences in western provincial cities from the situation in Rome and Italy, in particular arguing that their elites were more inclined to build tombs on their estates than in urban *Gräberstraßen*, especially from the second century AD onwards. It is the latter observation which I wish to develop here, since it has by no means exhausted the analytical potential of the topography of death. The types of analysis possible vary according to the differential adoption of the monument building 'habit' and the preservation and recording of evidence. The nuanced histories that can be written from the Campanian cities, Ostia and Rome depend on exceptional preservation conditions in which inscriptions and artwork are abundant and can often be related to the buildings from which they derive. This preservation more rarely pertains elsewhere. Individual monuments have endured, in more or less denuded form, in the places in which they were built, more commonly in North Africa but also, more rarely, on the northern shores of the Mediterranean and in northern Europe. Where they have collapsed, the protection of ruins from spoliation by subsequent colluviation sometimes allows more or less complete reconstruction, as at Sarsina in Umbria (Ortalli 2001). More typically, however, despoliation and destruction have taken their toll from the Roman period onwards, although to varying degrees: the frequency of barrows in the Hunsrück/Eifel compared to surrounding areas in western Germany, for example, is in part an artefact of their protection by forest cover. Collecting of epitaphs and funerary sculpture has also dismembered the surviving elements of tombs and divorced them from their original context. Where cemeteries have been satisfactorily investigated by modern standards, the areas even of the most extensive excavations are small in comparison to those occupied by cemeteries, and the key relationship, for present purposes, between tomb and road frontage has often not been documented. Only in exceptional cases have the majority of (surviving) burials of major cemeteries been excavated, in northern Europe most notably at Krefeld-Gellep and Wederath (Pearce 2002). Surveys at Kenchreai (Corinth) and Portus demonstrate the as yet underexploited potential for geophysics and other non-invasive techniques to examine cemeteries as (partly) monumental spaces on a scale not realistically to be tackled by area excavation (Keay *et al.* 2006; Rife *et al.* 2007).

As a consequence a *Gräberstraße* can only in rare cases be reconstructed in equivalent detail to the Italian sites exploited by von Hesberg and Zanker. The fragmentary knowledge of layout and the decontextualisation of monumental material (illustrated below in relation to Britain) oblige us to frame questions differently, but nevertheless there are two major directions in which analysis can be developed. First, the relationship of monumental tomb building to context can be more systematically examined. The apparent privileging of rural rather than urban contexts in the western provinces, especially where city territories were much larger, is often noted at a general level (see above and also, for example, Landes 2002; Moore 2007; Wigg 1993a and b) and can be exemplified in individual urban territories. In the cities of Gallia Narbonensis east of the Rhône, for instance, the presence of monumental tombs near villas or small towns as well as in urban cemeteries is well attested (Burnand 1975; Roth-Congès 1993). But the strength of association between tomb building and settlement type, whether town, 'agglomération secondaire'/'small town' or villa deserves much closer exploration. Given the extent of urban cemeteries, the attribution to an urban or rural setting is not always straightforward, but more importantly classification of context by 'urban', 'rural', or other category must not be allowed to obscure the broader setting. Villas, for example, are (by definition) located outside towns but villa distribution in Gaul and Britain often clusters around them (Millett 1990, 191–5; Woolf 1998, 158). As will be seen below, this point also pertains in the case of monumental tombs. Hitherto monumental public buildings and houses, especially rich *domus* and villas have been the primary sources for understanding provincial Roman settlements as social environments, as the limited exploitation of funerary data in recent synthetic treatment of Britain demonstrates (see below). Where discussed in this context, tombs are considered more often in the abstracted form of the 'epigraphic habit' rather than as funerary monuments, to measure the dynamism and/or complexity of urban societies (*e.g.* Woolf 1998).

The second approach advocated, though less fully developed in the case study below, is not separate from the first but requires a shift of perspective and scale. Unlike the distribution map- based analysis, "in which space is conceived of as a container abstracted from human affairs" (Parker Pearson 1999, 139), its focus lies on experience of the tomb's setting, insofar as this can be restored. An explicitly phenomenological approach to tombs has been more commonly applied in European prehistory (*e.g.* Tilley 1994), but the wealth of contextual information should allow equally rich exploration in the Roman period. Von Hesberg and Zanker's insights into the changing emphasis on tomb exterior and interior illustrate its potential, as does Koortbojian's (1996) discussion of the accumulating impression on the passer-by of civic, professional and ethical *exempla* presented in text and image along the street of tombs. Consideration of the non-funerary aspects of setting can add further nuance. Some tombs were placed at points where visibility and/or spatial association lent them an additional prestige. The edge of the city/*pomerium* appears to be one such privileged context, documented at Pompeii by both the placing of the most monumental tombs immediately beside the Herculaneum gate and in the general distribution of tombs for which the site was given as a civic honour (Kockel 1983; see also Lepetz and Van Andringa, this volume). A similar preference can be seen at other cities where monuments survive *in situ*, for example the tower tombs hard by the north gate and amphitheatre at Urbisaglia (Marche), where the *via Salaria Gallica* leaves the city, or by the Beneventum and Bovianum gates at Saepinum (Molise). The tomb of the Julii, adjacent to the triumphal arch at St Rémy

Figure 7.1 The view west and north over Autun and the Arroux valley from the Pyramide de Couhard. The Roman town lies under the modern city from left to centre (photo, Author).

(Glanum), exemplifies the same phenomenon beyond Italy. What is not clear is the importance of this space compared to others where general prominence or proximity to routes enhanced the visibility of a monument. Of many potential examples of this concern for broader impact, one of the most striking is the second century AD (?) 'Pyramide de Couhard' at Autun. Its mortared rubble core, on a spur by the road to Lyons, overlooks the town and a broad swathe of the Arroux valley to the north (Fig. 7.1). As first constructed, with cladding intact, it would have stood out against the hillside on which it stood. The situation of harbour cemeteries, as at Kenchreai, overlooking the Saronic Gulf (Rife *et al.* 2007) or overlooking Gaeta and the sea from Monte Orlando in the case of the tomb of G. Munatius Plancus illustrates the potential influence of marine as well as terrestrial settings on monument placing.

Beyond the cemeteries of cities and other agglomerations, the siting of tombs can be examined at various levels of resolution. A garden or orchard setting for many provincial as well as Italian tombs can be plausibly suggested from the stipulations in the so-called 'testament of the Lingon' (Le Bohec and Buisson 1991), but has not yet been identified archaeologically. The example of Biberist-Spitalhof (Vaud, Switzerland), demonstrates the potential for close integration of the tomb with the villa as monumental ensemble. Here the burial enclosure and *stele* were set up on the main longitudinal axis of the courtyard, *c.* 170m from the *pars urbana* but directly in its line of sight, visible only to an audience within the villa complex (Schucany 2000). At Newel and Nennig in Treveran territory on the Moselle tomb sites combined visibility both from the villa with which they are presumed to have been associated and from roads (Martin-Kilcher 1993). Where information on immediate environs is lacking, a widespread concern to ensure the visibility of tombs by their setting in prominent places and/or by major communication routes can be established: the recurring prominence of tower tombs in the countryside of Africa Proconsularis is a striking example (Moore 2007).

As well as their general visual impact on their setting, it may be possible to enquire into other associations prompted by tombs among passers-by. For example imperial mausolea at Rome, especially those of Augustus and Hadrian, were sited with an eye to their visual prominence and regard for the connotations of their setting. P. Davies

(2000) has shown their connection to previous funerary and other monuments in the city and beyond by juxtaposition, line of sight or echo of form. It is not implausible that other monumental tombs could provoke impressions beyond awe at their scale or situation. The famous verse epitaph on the tomb of the Flavii at Kasserine (Tunisia), built alongside other mausolea on the road from Theveste to Sufeitla, articulates the connections that might be prompted among those passing the tomb and (as imagined) for the statue of its occupant looking out over its environs (*Musa Lapidaria*, 199A 79–85; Groupes de Recherches sur l'Afrique Antique 1993). These connections are with the tomb's 'real' surroundings, endowed with the *munera Bacchi* by its occupant, seemingly an allusion to making the land productive through new water management and the introduction of viticulture, as well as with the monuments of the city of Cillium above. By its scale the tomb (so it claims) overshadows the plains and hills roundabout but recalls too the landmarks of empire, surpassing the obelisk of the Circus Maximus in Rome or the Pharos at Alexandria. The emphasis on filial piety and paternal achievement reminds us of the family association evoked by tombs and extends the family history to the history of its landscape setting, an account that may well have been contested, though we lack the other side of the story. The abundance of text in this case is exceptional, but nevertheless illuminates connections that could be prompted by context and form. It suggests the value of considering the relationship between tomb building and landscape modifications by clearance, reconfiguration of property holding or agricultural innovation. These connections seem at their starkest in semi-arid landscapes such as the Fazzan in southern Libya where better preservation makes clear the close juxtaposition of tombs, irrigation systems and cultivated land *c.* 500 BC–AD 500 (Mattingly 2007). Consideration of the spatial and chronological association with villas (and other structures, especially temples) may help to extend understanding of the extent to which groups manipulated landscapes to establish and advertise their power. Discussions of villas as monuments, especially in the north-west provinces, have so far focused primarily on the exploitation of interior space rather than broader visual impact (*e.g.* Scott 2000). Account should also be taken of Roman-period re-use of tombs and other structures of prehistoric date, a potential complementary or alternative strategy to connect a group within its setting (*cf.* Vermeulen and Bourgeois 2000). Given this lack of contextualising work, analysis of tomb setting is better discussed within the broader study of landscape change rather than in isolation, so receives less attention in the following case study, but its potential should be noted.

Burial monuments and their setting in Roman Britain

This section of the paper applies the questions outlined above to tombs in Britain as a case study. In writing the social and economic history of the province, burial practice has remained a relatively neglected area of study. Its evidence has been little used in many of the major syntheses and essay collections (Pearce 1999, 5–6), although it has recently enjoyed a higher profile (*e.g.* Creighton 2006; Mattingly 2006; Todd 2004). As noted above, funerary monuments have typically been considered in the context of the epigraphic habit and since most, like other inscriptions, derive from Roman garrisons, it is in relation to military communities that their significance has been discussed (*e.g.* Biró 1975; Cepas 1989; Hope 1997). One key observation, however, has been made which is important for the argument to be developed here, namely that both monuments and grave assemblages indicate that elite burials took place in a rural rather than urban setting in Roman Britain (Millett 1987; Philpott 1991; Struck 2000; Mattingly 2006, 478). This observation has been used to support an argument that British cities show only limited evidence of competition based on euergetism, an indication of the transformation of Iron Age aristocrats into Roman town councillors whose power remained substantially uncontested and for whom the primary context of display remained rural (Millett 1990). The following paragraphs summarise the evidence for monuments in the province and then explore their distribution in relation to the communities of southern Britain. (See the Appendix on pp. 153–4 for a list of Romano-British monuments discussed here and in the following pages, with references.)

The evidence available for study is very uneven and in comparison to other provinces, meagre in quantity and architecturally less sophisticated. Much more investigation has taken place of urban cemeteries than of any other site type (Pearce 1999, 25–26), although their burial beneath medieval and modern towns means that the survival of monument superstructures in particular is severely compromised. The closest to their 'original' context which can usually be reconstructed is re-use in Roman cemeteries (*e.g.* re-used sarcophagi at York) or fortifications (*e.g.* the fragments of the Gaius Iulius Alpinus Classicianus and other monuments in the bastions of London's city wall). Many discoveries are documented in antiquarian accounts of varying quality: the major cemeteries beneath the Railway station and Mount south of the *colonia* at York, recorded during obliteration by urban expansion and railway construction in the nineteenth century, provide a typical example (Jones 1984). In a rural context focus on the major residential buildings of villas has meant neglect of peripheral structures, including tombs. Better preserved rural funerary monuments typically attracted antiquarian interest, and knowledge of key tombs is compromised by limited documentation from their investigations (Jessup 1959; 1962). The lack of interest in excavating garrison cemeteries means that the many inscriptions originating from them are generally poorly contextualised: the limited information available from Hadrian's Wall is not atypical (Petts 2006). As elsewhere, better documented contexts are typically those of re-use, in Roman tombs (*e.g.* Brougham) or buildings (*e.g.* the walls of the legionary fortress at Chester).

To judge from limited intercutting between burials in many cemeteries, graves must have commonly been marked but the use of perishable materials and truncation of cemetery surfaces means evidence for markers rarely survives. The holes for wooden posts marking cremation burials at the St Stephen's cemetery in St Albans, in one case probably topped with a sheep's skull, or the mounds over the better preserved graves in feature 12 at Winchester Lankhills indicate likely common forms. It is likely that even substantial monuments have been lost to the plough or other post-depositional damage. At Stansted Duckend Car Park, for example, the distance between the two rich second-century cremation burials (25 and 26) suggests the existence of barrows of which all trace has disappeared. Since monuments commonly survive as foundations only, it is not always possible to attribute unreservedly a funerary function, the Shadwell 'tower' in east London illustrating this problem well. In other cases antiquarian records are suggestive but do not allow a precise attribution, most famously at 'Arthur's O'on' in Stirlingshire. This same problem applies to sculptural fragments (Blagg 2002). Practical limits to area excavation also mean that understanding of cemetery and monument context, especially around the public and small towns, will only ever be partial (Esmonde Cleary 1987). In some situations geophysical survey now lends the possibility of amplifying knowledge of the setting of individual monuments (*e.g.* M. Davies 2000; Astin *et al.* 2007) and cemeteries, especially in association with garrisons in upland Britannia (Petts 2006). The same techniques also have considerable potential to extend knowledge of cemeteries in Roman cities in the south not burdened with overlying medieval and modern occupation.

As elsewhere, so for Britain the different types of evidence for funerary monuments, inscriptions, art and structural types, have been considered in isolation. A synthesis is therefore lacking, although Manuela Struck (2000) has sketched key aspects, complementing Jessup's (1959; 1962) earlier studies. Before considering their spatial setting, the following discussion therefore outlines the range of monument forms. With the exception of the Classicianus tomb, British examples have not interested major recent surveys of funerary architecture (Gros 2001; von Hesberg 1992), but they fall into the main groupings documented elsewhere for the Roman world.

Many burials must have been marked in ways for which the evidence is now lost (see above). The simplest documented are markers in temporary materials, for instance four and six timber post structures over cremation burials at Hyde Street, Winchester and St Stephens, St Albans. More complex post-built structures, for example at Roughground Farm (Gloucestershire), may have played a temporary role in funerary rites or formed a timber framework for a burial mound. Much more numerous are inscribed stone markers, of which the freestanding *stele* is the most common type, though varying widely in size, scale and style of execution of text and image. The sometimes two metre high military tombstones bearing portraits, architectural framework and text account for the most monumental examples of these (Mattern 1989). Altars are rarer, the tomb of Classicianus being a so far isolated example of a type better known from Treveran territory in Gallia Belgica as well as the central Mediterranean. The stone used is usually local in origin where available and where not, as in London, derives from the same sources as those in other buildings, the use of limestone from eastern Gaul for the memorial of Facilis at Camulodunum, being a rare exception (Hayward 2006).

Grabgärten, tomb plots enclosed by banks, ditches or walls, are relatively common. They demarcated varying numbers of burials, from single tombs to the *c.* 80 cremations and 250 inhumations within the burial ground at Litlington in Cambridgeshire. Within these enclosures individual burials were sometimes distinguished by a further marker, as examples from Springhead (Kent) and Colchester show. Burials could also 'borrow' boundaries and markers by their association with other non-burial features, for example being placed on or in settlement and field enclosure ditches or entrances (Pearce 1999, 115–18).

The apparent abundance of the tumulus may be partly due to its lesser susceptibility to subsequent despoliation. In its main areas of distribution, the south-east and on the northern frontier, groups as well as individual examples have been documented, the eighteen within the hillfort at Borough Hill, Daventry being the largest so far recorded. The paucity of dating evidence and the frequency of Roman re-use of prehistoric barrows means that the mere presence of small quantities of poorly contextualised Roman period material is insufficient to confirm primary Roman construction. Within some, masonry- or tile-built cists shelter single burials, while others are revetted with walls which may be internally or externally buttressed. Tomb 1 at Keston, Kent, erected in *c.* AD 200, was an earth-filled circular drum contained by a buttressed stone wall. Surviving plaster suggests that its exterior was painted red and an inscribed fragment of white marble may derive from an epitaph from this or neighbouring tombs. These architecturally more sophisticated instances are much less common than in Gallia Belgica (*cf.* Wigg 1993a). Monumentality could also be 'borrowed' by re-using prehistoric monuments, either by insertion directly into the earlier tomb, as at the Neolithic long barrow at Uffington (Oxfordshire), or by burial close by, as near Bronze Age round barrows at Westhampnett (West Sussex), though rarely in comparison to some other provinces or post-Roman Britain (Vermeulen and Bourgeois 2000; Williams 1997).

In neighbouring provinces the 'tower tomb' ('mehrstöckige Aediculabau', 'tombeau à édicule sur podium') is the most frequently documented of mausoleum types, usually square or rectangular in plan, with its plinth supporting a multiple storey superstructure, a podium topped by a tholos or cella and pronaos with freestanding statues, or by a storey carrying relief sculpture. The pyramidal or pedimented roof often carried further decoration (Gros 2001; von Hesberg 1992). Foundations and sculptural fragments from garrisons (*e.g.* Brougham and Caerleon) as well as urban (*e.g.* Southwark) and rural sites (*e.g.* Langley, Kent) have been interpreted as possible instances. Within a walled funerary enclosure at Langley was the lower part of a nearly square (*c.* 3.8 x 4.3m) masonry monument and a circular foundation, 4.6m in diameter with evidence for painted plaster on the exterior of its superstructure, both perhaps the bases of such tombs. Relief-carved fragments associated with a rock-cut ledge above the Dee at Heronbridge (Cheshire) may also derive from a similar tomb, placed to maximise visibility from the river. The massive (*c.* 12m square) second-century AD foundation at Shorden Brae near Corbridge has been interpreted as the base of a tower tomb but its size, far exceeding the most substantial of the better documented continental examples, such as the tomb of the Julii at Glanum and similar structures (Roth-Congès 1993), suggests that it might be better interpreted as the foundations of a podium which supported a drum barrow.

The mausoleum at Lullingstone, Kent, perhaps the best documented of tombs built in the form of a Romano-Celtic temple, was constructed in *c.* AD 300 and had been demolished by the end of the fourth century. Its outer precinct was 12.2m square, the *cella* 6.4m x 5.2m, with a tomb chamber beneath. Evidence from Welwyn Hall in Hertfordshire reminds us that in some instances the interior and exterior of these were plastered and the fragments of a possible frieze, as well as carved sarcophagus, indicate the possibility of possible sculpted decoration. Most examples of the type have been found in south-east England, but excavations at Vindolanda on Hadrian's Wall have extended their distribution to the military area of the province. Given the difficulty of identifying a funerary function, it is not impossible that other Romano-Celtic temples served as mausolea or played a role in commemorative cult.

Fragments remind us of substantial monuments of unknown form which have been lost. For example the epitaph of the centurion T. Annius, used in the fourth-century rebuilding of the *praetorium* at Vindolanda, or *RIB* 233, a 1.2m wide panel from the tomb of a *strator consularis* from Irchester (Northamptonshire), derive from substantial mausolea of unknown form, as must sculptural fragments from statues of Minerva, a river god, slave girl, and a barbarian head re-used in the hypocaust flues of a fourth-century building at Stanwick, Northamptonshire. In general the iconographic repertoire of funerary sculpture in Britain is limited to the most commonly attested motifs in the western provinces, such as lions or pinecones (Blagg 2002; Mattern 1989).

Epigraphic formulae and limited evidence from excavation suggest that the *floruit* of monument construction lay in the second and third centuries AD (Hope 1997; Struck 2000). Funerary inscriptions were rarely cut after the mid-third century AD and few of the surviving funerary sculptures appear to date to later than this period. Nevertheless excavation of late Roman urban cemeteries shows that timber and masonry monuments continued to be constructed. The most impressive and best-preserved examples are the rectangular masonry chambers with painted decoration from Poundbury, Dorchester, but stone and timber-built tombs, as well as ditched enclosures and barrows have been recorded in other urban cemeteries at York, Gloucester, Winchester, Colchester and London and in small towns such as Shepton Mallet (Somerset) and Water Newton (Northamptonshire).

In mapping the evidence for monuments, inscriptions are easiest to assess. Figure 7.2 shows the number of epitaphs from the public towns of Roman Britain published in *RIB* and subsequently in the *Journal of Roman Studies* (to 1969) and *Britannia* (to 2005). The only other substantial group from a non-military site in the province derives

John Pearce

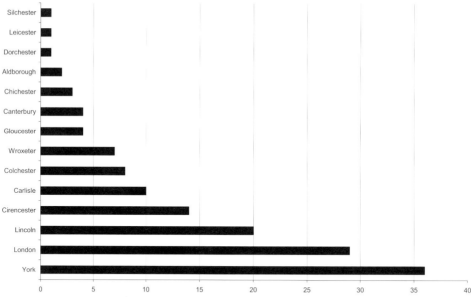

Figure 7.2 Numbers of funerary inscriptions from the towns of Roman Britain.

from Bath, where inscriptions and sculpture fragments have been recorded in modest numbers. The availability of suitable stone exerts some influence on the pattern but social factors are as, if not more, important, since the small total quantity is paralleled in the dearth of inscriptions related to the construction of urban public buildings (Blagg 1990; Mattingly 2006, 299). The 'ranking' of individual towns is prone to be substantially affected by new discoveries: two tombstones recently excavated at Gloucester (London Road) have increased the city's tally to six, a fifty per cent increase. Broader trends are therefore more reliable than differences between individual sites. In general, funerary inscriptions are best represented at London, York and Lincoln, which account for sixty per cent of the 140 instances documented. Mann's (1985) observation, re-iterated by Millett (1990, 117–100), that this small corpus of urban monuments is strongly skewed to particular groups, especially soldiers and individuals of non-insular origin, especially legionary garrisons in the case of Lincoln and York, continues to stand. There is very little evidence for members of the urban elite and their families, save at York and Lincoln, as Mattingly (2006, 304) notes. A wider range of monument types as the medium for epitaphs can also be documented at London and York, including *stelae*, coffins and statue bases (Fig. 7.3). Since the *Corpus Signorum Imperii Romani* (*CSIR*) for Britain is not yet complete, the distribution of funerary sculpture cannot yet be easily compared, but reference to volumes so far published and other surveys (Henig 2000) show it to be more abundant and varied in these same towns, as well, to a lesser extent, as Colchester and Carlisle.

For reasons discussed above, the context of these monuments is not easily established.

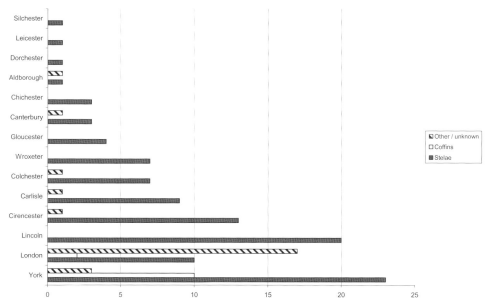

Figure 7.3 Types of funerary monument from Romano-British towns bearing inscriptions.

Limited evidence from Roman London suggests their presence throughout the areas of burial north of the Thames (Barber and Hall 2000). The clearest example of a monumentalised street of tombs has been excavated in Southwark at Great Dover Street, which revealed the foundations of closely spaced walled enclosures and other tombs adjacent to Watling Street, as well as fragments of funerary sculpture. The outlying 'tower' at Shadwell in east London, re-interpreted as a mausoleum associated with a second-century AD cremation cemetery, would have been clearly visible to those arriving in London via the Thames estuary. Limited evidence from York and Lincoln suggests the favouring of individual cemeteries for the construction of monumental tombs, best illustrated at the Mount/Railway station cemeteries at York (Esmonde Cleary 1987; Jones 1984).

The discussion of tomb typology showed that we should not rely on inscriptions and sculptural fragments alone to assess monument building. In the following paragraphs I take one case study, the territory of the Catuvellauni, with its centre at St Albans (Verulamium), to review the full range of evidence. I briefly compare the patterns to neighbouring urban territories but, as noted above, the uneven distribution of monument building in the province and its general greater frequency in south-east England should be remembered. The difficulties of establishing urban territories for this case study should also be acknowledged (Dunnett 1975; Rivet 1968, 145–8).

The *municipium* of Verulamium is arguably the best served in Britain for the study of Late Iron Age and Roman mortuary rituals, but the evidence is unevenly distributed. Of *c.* 1200 burials so far recorded, 900 are of first- to early third-century AD date, most from cemeteries south of the town (Niblett and Thompson 2005, 138–141). In the territory of the city substantial numbers of burials have also been excavated at the small town of Baldock (Hertfordshire) (Burleigh 1993) as well as more modest samples from other small towns, but only a small corpus of rural burials is so far recorded (Pearce 1999, 103–7).

The burials made in the King Harry Lane cemetery (late first century BC or early first century AD) are the earliest known from Verulamium. King Harry Lane is the largest documented cemetery of the pre-Roman centre, and may have served as a communal burial space for groups occupying dispersed settlement foci (Niblett and Thompson 2005, 36–37). With the establishment of a Roman urban plan, the separation between living and dead was perpetuated but reconfigured to place the latter outside the inhabited area. The primary use of the King Harry Lane cemetery ended in *c.* AD 60, roughly contemporary with the earliest use of the St Stephen's cemetery on Watling Street to the south (Niblett 1999, 400). Here some of the earliest burials were placed over a kilometre from the small pre-Flavian urban centre.

At both cemeteries the primary evidence for substantial funerary markers comprised the ditches that enclosed groups of interments, often with a focal burial at their centre. At St Stephen's these and the modest post-built structures marking a small number of tombs were placed adjacent to the road. In this instance, one of the few sites in Britain to have seen excavation of cemetery and road through it, there is no indication of a heavily monumentalised *Gräberstraße*. There are no certain epitaphs recorded in the very small corpus of inscriptions from the town and the sparse other evidence for monumental tombs includes a sculptural fragment, perhaps from the roof of a tower tomb, and a possible mausoleum detected on an aerial photograph near the road that runs to the north-east gate (Niblett and Thompson 2005, 145). The scarcity of local building stone is likely to have affected significantly the subsequent survival of masonry tombs and funerary inscriptions. The major exception to this dearth of monuments is the Folly Lane mortuary complex, a massive ditched enclosure *c.* two hectares in extent surrounding a wooden chamber, pyre and burial site, laid out probably in the immediate post-conquest period (*c.* AD 45–50) near the crest of the hill north-east of the town, contemporaneously with the earliest street plan. In the post-Boudiccan phase, after AD 60, a major period of monument building for the city, a temple was built over the pyre mound and the enclosure ditch re-cut. The contents of the shafts on the hill to the south suggest that the site remained a cult focus into the third century AD.

Within a zone seven to eight kilometres from the town further monuments have been documented (Fig. 7.4). These take a variety of forms, including a timber built enclosure excavated at Lindum Place, St Albans, barrows at Pickford Hill, Harpenden and probable tower- or temple-tombs from Wood Lane End (two) and Rothamsted, though in both latter cases a funerary function is plausible rather than proven. The Wood Lane End complex also included other buildings which may have accommodated cult activity, including a bath-house and other buildings suitable for collective use. Its use lasted

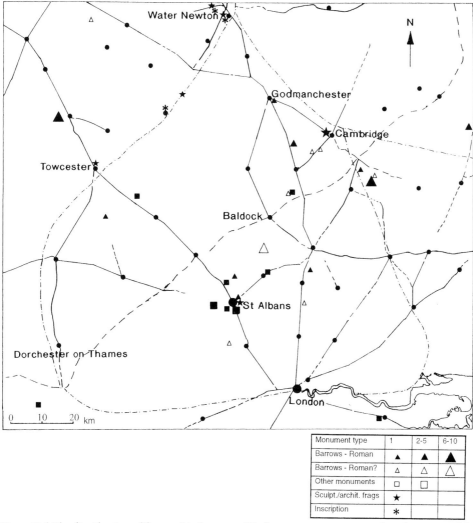

Figure 7.4 The distribution of first to third century AD funerary monuments within the civitas of the Catuvellauni (plan, Author). The line of dots and dashes indicates the possible civitas boundary.

during the second century AD, during which time the first tomb was demolished and its materials probably re-used in the second. The tower tomb, if correctly identified as such, was likely to be visible over a wide area of the plateau west of St Albans, indeed from as far away as Folly Lane on the other side of the valley of the Ver, as well as from the Silchester road which passed to its south.

Beyond Verulamium, monumental burials from large cemetery excavations are lacking: in this connection the negative evidence, save for occasional post-built structures, from the very extensive excavations of cemeteries at Baldock in Hertfordshire, seems significant. Fragments of funerary sculpture and single inscriptions are associated with the cemeteries of small towns in the north-western part of the *civitas*, including Irchester (see above) and Water Newton, the latter also with evidence from aerial photography suggesting the existence of mausolea (Burnham and Wacher 1990, 91). These may reflect the greater availability of stone in this area, especially Barnack Rag. In the northern part of the territory, near the boundary with the Trinovantes and Iceni in a zone around and between the small towns of Great Chesterford, Cambridge and Godmanchester, is a second, more abundant cluster of monuments, primarily barrows, none of which has been examined by modern excavation.

The immediate settings of these monuments are patchily documented and deserve fuller exploration. Some were constructed in seeming isolation (*e.g.* Welwyn, Hertfordshire), others in association with larger cemeteries (*e.g.* the walled cemetery at Litlington, Cambridgeshire). Many were sited with a concern to enhance their visibility, either in prominent locations (*e.g.* the Limlow Hill barrow, Cambridgeshire), adjacent to roads (*e.g.* Emmanuel Knoll nr Godmanchester) or at points visible from the latter: the temple-mausoleum at Bancroft (Buckinghamshire) would have been visible from Watling Street 2.5 km to the south-east. The latter also overlooked the villa in the valley beneath, the construction of tomb and house being very roughly contemporaneous (late first to late second century AD). The siting of some monuments privileges a particular view which needs further examination: the Bartlow Hills, for example, among the largest of provincial Roman barrows, overlook the area to their north and east but their position towards the base of a gentle slope of the valley of the Granta makes them less visible from other directions.

Similar patterning in the distribution of monuments can be documented in the territories of neighbouring cities. Mapping the distribution of some 'elite' grave indicators, including barrows and mausolea, led Manuela Struck (2000, 89–93), like others, to emphasise their rural location, but when the distribution of towns is taken into account her maps clearly show similar clustering to that identified for the Catuvellauni. Among the Trinovantes, late Iron Age and conquest period monumental burials cluster around Camulodunum at Lexden (a barrow of the last decade of the first century BC), Stanway (massive ditch-bounded mortuary complexes, AD 40–60) and, perhaps, Gosbecks (Crummy *et al.* 2007). The development of an extra-mural sanctuary with a theatre at the latter has analogies to the Folly Lane sequence but the burial connection is unproven (Creighton 2006, 134–5). In the Roman period, monumentalised cemeteries nearer the city can also be documented, in particular in the zone around the crossroads west of the Balkerne gate. Here monument building, including tombstones and mausolea, continues from the mid first century AD *stelae* of Facilis and Longinus (*RIB* 200 and 201) to at least the late third/early fourth century AD tower(?) tomb excavated on Lexden road in 2005. The location of the Mersea Island barrows in the colony's *territorium*, one on its south coast, the other overlooking the channel between the estuaries of the Blackwater and Colne to the north, recalls the importance of views over water as well as land noted elsewhere. In the territory of the Cantii there are groups of monuments towards the western periphery of the *civitas* between the small towns at Darenth and Rochester, as well as in the east around Canterbury. Whether the mausolea (and associated villas) at Lullingstone and Keston should be associated with London or with these small towns cannot be established, but they are also in a peripheral location with respect to urban territories. Many of these tombs were sited with a concern for visibility. The Holborough barrow was situated on the final crest of a spur overlooking the Medway valley, at Keston the prospect from the tombs takes in the villa below and the valley to the south and at Langley the enclosure was prominently sited on a hill by the Roman road between Rochester and Hastings. It is worth briefly noting here that the importance of this peri-urban setting is also demonstrated in the distribution of the most substantial and most varied burial assemblages in some southern *civitates* (Pearce 1999, 141–44).

What is the significance of these different zones of monumentalisation, centred on *civitas* capitals and also on some small towns? From differences in the culture of euergetism, Martin Millett (1990, 80–91) has argued for a distinction in terms of social complexity and degrees of competition between the *civitates* which often developed from Iron Age centres, such as St Albans, and the newly founded *coloniae*, especially London, York and Lincoln. As noted above, in this model the former are primarily governed by an elite which remained in power over the conquest transition, the Roman town councillors comprising a limited oligarchy with little challenge to its position because of the lack of alternative routes to wealth and status. The latter towns, by contrast, can be argued to have been more open and dynamic social environments, with competition driven by the multiple routes to power, status and wealth provided by connection to provincial administration, economic opportunities related to long distance trade networks, and through the mixing of populations from varied backgrounds, soldiers, other extra-provincials and those Britons drawn to new opportunities. The lack of villas around London and York, in contrast to their clustering around many *civitas* capitals, has been attributed to the lack of integration of these towns with their hinterlands (Millett 1990, 88).

At first view the funerary evidence appears to provide some support for this bipartite model. The epigraphic and artistic evidence suggested a more intensive monumentalisation of cemetery space for London, York and Lincoln, related to social factors identified above and to greater familiarity with the epigraphic habit and languages in which inscriptions were written. Woolf (1998), noting similar variation in the epigraphic habit between Gallic cities, invokes similar arguments, but it is important to note that the most substantial samples of inscriptions from Gaul (*e.g.* Lyons, Trier, Langres) are much larger (greater than a factor of 10) than those of London and York. This difference from analogous sites in neighbouring provinces has not received as much attention as it deserves, though direct comparison is difficult because of varying access to building stone and, arguably, the exponentially greater

Figure 7.5 The view from the cavea of the theatre at Verulamium looking north-east to the north side of the Ver valley. The Folly Lane temple would have stood to the right of the hospital building on the skyline (photo, Author).

scale of the destruction of archaeological remains from London in comparison to those continental sites.

However when the analysis widens to take into account the full range of monument types and the broader peri-urban zone this distinction becomes less clear-cut. The emphasis of previous commentators (see above) on the rural setting of burial display is, to some extent, accurate in its characterisation of the immediate environs but neglects the bigger picture. Monumental tombs can be documented, in small numbers at least, in urban cemeteries. At St Albans the Folly Lane complex, the most substantial mortuary area that has so far come to light, was transformed into a major civic monument, speculatively perhaps the grafting of the history of an individual lineage onto that of the broader community through a 'founder' cult. Niblett (1999, 416–7) and Creighton (2006, 125) have argued that it is linked by a processional route to the theatre, adjacent temple and Branch Road baths in the city's festivals, Creighton also arguing that the same may be true of other early sanctuaries on the margins of other cities (Fig. 7.5). For several kilometres beyond the urban cemeteries of Verulamium the landscape was punctuated by monumental tombs, some of which had facilities for communal ceremony (*e.g.* Wood Lane End). This distribution is similar to, though quantitatively less significant than, the clustering of villas around most of the public towns documented by Millett (1990, 191–95). Since the tombs to some extent predate the phase in which villas reach their most monumental form, they indicate the longevity of the attachment of elites to urban centres. A classification of tombs as 'urban' or 'rural' categories obscures this aspect of the distribution pattern. A more helpful perspective is offered by Hurst (1999), who 'walks' the reader from the centre of the city (in his case study *Glevum* – Gloucester) to its margins in order to visualise the texture of urban space. If we extend that walk at Verulamium then we extend the space of display into a hinterland that is no longer a suburb but is nonetheless studded with tombs and villas, both perhaps calling attention to family status and ancestry. In this area the visibility of tombs from a distance is a recurring characteristic, as is the variety of forms, which may lend greater distinctiveness and memorability to individual instances. The different forms may carry varied connotations. Temple-mausolea echo the major urban sacred buildings and may have prompted associations between the divine status of the latter and divine/heroised occupants of the former, a blurring which can be documented in other Roman tomb types. The polysemic quality of the tumulus, echoing the greatest tombs of Rome and local prehistoric forms, has been remarked on by others (*e.g.* Wigg 1993a).

In general, therefore, the understanding of urban society as seen through funerary evidence requires recalibration. The spatial modes may differ, the monuments of some cities being concentrated in the urban cemeteries proper, especially London and York, those of others in the broader peri-urban area. These are not the only privileged spaces of burial display. The significance of some minor centres and *civitas* peripheries as zones of burial display has also emerged from the case study, in particular in Britain in a tract of territory on the boundaries of the Catuvellauni, Trinovantes and Iceni. These minor centres and peripheral zones have been characterised as significant alternative foci of social and economic power in the late Roman period when central municipal elites may have exercised decreasing and less spatially extensive authority. This characterisation is based on evidence of investment in public buildings, primarily walled circuits, the clustering of villas and also with a significant economic role as markets and production centres (Millett 1990, 145–50). The funerary evidence suggests that these were already dynamic and competitive zones before the late Roman period.

The limitations and weaknesses of this characterisation should be acknowledged. Since some areas of Roman Britain, especially the *civitates* of north and west do not adopt the forms of funerary display discussed here, it applies to only part of the province. Where a monument building culture can be identified, the poverty of dating evidence and the uncertain attribution of a funerary character to some monuments has been indicated. Even more difficult to establish is the period for which tombs continued to stand as monumental markers. A handful of better documented instances shows that their 'afterlife' need last no more than a century or so (*e.g.* Bancroft, Welwyn Hall). The 'pristine' appearance frequently presented in reconstruction images certainly needs further testing against better archaeological (and archaeobotanical) samples. The distribution patterns and the observations concerning visibility of individual monuments need fuller assessment using GIS to test the impressionistic assessment given here. This is better undertaken in tandem with a broader assessment of the visual aspect of urban and rural built environments. The approach advocated here can also be more fully applied in neighbouring regions with a richer monumental culture, and in this context it is worth noting that in Gaul too there are indications that this peri-urban zone is as significant as it is in Britain for display through funerary monuments. In Aquitaine, for instance, Sillières and Soukassian (1993) emphasise the rural setting of tower tombs, but their distribution map shows a clear clustering on the cities of Auch and St Bertrand de Comminges. At Avenches in Switzerland in the 'En Chaplix' zone two *fana* and two richly decorated *exedrae*, all set within enclosures, face each other *c.* 500m from the walls across the route that links the city to its port on Lake Morat, (Bossert 2002; Castella 1993). The excavators argue for these to have been linked to a suburban villa, but arguably their form and decorative detail extend urban monumentality into this peri-urban space. Treveran territory in Gallia Belgica would provide a case study of particular potential richness. Its monuments are as typologically diverse as those of any provincial setting, including barrows of varying architectonic sophistication, tower and temple tombs, a mass of sculpted monuments and inscriptions, carved monoliths and *Grabgärten* (Cüppers 1990; Freigang 1997). They are distributed across the territory, in association not only in the environs of Trier but also with small towns (*e.g.* Wederath-*Belginum*, Neumagen, Arlon), and rural estates.

Conclusion

Despite the limitations as a case study of Britain's Roman-period funerary monuments in their quantity, typological range and survival, nevertheless their distribution and setting have allowed insights into social dynamics in town and country. When the full range of evidence is considered, a range of patterns can be seen in the placing of the dead, including monumentalised *Gräberstraßen* for some towns, a halo of funerary monuments and villas in the environs of others and zones of monument building on the peripheries of urban territories. Whatever the setting, many tombs were built with a view to their local and wider visual prominence. Where it can be measured, their 'afterlife' often seems to have been short-lived compared to the villas with which they were often associated, especially where constructed of re-usable masonry. The impressionistic basis for some of the observations made has been acknowledged and ways to extend and strengthen the approach have been proposed. But the results even in a province with limited monumentality in its tomb building suggest that in the many provinces where this aspect of Roman funerary culture was more substantially developed, the prospects for a topography of the dead should be concomitantly richer.

Acknowledgements

My principal thanks are to the editors for their invitation to speak at the conference and in particular for their forbearance in waiting for a long-delayed contribution. They are also due to Martin Millett, the supervisor of the doctoral thesis in which the approach presented here was developed, and to participants at the Sheffield and previous conferences in London and Rome for their comments.

Appendix – a list of Romano-British monuments discussed with references

For the following monuments on which fieldwork primarily took place prior to the 1960s, Jessup's 1959 article remains the key synthesis, supplemented by a further paper in 1962.

Barrows: Emmanuel Knoll [Cambs]; Holborough [Kent]; Limlow Hill [Cambs]; Mersea Island [Essex]; Pickford Hill, Harpenden [Herts]; Riseholme [Lincs]

   Other tombs: Langley [Kent]; Litlington [Cambs]; Rothamsted [Herts]

The following sites have been subject to more recent fieldwork or analysis:

'Arthur's O'on' [Stirlingshire] (Wigg 1993c)
Bancroft [Bucks] (Williams and Zeepvat 1994)
Bartlow Hills [Cambs] (Astin *et al.* 2006)
Borough Hill, Daventry [Northants] (Brown 1977)
Brougham [Cumbria] (Cool *et al.* 2004)
Caerleon Lodge Hill [Gwent] (Evans and Maynard 1997)
Colchester Balkerne Gate [Essex] (Brooks 2006)
Colchester Stanway [Essex] (Crummy *et al.* 2007)
Heronbridge [Cheshire] (*Britannia* 36, 2005, 422–3)
Keston [Kent] (Philp *et al.* 1991; Philp *et al.* 1999; *Britannia* [2006] 37, 467).
London, Classicianus altar (Grasby and Tomlin 2002)
London, Shadwell (Lakin 2002)
Lullingstone [Kent] (Meates 1979; 1987)
Roughground Farm [Glos] (Allen *et al.* 1993)
St Albans Folly Lane [Herts] (Niblett 1999)
St Albans St Stephens [Herts] (Niblett and Thompson 2005)
Shorden Brae [Northumberland] (Daniels and Gillam 1961)
Stansted [Essex] (Havis and Brooks 2004)
Stanwick [Northants] (*Britannia* [1990] 21, 253; *Britannia* [1991] 22, 285)
Uffington [Oxon.] (Miles *et al.* 2003)
Vindolanda – T. Annius epitaph and temple-mausoleum [Northumberland] (Birley 1998; R. Birley, Vindolanda Trust, *pers. comm.*)
Westhampnett [West Sussex] (Fitzpatrick 1997)
Welwyn Hall [Herts] (Rook *et al.* 1984; T. McDonald, Hertfordshire Archaeological Trust *pers. comm.*)
Winchester Lankhills [Hants] (Clarke 1979)
Wood Lane End [Herts] (Neal 1984)

Bibliography

Abbreviations

Lex Ursonensis   Crawford, M. H. (1996) *Roman Statutes*, Bulletin of the Institute of Classical
                   Studies Supp. 34: London (*no. 25*).
RIB   Collingwood, R. G. and Wright, R. P. (1965) *The Roman Inscriptions of
                   Britain.* Volume 1. *Inscriptions on Stone.* Oxford: Clarendon.
CSIR   *Corpus Signorum Imperii Romani,* Vol. 1 (Britain). Oxford: Oxford University
                   Press (1977–).
Musa Lapidaria   Courtney, E. (1995) *Musa Lapidaria. A selection of Latin verse inscriptions.*
                   Atlanta: Scholars Press.

Allen, T. G. *et al.* (1993) *Excavations at Roughground Farm, Lechlade, Gloucestershire: a Prehistoric
    and Roman Landscape.* Oxford: Oxford Archaeological Unit/OUCA.
Astin, T. *et al.* (2007) Resistivity imaging survey of the Roman barrows at Bartlow,
    Cambridgeshire, UK. *Archaeological Prospection* 13, 1–14.
Barber, B. and Hall, J. (2000) Digging up the People of Roman London. In I. Haynes *et al.*
    (eds), *London Underground: the Archaeology of a City,* 102–120. Oxford, Oxbow.
Bayard, D. and Massy. J.-L. (1983) *Amiens Romain: Samarobriva Ambianorum.* Heilly, Revue
    Archéologique de Picardie.
Birley, A. R. (1998) A new tombstone from Vindolanda. B*ritannia* 29, 299–306.
Biró, M. (1975) The inscriptions of Roman Britain. *Acta Archaeologica Academiae Scientiarum
    Hungaricae* 27, 13–58.
Blagg, T. F. C. (1990) Architectural munificence in Britain: the evidence of inscriptions.
    Britannia 21, 13–31.
Blagg, T. F. C. (2002) *Roman Architectural Ornament in Britain.* Oxford, Hadrian Books.
Bossert, M. (2002) *Die figürlichen Skulpturen der Nekropole von Avenches – En Chaplix (VD):
    nördlicher und südlicher Grabbezirk.* Aventicum XII. *CSIR* Schweiz, Bd. I, 3.
Brooks, H. (2006) *A Roman temple-tomb at Colchester Royal Grammar School, 6 Lexden Road,
    Colchester, Essex. August–September 2005,* http://cat.essex.ac.uk/reports/CAT-report-0345.
    pdf (last accessed 1st December 2008).
Brown, A. E. (1977) The Roman barrow cemetery on Borough Hill, Daventry. *Northamptonshire
    Archaeology* 12, 185–190.
Burleigh, G. (1993) Some aspects of burial types in the cemeteries of the Romano-British
    settlement at Baldock, Herts., England. In M. Struck (ed.), *Römerzeitliche Gräber als
    Quellen zur Religion, Bevölkerungsstruktur und Sozialgeschichte,* 41–50. Mainz, Johannes
    Gutenberg Institut für Vor- und Frühgeschichte.
Burnham, B. and Wacher, J. (1990) *The Small Towns of Roman Britain.* London, Batsford.
Burnand, Y. (1975) *Domitii Aquenses: Une famille de chevaliers romains de la region dAix-en-
    Provence: Mausolée et domaine.* Paris, Boccard.
Carroll, M. (2006) *Spirits of the Dead: Roman funerary commemoration in western Europe.*
    Oxford, Oxford University Press.
Castella, D. (1993) Un sanctuaire augustéen autour d une sépulture à incinération à Avenches,
    Canton de Vaud (Suisse). In M. Struck (ed.), *Römerzeitliche Gräber als Quellen zur
    Religion, Bevölkerungsstruktur und Sozialgeschichte,* 229–245. Mainz, Johannes Gutenberg
    Institut für Vor- und Frühgeschichte.
Cepas, A. (1989) *The North of Britannia and the North-West of Hispania: an epigraphic comparison.*
    Oxford, British Archaeological Reports.

Clarke, G. (1979) *Pre-Roman and Roman Winchester, Part 2: The Roman Cemetery at Lankhills.* Oxford, Clarendon Press.

Cool, H. E. M. *et al.* (2004) *The Roman Cemetery at Brougham, Cumbria: Excavations 1966–67.* London, Society for the Promotion of Roman Studies.

Creighton, J. (2006) *Britannia. The Creation of a Roman Province.* London, Routledge.

Crummy, P. *et al.* (2007) *Stanway: an Elite Burial Site at Camulodunum.* London, Society for the Promotion of Roman Studies.

Cüppers, H. (1990) *Die Römer in Rheinland-Pfalz.* Stuttgart, Theiss.

Daniels, C. M. and Gillam, J. P. (1961) The Roman mausoleum on Shorden Brae Beaufront, Corbridge, Northumberland. *Archaeologia Aeliana* (4th series) 39, 37–63.

Davies, M. (2000) Death and social division at Roman Springhead. *Archaeologia Cantiana* 121, 157–169.

Davies, P. (2000) *Death and the emperor.* Cambridge, Cambridge University Press.

Dunnett, R. (1975) *The Trinovantes.* London, Duckworth.

Esmonde Cleary, A. S. (1987) *Extra-Mural Areas of Romano-British Towns.* Oxford, British Archaeological Reports.

Esmonde Cleary, A. S. (2000) Putting the dead in their place: cemetery location in Roman Britain. In J. Pearce, M. Millett and M. Struck (eds) *Burial, Society and Context in the Roman World,* 127–142. Oxford, Oxbow.

Evans, E. M. and Maynard, D. J. (1997) Caerleon Lodge Hill cemetery: the Abbeyfield site 1992. *Britannia* 28, 169–244.

Ferdière, A. (ed.) (1993) *Monde des morts, monde des vivants en Gaule rurale.* Tours, Université de Tours.

Fitzpatrick, A. P. (1997) *Archaeological excavations on the route of the A27 Westhampnett bypass, West Sussex, 1992. Vol. 2. The late Iron Age, Romano-British, and Anglo-Saxon cemeteries.* Salisbury, Trust for Wessex Archaeology.

Freigang, Y. (1997) Die Grabmäler der gallo-römischen Kultur im Moselland. Studien zur Selbstdarstellung einer Gesellschaft. *Jahrbuch des Römisch-Germanischen Zentralmuseums Mainz* 44.1, 278–440.

Grasby, R. D. and Tomlin, R. S. O. (2002) The sepulchral monument of the procurator C. Julius Classicianus. *Britannia* 33, 43–76.

Gros, P. (2001) *L'architecture romaine du début du IIIe siècle av. J-C. à la fin du Haut-Empire. Vol. II, Maisons, palais, villas et tombeaux.* Paris, Picard.

Groupes de Recherches sur l'Afrique Antique (1993) *Les Flavii de Cillium. Etude architecturale, épigraphique, historique et littéraire du mausolea de Kasserine.* Rome, École Française.

Havis, R. and Brooks, H. (2004) *Excavations at Stansted Airport, 1986–91.* Volume 1: *prehistoric and Romano-British.* Chelmsford, Essex County Council.

Hayward, K. M. J. (2006) A geological link between the Facilis monument at Colchester and first-century army tombstones from the Rhineland frontier. *Britannia* 37, 359–363.

Haynes, I. *et al.* (eds), *London Underground: the Archaeology of a City.* Oxford, Oxbow.

Henig, M. (2000) Art in Roman London. In I. Haynes *et al.* (eds), *London Underground: the Archaeology of a City,* 62–84. Oxford, Oxbow.

von Hesberg, H. (1992) *Römische Grabbauten.* Darmstadt, Wissenschaftliches Buch- gesellschaft.

von Hesberg, H. and Zanker, P. (1987) Einleitung. In von H. Von Hesberg and P. Zanker (eds), *Römische Gräberstraßen – Selbstdarstellung, Status, Standard,* 9–20. Munich, Bayerische Akademie der Wissenschaften.

von Hesberg, H. and Zanker, P. (eds) (1987) *Römische Gräberstraßen – Selbstdarstellung, Status, Standard.* Munich, Bayerische Akademie der Wissenschaften.

Hope, V. (1997) Words and pictures: the interpretation of Romano-British tombstones. *Britannia* 28, 245–258.

Hope, V. (2001) *Constructing Identity: The Roman Funerary Monuments of Aquileia, Mainz and Nîmes.* Oxford, John & Erica Hedges.

Hurst, H. R. (1985) *Kingsholm.* Gloucester, Gloucester Archaeological Publications.

Hurst, H. R. (1999) Topography and identity in Glevum colonia. In H. Hurst (ed.) *The Coloniae of Roman Britain: new studies and a review*, 113–135. Portsmouth, R.I., Journal of Roman Archaeology.

Jessup, R. F. J. (1959) Barrows and walled cemeteries in Roman Britain. *Journal of the British Archaeological Association* 22, 1–32.

Jessup, R. F. J. (1962) Roman barrows in Britain. In J. Bibauw (ed.) *Hommages à Marcel Renard* (3 vols), 853–867. Brussels, Collections Latomus.

Jones, R. F. J. (1984) The cemeteries of Roman York. In P. Addyman and V. Black (eds) *Archaeological Papers from York Presented to M. W. Barley*, 34–42. York, York Archaeological Trust.

Keay, S. *et al.* (2006) *Portus: An Archaeological Survey of the Port of Imperial Rome.* Rome, British School at Rome.

Kockel, V. (1983) *Die Grabbauten vor dem Herkulaner Tor in Pompeji.* Mainz, Philipp von Zabern.

Koortbojian, M. (1996) *In commemorationem mortuorum*: text and image along the Streets of Tombs. In J. Elsner (ed.) *Art and Text in Roman culture*, 210–234. Cambridge, Cambridge University Press.

Lakin, D. *et al.* (2002) *The Roman tower at Shadwell, London: a re-appraisal.* London, MoLAS.

Landes, C. (ed.) (2002) *La mort des notables en Gaule romaine.* Lattes, Musée archeologique Henri-Prades.

Le Bohec, Y. and Buisson, A. (eds) (1991) *Le Testament du Lingon.* Lyon/Paris, de Boccard.

Leveau, P. (1987) Nécropoles et monuments funéraires à Caesarea de Maurétanie. In von H. Von Hesberg and P. Zanker (eds), *Römische Gräberstraßen – Selbstdarstellung, Status, Standard*, 281–90. Munich, Bayerische Akademie der Wissenschaften.

Mackinder, A. (2000) *A Romano-British cemetery on Watling Street.* London, MoLAS.

Mann, J. (1985) Epigraphic consciousness. *Journal of Roman Studies* 75, 204–206.

Martin-Kilcher, S. (1993) Situation des cimetières et tombes rurales en Germania Superior et dans les régions voisines. In A. Ferdière (ed.), *Monde des morts, monde des vivants en Gaule rurale*, 153–164. Tours, Université de Tours.

Mattern, M. (1989). Die reliefverzierten römischen Grabstelen der Provinz Britannia. Themen und Typen. *Kölner Jahrbuch für Vor- und Frühgeschichte* 22, 707–801.

Mattingly, D. (2006) *Imperial Possession: Britain in the Roman Empire: 54 BC–AD 409.* London, Allen Lane.

Mattingly, D. (2007) The African way of death: burial rituals beyond the Roman empire. In D. Stone and L. Stirling (eds), *Mortuary landscapes of North Africa*, 138–163. Toronto, University of Toronto Press.

Meates, G. W. (1979/1987) *The Roman Villa at Lullingstone, Kent.* Vols. 1 and 2. Maidstone, Kent Archaeological Society.

Meffre, J.-C. (1993) Lieux sépulcraux et occupation du sol en milieu rural dans la cité antique de Vaison sous le Haut-Empire. In A. Ferdière (ed.), *Monde des morts, monde des vivants en Gaule rurale*, 371–387. Tours, Université de Tours.

Miles, D. *et al.* (2003) *Uffington White Horse and its Landscape. Investigations at White Horse Hill Uffington, 1989–95 and Tower Hill Ashbury, 1993–4.* Oxford, Oxford Archaeology.

Millett, M. (1987) An early Roman burial tradition in Central Southern England. *Oxford Journal of Archaeology* 6, 63–68.

Millett, M. (1990) *The Romanization of Britain*. Cambridge, Cambridge University Press.

Moore, J. (2007) The mausoleum culture of Africa Proconsularis. In D. Stone and L. Stirling (eds), *Mortuary landscapes of North Africa*, 75–109. Toronto, University of Toronto Press.

Morris, I. (1992) *Death Ritual and Social Structure in Classical Antiquity*. Cambridge, Cambridge University Press.

Neal, D. S. (1984) A sanctuary at Wood Lane End, Hemel Hempstead. *Britannia* 15, 193–217.

Niblett, R. (1999) *The Excavation of a Ceremonial Site at Folly Lane, Verulamium*. London, Society for the Promotion of Roman Studies.

Niblett, R. and Thompson, I. (2005) *Alban's buried towns. An assessment of St Albans Archaeology up to AD 1600*. Oxford, Oxbow/English Heritage.

Ortalli, J. (2001) Il culto funerario della Cispadana romana. Rappresentazione e interiorità. In M. Heinzelmann *et al.* (eds) *Römischer Bestattungsbrauch und Beigabensitten*, 215–242. Reichert, Rome/Wiesbaden.

Parker Pearson, M. (1999) *The Archaeology of Death and Burial*. Stroud, Sutton.

Pearce, J. (1999) *Contextual archaeology of burial practice: case studies from Roman Britain.* Unpublished Ph.D. thesis, Durham University.

Pearce, J. (2000) Burial, society and context in the provincial Roman world. In J. Pearce, M. Millett and M. Struck (eds), *Burial, Society and Context in the Roman World*, 1–12. Oxford, Oxbow.

Pearce, J. (2002) Ritual and interpretation in provincial Roman cemeteries. *Britannia* 33, 373–8.

Pearce, J., Millett, M. and Struck, M. (eds) (2000) *Burial, Society and Context in the Roman World*. Oxford, Oxbow.

Petts, D. (2006) Burial on Hadrians Wall. In M. Symonds (ed.) *Hadrians Wall Research Framework*, Durham University/Durham County Council, http://www.dur.ac.uk/resources/archaeological.services/research_training/hadrianswall_research_framework/project_documents/Burial.pdf. (last accessed 1st December 2008).

Philp, B. *et al.* (1991) *The Roman Villa Site at Keston, Kent: First Report (Excavations 1968–1978)*. Dover Castle, Kent Archaeological Rescue Unit.

Philp, B. *et al.* (1999) *The Roman Villa Site at Keston, Kent: Second Report (Excavations 1967 and 1978–1990)*, Dover Castle, Kent Archaeological Rescue Unit.

Philpott, R. (1991) *Burial Practices in Roman Britain. A survey of grave treatment and furnishing A.D. 43–410*. Oxford, British Archaeological Reports.

Rife, J. L. *et al.* (2007) Life and death at a port in Roman Greece: The Kenchreai Cemetery Project 2002–2006. *Hesperia* 76, 143–181.

Rivet, A. L. F. (1968) *Town and Country in Roman Britain* (2nd ed.). London, Hutchinson.

Rook, A. G. *et al.* (1984) A Roman mausoleum and associated marble sarcophagus and burials from Welwyn, Herts. *Britannia* 15, 143–162.

Roth-Congès, A. (1990) Les voies romaines bordées de tombes. *Journal of Roman Archaeology* 3, 337–351.

Roth-Congès, A. (1993) Les mausolées du sud-est de la Gaule. In A. Ferdière (ed.), *Monde des morts, monde des vivants en Gaule rurale*, 90–96. Tours, Université de Tours.

Schucany, C. (2000) An elite funerary enclosure in the centre of the villa of Biberist-Spitalhof (Switzerland) – a case study. In J. Pearce, M. Millett and M. Struck (eds), *Burial, Society and Context in the Roman World*, 118–126. Oxford, Oxbow.

Scott, S. (2000) *Art and society in fourth-century Britain: villa mosaics in context.* Oxford, Oxford University School of Archaeology.

Sillières, P. and Soukassian, P. (1993) Les piles funéraires du sud-ouest de la France: état de recherches. In A. Ferdière (ed.), *Monde des morts, monde des vivants en Gaule rurale,* 299–306. Tours, Université de Tours.

Stirling, L. and Stone, D. (eds) (2007) *Mortuary landscapes of North Africa.* Toronto, University of Toronto Press.

Struck, M. (ed.) (1993) *Römerzeitliche Gräber als Quellen zur Religion, Bevölkerungsstruktur und Sozialgeschichte.* Mainz, Johannes Gutenberg Institut für Vor- und Frühgeschichte.

Struck, M. (2000) High status burials in Roman Britain (1st to 3rd century AD) – potential of interpretation. In J. Pearce, M. Millett and M. Struck (eds), *Burial, Society and Context in the Roman World,* 85–96. Oxford, Oxbow.

Tilley, C. (1994) *A Phenomenology of Landscape. Places, Paths and Monuments.* Oxford, Berg.

Todd, M. (2004) *Companion to Roman Britain.* London, Routledge.

Vermeulen, F. and Bourgeois, J. (2000) Continuity of prehistoric burial sites in the Roman landscape of Sandy Flanders. In J. Pearce, M. Millett and M. Struck (eds), *Burial, Society and Context in the Roman World,* 143–161. Oxford, Oxbow.

Wigg, A. (1993a) Barrows in north-eastern Gallia Belgica: cultural and social aspects. In M. Struck (ed.), *Römerzeitliche Gräber als Quellen zur Religion, Bevölkerungsstruktur und Sozialgeschichte,* 371–380. Mainz, Johannes Gutenberg Institut für Vor- und Frühgeschichte.

Wigg, A. (1993b) *Grabhügel des 2. und 3. Jahrhunderts n. Chr. an Mittelrhein, Mosel und Saar.* Trier, Rheinisches Landesmuseum.

Wigg, A. (1993c) Zu römerzeitlichen Grabhügeln mit gemauerter Grabkammer in Großbritannien. *Germania* 71.2, 532–538.

Williams, H. (1997) Ancient landscapes and the dead: the re-use of prehistoric and Roman monuments as early Anglo-Saxon burial sites. *Medieval Archaeology* 41, 1–32.

Williams, H. (1998) The ancient monument in Romano-British ritual practices. In C. Forcey, J. Hawthorne and R. Witcher (eds) *TRAC 1997, Proceedings of the Seventh Annual Theoretical Roman Archaeology Conference,* 71–86. Oxford, Oxbow.

Williams, R. J. and Zeepvat, R. J. (1994) *Bancroft: a Late Bronze Age/Iron Age Settlement, Roman Villa and Temple/Mausoleum.* Aylesbury, Buckinghamshire Archaeological Society.

Woolf, G. (1996) Monumental writing and the expansion of Roman society in the early empire. *Journal of Roman Studies* 86, 22–39.

Woolf, G. (1998) *Becoming Roman: the Origins of Provincial Civilization in Gaul.* Cambridge, Cambridge University Press.

Zanker, P. (2000) The city as symbol: Rome and the creation of an urban image. In E. Fentress (ed.) *Romanization and the City. Creation, transformation and failure,* 25–41. Portsmouth, R.I., Journal of Roman Archaeology.

8

The mechanics of social connections between the living and the dead in ancient Egypt

Martin Bommas

Life in ancient Egypt was distinctively influenced by funerary belief and the way that death was treated in Egyptian culture. The knowledge of funerary rituals provided a common understanding of the possible interaction between human and divine. Funerary belief also fuelled the prospects of those who had increasing expectations of prosperity and eternal youth in the hereafter. Contact was made with the dead during burial processions, funerary festivals and the like (Fig. 8.1). However, a spacious tomb at the desert edge, equipped with funerary goods and highly skilled priests performing the funerary rites necessary to ensure a successful life in after death, was within the reach only of a lucky few. When dealing with death in ancient Egypt, modern Egyptology is still dependant on textual and archaeological sources left behind mainly by the elites, although, since the end of the twentieth century, an interest in the life and death of the non-elite population is apparent.[1] This article aims at presenting a survey of roughly 3000 years of interaction between

Figure 8.1 The necropolis of Qubbet el-Hawa, Aswan. The structure at the foot of the hill is a middle class tomb of the early Middle Kingdom. The first row of tombs dates to the Old and Middle Kingdom, while the buildings on the top of the hill are a Coptic monastery (left) and a tomb of a Muslim sheikh (right). The causeway in the centre of the photograph leads to the tomb of Chunes and it was initially used during his funerary procession (photo, Author).

the living and the dead in ancient Egypt. By using archaeological as well as written sources, focus will be placed on the mechanics that were established in order to live through the dead.

Defining Egyptian funerary culture

The unquestioned relevance of sources relating to funerary belief has led to the controversial assumption, possibly influenced by the overwhelming numbers of large-scale funerary monuments in ancient Egypt, that the Egyptians established a funerary *religion* (Riggs 2005, 26–36; Gee 2006, 85). But socially stratified funerary belief is only one part of Egyptian *religion*, a word that did not even exist in the Egyptian lexicon.[2] Returning the modern word *religion* to its original Latin (*religio*) meaning – the belief in a superhuman controlling power to be worshipped –, it soon becomes evident that Egyptian funerary belief is more closely related to funerary *cult*, a system of religious devotion of the deceased and his survival in the form of a glorified spirit. It was Dario Sabbatucci (1988, 57) who – on a general level – contextualised religion by exploring the integration of specific religious aspects in any given culture and society. Whether or not one shares the views of phenomenologists or historians, one must differentiate between ethnic and universal religions. Ancient Egyptian religion was always an ethnic one, limited to the borders of Egypt and restricted to the nation of Egypt. It was not until Isis became a Greek goddess and conquered the Aegean (fourth to third centuries BC), the Mediterranean (third century BC – fourth century AD) and later an area stretching from modern Pakistan to Yorkshire (first to fourth centuries AD), that Egyptian ideas contributed to the development of a concept we can describe as the first universal religion.

Understanding Egyptian funerary culture as funerary religion is deeply rooted in a phenomenological understanding of religion as an absolute quantity. But this ignores the deep roots between religion and culture. Recognising that religion, especially ethnic religion, has an historical dimension means that we can accept religion as one of the main factors of culture from an independent point of view, one that excludes our own religious opinion(s) and ideas from our own cultural background.

Taking into account the fact that no religion is static and that an historical perspective is essential in view of the ethnically limited character of Egyptian religion, the discussion of how ancient Egyptians lived through the dead will proceed here in chronological order. The entire history of ancient Egyptian funerary culture will be explored, because the topic of living through the dead is a novel one and because we are dealing with a development of thought rather than with a canonical concept of unchanging character.

The power of knowledge

Through an investigation of pharaonic textual sources, it is apparent that the average Egyptian must have had a fairly good knowledge of the various ways to reach the hereafter, without really knowing much about the afterlife itself. Texts painted on the ceilings of Theban Tombs of the New Kingdom illustrate this dichotomy.[3]

Because in ancient Egypt the living and the dead were part of the same and inseparable community (Baines 1991), the dead were believed to play an essential role in the world of the living. But if the Egyptians had little idea of the hereafter, how would they be able to approach the dead, address them, write to them, and live through them? The chief response to the dead was grounded in ritualistic actions, such as sacrifice, magical rites, and festivals, all of which were privileges of the dead to which people aspired throughout their lives. In creating and maintaining social connections with the dead, recitations, offerings

Figure 8.2 Tomb of Nebenma'at, TT 219 (20th Dynasty, c. 1100 BC). A priest in the role of Anubis bends over the mummy of the deceased during the Ritual of Opening Mouth. The hieroglyphic inscription in the background gives the recitation of the priest in direct speech (photo, Author).

and sacrifice[4] were the only means by which one could be recognized by the deceased. Funerary literature, to be read *by* the deceased himself to ward off the dangers of the afterlife, as well as recitation literature that was read *for* the deceased by priest in divine roles (Fig. 8.2), was in the hands of highly skilled cult personnel. It is important to understand that both types of texts contained restricted knowledge kept and handed down to future generations by priests who would not allow their priestly knowledge to appear on the outer walls of tombs. These texts needed to be mobile in order to keep the secrets in the possession of the priests or the deceased; they were, therefore, written on papyri or stored in burial chambers. While recitation texts were entirely in the hands of lector priests, spells containing funerary literature accompanied the deceased, thus being inaccessible to the public. Some copies of the Book of the Dead were inserted among the folds of the mummy bandages so that the deceased would have the spells close at hand (James 1985, 8), while some spells from the same book were written on mummy bindings to provide cheaper alternatives to costly papyrus versions (Ritner 1988, 226*f*.). Those who wrote these texts (such as the Book of the Dead) sometimes had little knowledge of what they were copying, as orthographic errors in some of the manuscripts make clear.

Dead, but alive

The relationship between the living and the dead in ancient Egypt was bridged by an idea that at first seems a paradox: someone who was buried according to funerary ritual was not thought to be leaving this world dead, but alive. There are a few spells in the early Pyramid Texts (*c.* 2350 BC) which turn this concept into passages of proverbial character when addressing the glorified deceased, as in PT 213:

> Oh Osiris N,
> you do not leave being dead
> it is alive that you leave
>   (Sethe 1908, 81 [=Pyr. §134a]; Assmann 2002, 367).

Later recitation texts continue to address the deceased using the same topos but offer variants as well, such as Coffin text spell 67 (*c.* 2000 BC):

> Oh Osiris N,
> It is not being dead that you die,
> And I shall not let you die of death
>   (De Buck 1935, 287a–b).

It was not physical death Egyptians were anxious about, as it was thought to be a mere transitory condition on the way to a much more enjoyable state as a glorified spirit in the afterlife. Dying a second death was a much more frightening idea: the deceased would be attacked by Seth – the notorious trickster and brother, as well as murderer, of Osiris – and would lose his status and place in the afterlife forever. The fact that the dead were not really dead but living a life in the hereafter made death negotiable and opened possibilities for social connectivity between the living (in this world) and the dead. The concept of living alongside the dead was made possible by accepting the fact that the dead were alive.

Old Kingdom I: Funerary customs according to the myth of Osiris

Due to the lack of textual and archaeological evidence it is nonetheless difficult to say whether the ancient Egyptians lived *through* the dead and not only lived *with* the dead. Important here is the principle *do ut des* – "I give so that you may give" – which is one of the prominent features of Egyptian cult practice (Assmann 1990b, 186). During the Old Kingdom (*c.* 2686 BC–2181 BC) this principle is only employed if man deals with the gods, for instance in the context of an offering. Understanding reciprocal exchange as a key focus of social relationships throughout antiquity, the relationship between man and the divine is most prominently expressed by the exchange of goods which forms part of a silent ritual; the making of an offering implies a person's expectation of receiving something in return (Mauss 1990). With the development of the myth of Osiris and the formalisation of this process during the reign of King Snofru (*c.* 2260 BC), kings as well as private individuals could be transformed into a god in the afterlife by means of customized recitations, thus following the model of the mythical antecedent Osiris. According to the myth, Osiris ruled as king of Egypt before he was killed by his brother Seth. His wife Isis collected the limbs of his dismembered body at the banks of the river Nile. By re-membering Osiris physically and with the help of lamentations, Isis created what can be described as the process of mummification that went hand-in-hand with recitations. Thus, ritualistic actions enabled Osiris to reach the afterlife and become the ruler of the realm of the dead. This remarkable development paved the way for every deceased person to benefit from funerary rituals and glorifications (Assmann 1990a), to become Osiris NN in the hereafter,[5] and – as a consequence – to be treated as a god. Since offerings were widely regarded as structuring relationships between mortals and immortals, the result of this progressive change was to expand the principle of *do ut des* to the dead of non-royal status. This concept, however, is revolutionary: myth does not provide the background for the dead acting for the living because Osiris, the mythical role-model, remains thoroughly passive[6] in the funerary texts of the Old Kingdom. Therefore, the concept of living through the dead and accepting their favours is based on religious practice rather than theology. There is no reason to believe that this idea changed before the New Kingdom (1575–1069 BC). Hymns to Osiris in that period show that he was no longer seen as a passive god only interested in his own matters. A *stele* kept in the Louvre (C 286) clearly points to the fact that Osiris, the deceased *par excellence,* is seen as a ruler of this world, one who is adored by the living as supplier of life, when described as:

> (...) north-wind, Nile, flood,
> all plants, all vegetables,
> the corn-god, he gives all his herbals,
> food from the earth,
> he serves to satisfy hunger and gives it into all lands
>   (Assmann 1975, 447).

As we shall see below, this new thought – paralleled by other hymns to Osiris with similar expressions – introduced to theology the popular concept of the caring dead in later periods. During the Old Kingdom, however, when myth became codified by the attempts to create written tradition, only ritual played a key role in expressing the interaction between the living and superhuman powers. As such, religion and magic are two sides of the same coin as the following demonstrates.

Old Kingdom II: Appeal to the Living

The contact of the dead with the living is by no means limited to specific occasions. In a more general approach, communication is made possible where the walls of a tomb or even *stelae* are used to attract the attention of passers-by (Fig. 8.3). However, the 'Appeal to the Living' (Müller 1975; Lichtheim 1992, 155–190) does not appear before the 5th Dynasty (*c.* 2400 BC). The Stela Florence 1540 (Fig. 8.4), dating to the 11th–12th Dynasty (*c.* 1940 BC), has all the key features of such texts:

> Oh you, who are living on earth,
> every scribe, every lector-priest, every magistrate,
> who will pass by this noble (tomb),
> while you love, that Osiris, the Lord of Life and Ruler of Eternity will be favourable to you.
> May you say:
> 'Thousands of bread and beer,
> Thousands of oxen and fowl,
> Thousands of offerings and provisions on the altar of the Lord of Eternity for the ka[7] of the Keeper of the Bows Nefer-en-ij',
> because it is more effective for the one who does, than for the one for whom something is done:
> A breath for a spell, which is effective for the dead is not something one becomes tired of.
> I am one who is dead and who can listen to someone,
> one who repays the good which is done for him
>   (StFlorence 1540 = Inv.no. 2590; Bosticco 1959, 29*f.* and fig. 24; Sethe 1983, 88.12–18; Bommas 2009).

The relevant passage in this prayer is "…because it is more effective for the one who does, than for the one for whom

Figure 8.3 Façade of the tomb of Herkhuf (35n), Qubbet el-Hawa, Aswan (c. 2287–2278 BC). Herkhuf (left) receives a funerary offering by his eldest son. Inscriptions as well as visual art in the open courts of Egyptian tombs aimed at attracting passers-by (photo, Author).

something is done." Acting for the dead goes hand in hand with a benefit for the living, or in other words: the dead act for the benefit of the still-living descendants. As shown above, this concept involves magic to make things happen which usually are beyond human control.

Sacrifice as impetus for the principle of Ma'at

In ancient Egypt, the principle of truth, justice and harmony of the universe is personified by Ma'at, a goddess that is usually portrayed as a seated woman wearing an ostrich feather. Although Ma'at was the only principle that embodied the concept of justice, an inscribed *stele* of King Neferhotep (*c.* 1700) gives the only known Egyptian definition of the term Ma'at:

> The reward for one who does consists of what is done for him.
> This is Ma'at in the opinion of god
> (Mariette 1869, 30, line 40).[8]

This passage is clear about the fact that Ma'at emerges from god[9] who defines it. But this concept is at least 700 years older than its first appearance in this royal inscription, as the Florence *stele* reveals. Furthermore, inscriptions such as the Appeal to the Living (see above) contain definitions of Ma'at and illustrate the concept of reciprocity. As a consequence, this can only mean that Ma'at must be viewed as a moral value for both the living and the dead. It seems to appear as a product of the dynamism of funerary belief, underlined by the fact that the nameless god mentioned

Figure 8.4 Stela Florence 1540. 'Appeals to the Living' form a genre of texts in its own right. Mostly inscribed on stelae, The Keeper of the Bows Nefer-en-ij invites passers-by to recite an offering spell on his behalf, promising to "repay the good which is done for him." These funerary texts are neither funerary literature nor recitation texts. Their only purpose is to make contact with the living and to provide the living with a point of reference if they need someone to listen to their pleas and become active on their behalf" (Bosticco 1959, 29–30 and fig. 24) (photo courtesy of Dr M.C. Guidotti, Archaeological Museum of Florence).

on the aforementioned *stele* of Neferhotep can be no-one else but Osiris.[10] There can be no doubt that the Egyptian concept of reciprocity, derived from sacrifice as the main element of Egyptian funerary belief, was likely to have been the starting point for the concept of social connectivity embodied in the term of Ma'at.[11]

Accordingly, Appeals to the Living, funerary offerings, and speech acts addressed to someone unknown promoted the idea of Ma'at as order in the world. Speech acts (recitals) together with physical actions (manual) are integral parts of what can be called ritual. In ancient Egypt, however, ritual is the only means by which the order of the world can be restored successfully, be it the world of the living or the world of the dead. On the level of personal religion, a speech act following the rules of Ma'at is a prayer, signifying an individual approach to either god or the deceased. Appeals to the Living, which are prayers by themselves, are essential to establish the idea of reciprocity involving two parties on the basis of consent. However, the absence of prayers would lead to an early end. In the Teaching of Papyrus Insinger, dating to the first century AD, the importance of a prayer is made clear:

> He who is mean to his people dies without prayers being said for him
>   (trans. Lichtheim 1980, 198).

Acting through words

It must be assumed that the Appeals to the Living placed on *stelae* and tomb façades did not necessarily have to have a literate audience to be effective. In ancient Egypt, tomb decoration forms part of a cosmos of its own in which every piece – however small – has a function and never stands without context. The Appeals to the Living cannot be understood as isolated texts. They form part of a much wider picture and therefore must be understood as performative texts (Fig. 8.2). These texts are self-reflective and they must neither be constantly read nor spoken to be effective. They must only be read once; according to the speech act theory of John L. Austin (1962), a word once uttered can evoke or even replace action. However, the restrictive nature of written words must lead to a process of decoding, the outcome of this process not always being predictable and possibly resulting in a gap between script and thought (Shillingsburg 2006, 41). An ancient Egyptian attempt to solve this dilemma was to involve images which reached the observer on the broader and more elaborate basis of social conventions. In the case of the Florentine *stele* mentioned above, this image consists of nothing more than the deceased standing beside the inscription. The direction of the hieroglyphs, however, leaves no doubt that the words are spoken by the deceased himself. Furthermore, the deceased is depicted without any funerary equipment such as offering tables, thus making clear that he has not yet received offerings from a living passer-by and is inviting one to come along and perform this act. It can be argued that even illiterate "readers" were able to decode the meaning of such *stelae*. The decoration of the tomb-facade of Herkhuf (Fig. 8.3) uses the same method to inform passers-by.

Middle Kingdom I: "Do for the one who does for you"

The relationship between the dead and the living was ruled by the concept of social connectivity based on Ma'at, the principle of truth and justice (Assmann 1990b). A nearly endless series of texts, mostly teachings and so-called *belles lettres*, exemplify what it meant to live a life according to Ma'at. These texts include the Tale of the Eloquent Peasant (Parkinson 1998, 54–88) and the Dispute Between a Man and His Ba (Parkinson 1998, 151–165). In fact, this topic becomes so prominent during the Middle Kingdom (*c.* 2055–1650 BC) that it can be regarded as one of the key features of written culture at the beginning of the second millennium BC.[12] The ideal of acting according to the rules of Ma'at implies reciprocity between the one who does and the one for whom something is done. The concept, as such, is necessarily more elaborate in terms of social interaction than the *do ut des* principle (see p. 162). Widely regarded as a moral value (Lichtheim 1992, 48), the principle of Ma'at does not involve *a priori* ritualistic actions to structure relations between living humans; it is omnipotent and unlimited. The Eloquent Peasant has this passage to clarify what is meant:

> Do not push back someone, who addresses you begging
> but step back from hesitating to let your utterance be heard.
> Do for the one who does for you
>   (B2, 106–108, Vogelsang and Gardiner 1908, Pl. 22).

It is important to note that only those who led a life according to Ma'at would pass the final judgement and reach the hereafter, as depicted for instance on the Papyrus of Ani (Faulkner 1985, 14). Within this image, emblematic and central for the understanding of Egyptian funerary belief as it appears to be, the feather of Ma'at (p. 165) is confronted with the heart of the righteous man. In the tomb of Petosiris it is stated:

> No one reaches it (*i.e.* the West, where the dead live) if his heart was not truthful in doing Ma'at.

But Ma'at is not something which vanishes in the netherworld or leaves the dead. It stays with them as the Eloquent Peasant states:

> Ma'at will be eternal,
> She will descend to the netherworld at the hand of someone who did her.
> He will be buried and united with the earth,
> But his name will not be extinguished on earth,
> But he will be remembered because of the good (deeds)
>   (B1, 307–311, Vogelsang and Gardiner 1908, Pl. 17).

And furthermore:

> Say Ma'at, do Ma'at,
> because she is great and mighty.
> She is constant, her power is proven,
> she alone leads to being supplied in the hereafter (ỉmȝḫ.w)
>   (B1, 320–322, Vogelsang and Gardiner 1908, Pl. 17).

From here it seems to be only one short step to applying the principle of connectivity to the dead; it is thoroughly convincing to follow the example of someone who did right and is approved of having done so by divine judgment. The Book of the Dead, chapter 125, gives all the judicial details of a personal plea accompanying this approval (Faulkner 1985, 29–34), while images sometimes illustrate the process. The dead are divine, as stated before, however it is not their divine status which attracts the living but their truthful life, as the Teaching of Merikare reveals:

> Eternity means being there
> (...) he who reaches it without transgression
> will be there like a god,
> striking out like the Lords of Eternity (*i.e.* the dead)
>   (Quack 1992, 157).

In the light of these texts, living through the dead – those who have reached the afterlife and who strike out as the Lords of Eternity – is of utmost importance. Living through the dead during the Middle and New Kingdoms is a moral imperative, thus upholding the dead as a good example for a righteous life.

Middle Kingdom II: Letters to the Dead

A remarkable group of twenty texts – all deriving from cemeteries and forming a literary genre in itself – helps to shed some light on the relationship between the living and the dead. What is remarkable about these testimonies is that they focus on the importance of living *through* each other. The texts in question do not reflect official attitudes and codes, but instead are individual expressions of personal approaches to the world of the dead. Using papyrus, linen or drinking cups as a medium, private inscriptions were placed on the offering tables in the tombs of the addressees. This led the first editors of these texts to coin them Letters to the Dead (Gardiner and Sethe 1928; Ritner 1993, 180–183; Verhoeven 2003, 31–51).

These letters did not address just any dead relative. If so, this would have included those who failed to maintain the status of a good spirit and happened to die "a second death" (p. 162). Those dying a second death are called *mwt.w*, "dead ones". They are not helping spirits, but condemned demons who spend a restless and dislocated life suffering from a *damnatio memoriae*, or a damnation of memory, in the netherworld. The letters to the dead instead address the glorified spirits (ꜣḫ or ꜣḫ iqr, Demarée 1983), who were thought to be able to intercede in personal matters, such as injustice, legal affairs, infertility etc. (Baines 1991, 153–155). Some of these letters make the dead responsible for bad luck and aim at warding them off. A hieratic inscription on the outside of a drinking cup from the *necropolis* of Qua contains a text of a son who wrote to his deceased mother asking her for help against the dead Sobekhotep. This plea clearly illustrates that the relations between the living and the dead were not always without tensions and that men and gods took issue with injustice:

> Shepsi adresses his mother Iyu. This (letter) is a reminder of this which you said to me (…) If only you would decide between me and Sobekhotep, whom I brought from another town to be buried in his town among his tomb-companions, having given him funerary clothing. Why does he act against me, your son? I have neither said nor done anything wrong to him. Wrongdoing is painful to the gods (London, University College UC 16163, after Strudwick 2005, 183).

The essential questions however are, firstly, how were the dead able to "read" these letters and, secondly, what made the writers sure that the inscriptions on drinking cups were really received by the dead? The answer to these questions can be seen in the location of the writing itself. Let us look at drinking cups on which something was written. They were not used simply because more expensive papyrus might not have been available, but were intentional choices determined by the function of the cups. By using cups and filling them with water, the written inscriptions on them could be swallowed by the deceased. In this way, the contents of the letter would be incorporated into the addressee's own personal sphere (Bommas 1999, 53–60). In fact, the liquid would evaporate after a short while and the returning donator could interpret from the empty cup that the deceased had already "read" and digested the letter addressed to him.

The Egyptians believed in the power of the ꜣḫ-spirits and their positive or negative influence on persons and events. In the much later Teaching of Ani (*c.* 960 BC) this concept is suggested by focussing on the spirits of the dead responsible for inexplicable disturbances of every-day life:

> Pacify the demon: do what he desires.
> Be pure for him from his abomination
> that you might be safe from his many afflictions.
> He is responsible for all destructions.
> Cattle taken in the fields? It is he who acted likewise.
> As for every loss in the threshing floor or in the field,
> "The ꜣḫ –spirit is it", one says.
> When he places disturbance in a household, the hearts are set apart.
> They all pray to him, too
> (Quack 1994, 324*f*.; Ritner 1993, 180, n. 835).

Returning to the discussion of performative texts within the context of social connectivity (p. 166), we can conclude that, when contact is made in public, performative texts ensured eternal validity. If this contact between the living and the dead was in a more private context (as in the Letters to the Dead), texts affect the body of the dead in a more physical way, either by being swallowed by them or by being dressed with them and only short-term results can be achieved.

New Kingdom I: Celebrating with the dead

In ancient Egypt a local remembrance festival for the dead was introduced in Thebes during the rule of Hatshepsut *c.* 1450 BC (Schott 1953; Wiebach 1986, 263–291; Strudwick 1999, 78–90), most probably following the Festival of Osiris at Abydos, which had become a centre of elite pilgrimage already during the Old Kingdom (Yoyotte 1960; Franke 1984). On the occasion of the Beautiful Festival of the Valley, however, the living celebrated together with the dead at nightly banquets within the Theban *necropolis*. Here, the worlds of the dead and the living intermingled with each other. During this two-day festival, important third and fourth parties were involved in the celebrations, namely the Theban gods and the dead and living kings. Amun made his way from his temple at Karnak (Fig. 8.5) to the Nile, where, in the early versions, he crossed over to the west bank to visit the mortuary temple of Hatshepsut in Deir el-Bahari (Fig. 8.6). In later times other mortuary temples of dead kings were made part of this festival. Amun would rest within the temple of the reigning king and spent the night in his sanctuary. Following Amun, who visits "the gods of the West", high-ranking officials, civil servants and the rest of the Theban population reached the private *necropolis* to gather in large banquets within the open courtyards of tombs (Schott 1953, 5–9; Wiebach 1986, 265). By replacing the ancient ritualistic offering meals of the Old and Middle Kingdoms with an earthly gathering during the New Kingdom (1550–1069 BC), a future tomb owner celebrated together with the dead during his lifetime, while after his death his successors would do the same to honour his memory. The intimate meeting of the living, the dead, the gods and kings make this Theban festival a comprehensive religious festival *par excellence*; the divisions between these four groups were abandoned as part of this annual ritual. Moreover, this festival played a crucial role by offering an opportunity for those who wanted to meet Amun and other gods in his entourage. This role is made clear by a song dating to the second half the 15th century BC that was originally performed during the Beautiful Festival of the Valley, involving harpists and dancing girls and emphasising Amun as a personal protector god:

> Your lord is [Amun],
> the good father,
> the lord of the entire land.

Figure 8.5 (left) The temple of Karnak. Cult centre of Amun of Thebes since 2100 BC, this temple became one of the most important religious centres in Egypt during the New Kingdom. The Great Hypostyle Hall, built during the reign Seti I (1294–1279 BC), was connected with the king's mortuary temple at the west bank of the Nile. He not only reinforced the tradition started by Queen Hatshepsut but provided a splendid setting for the Beautiful Festival of the Valley during the later New Kingdom (photo, Author).

Figure 8.6 (below) Temple of Hatshepsut (1473–1458 BC). Hatshepsut built her terraced style temple set against a cliff wall. The north side of the court of the upper terrace was decorated with scenes of the Beautiful Festival of the Valley procession, the infrastructure of which focused on the causeway (cp. Fig. 8.1) (photo, Author).

He who protects is you
and we shall fear no one.
The sweet father
[...]
  (Caminos and James 1963, 31 and Pl. 23; Kucharek 2000, 77–80).

What makes this text so remarkable is the context in which it was presented. It forms part of a scene in a rock-cut chapel at Gebel es-Silsilah, one of thirty-two mock tombs one hundred miles south of Thebes that were never meant to contain a burial. These chapels, however, display a decoration very similar to contemporary Theban tombs. They were intended to recall the idea of a tomb within easy reach of the annual inundation of the Nile, which was believed to bring fertility and to guarantee prosperity for the deceased buried in Thebes (Bommas 2003, 88–103). Personal religion formed a vital part of a festival during which the living imagined the dead in the procession of the gods; this text offers a unique insight in the close relationship of the living and the gods they met with the help of Amun.

New Kingdom II: Statues of the dead in temples

As we have seen, it was not only the gods of this world who became involved with the dead, but also Osiris, the role model of the dead, who was perceived in hymns as responsible for the prosperity of the living (p. 162). It is not until the New Kingdom, however, that such a constellation arose, pointing to the fact that the worlds of the living and dead were closer to each other than in any other period before this. This concept is supported by the development of intermediary statues (Fig. 8.7; Clère 1968, 135–148; Clère 1969, 1–4) in temple forecourts during the New Kingdom (Pinch 1993, 333–334). The owners of these statues took over the task of conveying prayers to the gods for those who were not allowed to enter the interior of a temple unless a spell was said on their behalf (Luiselli 2006, 46–49). On one of these statues, erected by Amenophis, son of Hapu, in the court before the tenth pylon of Karnak, it says:

Figure 8.7 Intermediary statue of the Royal Butler Tiau. The inscription points out that Tiau is presenting himself as a musician of the goddess Hathor, "who listens to the petitions of every young girl (...)," thus giving a fine example not only of the practice of personal religion but also about how the living were in need of the dead to make their prayers heard (after Pinch 1993, 333 and plate 40).

> Oh, people who are in Karnak and wish to see Amun,
> come to me! I will pass on your prayers!
> (...)
> Make funerary offerings for me,
> call my name every day like it is done for a praised one
>   (Helck 1958, 1835, 3–9).

If a prayer needed to be heard by the gods, the dead were invited by the living to approach the deities who otherwise remained hidden. During the New Kingdom, living through the dead meant praying to the gods with the help of intermediaries. This intervention, however, was only possible after the dead came much closer to the divine world than had been the case in earlier periods. This concept laid the foundations for the following periods, when the living and the dead acted for each other under the guidance of the gods in a more immediate way.

Late Period: Teachings

During the Late Period (664–317 BC) and the Graeco-Roman Period (310 BC–AD 313) the relationship between the living and the dead was negotiated more explicitly as standing in for each other. What is important to note, however, is the fact that the inner self, represented by a guiding god, appears as an independent protagonist, as demonstrated by this passage in the Demotic Papyrus Berlin 24195 (*non vidi*):

> But this does not mean that the one who acts does for someone who does not act.
> It rather means that Re acts in the sky
> and observes the one who acts.
> He rewards the one for the deed who did it
>   (cited after Assmann 1990, 67).

This concept is hardly astonishing given the fact that gods are thought to inhabit man and make the living behave and act under their divine influence. Moreover, the good deeds of a man are counted before the final Judgment of the Dead, a heavenly institution to which the deceased travelled in the barque of Ra. If during this procedure the heart of a dead person failed to be in balance with Ma'at, he or she was not allowed to enter the netherworld. Good deeds, however, although observed by the gods, should not be done in private, as the Teaching of Ani reveals:

> Lay down water for your father and your mother,
> who rest in the valley (*i.e.* the *necropolis*).
> Righteous is (a libation of) water made for the gods,
> briefly: they accept it.
> Do not let it become unnoticed in public that you do it:
> then your son will do the same for you
>   (Quack 1994, 289–90).[13]

According to this text, good deeds are performed in public places, in this case the *necropoleis* of the New Kingdom. This development runs parallel with the rise of the divine presence at burials (p. 170), thus the contact between the living, the gods and the dead became increasingly close. In this context, the offering of water is one of the key rituals carried out for the dead, especially during the Late Period. The mythical antecedent for travelling the roads to the *necropolis* must be seen in the procession of Amenope, who set off once a week from his temple in Luxor to Djeme (ancient Medinet Habu) on the West Bank to carry out a libation for his divine ancestors (Bommas 2005b, 261). This cyclically repeated Ritual of Djeme became increasingly important during the Greek Period when Choachytes – a word that corresponds to the Egyptian wȝḥ mw, "one who offers water" (Bommas 2005b, 262) – made this ancestor ritual one of the most prominent. It had undeniable features of a religious "industry": by repeating the offering of water in the name of Amenope, paid priests acted as guarantors of the duration and cosmic integration of the dead. Already during the Ramesside Period (1292–1070 BC) wȝḥ mw, the "offering of water" had become important and socially accepted enough to be taken as a common excuse for staying home from work, although a contemporary calendar of lucky and unlucky days seems to mention a particular day for it.[14]

This remarkable passage in the Teaching of Ani underlines not only the general importance of giving offerings to the dead but explains what the dead are able to give in return: they stand in for the offerer's interest after his own physical death if heirs fail to carry out the burial according to the rule. This worst case scenario is resignedly summarized in the Teaching of Ankhsheshonqi (pBM EA 10508, 21.20) of late Ptolemaic date:

> Better (is) a statue of stone than a foolish son!
>   (trans. Lichtheim 1980, 176).

Giving offerings to the deceased – whether or not personally known – means living through them. The means of communication are goods[15] to be offered, and the advantage guaranteed by the deceased completes the act of reciprocity in which the exchange of goods is accepted as a medium of social connection. It lies in a person's self-interest to sustain the dead if he wants to live through them.

Roman Period: Exposed mummies?

The latest example of living through the dead in this survey of ancient Egypt is of Roman date (31 BC–AD 313). Even during the Third Intermediate Period (1069–664 BC) the dead were no longer necessarily buried in *necropoleis* at the desert edge and royal tombs began to spring up in temple precincts such as Tanis (Fig. 8.8), Sais, Medinet Habu, Mendes (Bommas 2005a, 63) and Ashmunein (Spencer 2007, 49–51). In this way, the dead came much closer to the world of the living than in earlier periods. One may even assume a novel development within funerary belief and customs.[16] With the concept of Amun as a sovereign (*e.g.* pBoulaq 17, 2.2–3; Luiselli 2004, 2) residing over tombs and other earthly aspects of a burial (Bommas 2005a, 55–57), it is plain to see why these aspects of funerary customs were revisited during the Late Period, especially after burial had become so clearly a phenomenon of this world (Assmann

1995, 281–293). More explicit relations between the living and the dead acting through each other in a less formal way become factors of every-day life once offering rites had become public affairs (p. 172).

In ancient Egypt the dead had always enjoyed strong ties with the private homes they inhabited while alive, and many texts containing the *topos* of a *retour à la maison*

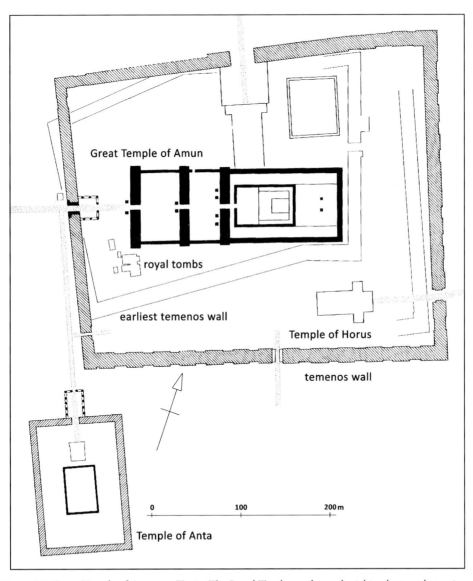

Figure 8.8 Great Temple of Amun at Tanis. The Royal Tombs are located within the temple precinct, south of the first pylon (after 1070 BC) (after Bommas 2005a, 56).

illustrate this (Assmann 2005, 264–268). This idea, however, was always part of the virtual world of the dead celebrated by wishes. This example taken from a Coffin Text from the Middle Kingdom (Coffin Texts, Spell 697, *c.* 2000 BC) illustrates the point:

> (May he give) that N may enter his house and visit his nestlings,
> that he does pleasant things in the small wood together with those on earth
> for ever and ever
>   (De Buck 1956, 331k–l).

During the New Kingdom, the return to the home of the living was made possible if the dead could manage to open the mountain which housed their homes in the hereafter:

> May you open the mountains of the *necropolis*,
> that you may see your house of the living.
> May you hear the sound of song and music
> in your country home within this.
> May you be a protection for your children
> for ever and ever
>   (Assmann 2005, text NR.5.1.3).

This passage from Theban Tomb 82 (*c.* 1420 BC) clearly points out the double interest in a dead person being capable of returning home: the deceased wants to partake in the life he is missing, and, by the same token, the living acquire protection by their ancestor's 3ḫ-spirit.[17]

In Roman times this relation between the living and the dead became even closer when the practice developed of keeping mummified bodies not just in the *necropolis*, but also on display in large banquet halls of tomb houses, before they were carried (sometimes several years later) to their final burial place.[18] This led Diodorus (1.91), who travelled in Egypt between 60 and 57 BC, to believe that "the dead seem to live together with those who looked at them." This practice, however, excluded the bodies of newborn children, especially female infants who often were exposed to die (Lewis 1983, 55).

In fact, in Roman times, mummies were no longer represented as Osiris with a generic mummy-mask but with individualised portrait features of the deceased as a young person (Dioxiadis 1995; Borg 1996). A few literary sources of Greek and Roman times refer to this practice (Borg 1998, 77–79), however it is not likely to have developed before the third century BC and it was certainly due to the changed relationship between gods and men in earlier times (p. 170). In a poem of the first century AD by Silius Italicus (*Punica* XIII, 468–476) mention is made of the burial of Appius Claudius by Scipio in Rome. The Roman text wrongly suggests that mummies were kept at home:

> The people of Egypt lock the standing bodies in (a sarcophagus of) stone after death,
> which they praise and neither at table do they keep the bloodless shadows apart.

Such sources seem to be a testimony to the love and affection felt for the ancestors by the living and they highlight their wish to keep the mummies of their relatives in this world as long as possible. This is, however, only one side of the coin. As a matter of fact, expensive mummies, mostly with costly mummy portraits, often seem to have been a family's most substantial financial investment. No wonder that full control of their whereabouts was crucial. It is interesting to note that these mummies were often mortgaged, as Diodorus (1.92) reports. The earliest record of this legal custom (Römer 2000, 152–153) can be found in Herodotus (*Histories* 2.136) in the fifth century BC, the Greek historian clearly stating that the living, when they pawned complete burials, were making ends meet through their dead ancestors in times of hardship:

> They said that during his (*i.e.* Asychis' = Sheshonq I's) reign there was a severe financial recession and so a law was passed that a person might use his father's corpse as security to take out a loan. There was a rider to the law, however, to the effect that the lender also became the proprietor of the whole of the borrower's burial-plot, so that if the mortgagee refused to pay back the loan, as a penalty neither he nor any other member of his family could have access on their deaths to burial in the family tomb.[19]

Summary

Based on the concept of Ma'at, early attempts to live through the dead during the Old Kingdom are to be seen in the light of social connectivity between those who inhabited this world and the hereafter as part of the same community. The concept of reciprocity, expressed by ritualistic actions, public performances (Appeals to the Living addressing the living) and private sacrifice (Letters to the Dead addressing the dead), guaranteed strong links between both worlds to the benefit of the one who acts for the dead. Living through the dead entailed a high level of maintenance of the dead. As encounters with the dead began to be of a more public nature in the New Kingdom and thereafter, closer relations with the dead became an increasingly important factor of everyday life. The deceased were engaged as intermediaries between gods and men by an offering spell said on their behalf. Acting for the deceased became less formal and increasingly industrialized at the same time. From the early eleventh century BC, mummified bodies could be buried in temple precincts of non-funerary divinities, and in the Greek and Roman periods they were even displayed in public, thus enabling the living to be protected by the deceased through living and eating together with them in the banquet halls. The spatial closeness of the dead in the world of the living now offered the possibility of control of the living, but the survivors and descendants of the dead were also protected by them. This concept of social connection, however, required the commitment of the living to act reciprocally and perform ritual actions that would secure a foreseeable outcome. The Egyptians not only lived with the dead but included them in their ideas about everyday life to such an extent that living through each other became possible. One of the reasons for the overwhelming success of this aspect of ancient Egyptian funerary cult might be seen in the introduction into the Egyptian pantheon of gods who controlled the reciprocal togetherness of the living and the dead.

Notes

1 The most convincing material that sheds some light on the social stratification of burial customs during the Middle Kingdom (*c.* 1960–1760 BC) has been found in the area of Aswan, with rock-cut tombs of the elite at the necropolis at Qubbet el-Hawa (Willems 1996, ch. 2); high middle-class, but illiterate, burials on the Western part of the Island of Elephantine (Seidlmayer 2003, 60–74); and lower-class burials for those who were buried in abandoned houses (Schultz and Schmidt-Schultz 1993, 186). For a more general introduction see Willems 2001. Herodotus (2.85–88) was the first to draw attention to the social stratification of death in ancient Egypt.

2 Most languages do not have their own word for religion (Antes 1978, 184ff.) with the exception of the Dutch word *godsdienst, used* alongside *religie.*

3 These texts have not been studied in detail so far; for a preliminary overview, however, see Assmann (2005, ch. 5). It is interesting to note that funerary literature, destined to be read by the deceased to ward off enemies and other dangers in the other world (as stated in the large corpora of funerary texts, such as the so-called Pyramid Texts, Coffin Texts and the Book of the Dead) had hardly any positive impact on the personal feelings towards an existence in the next world. It can be assumed that funerary texts where not read by a general audience during lifetime.

4 Blood sacrifice, as in Graeco-Roman religion, plays only a virtual role in pharaonic Egypt, due to its high economic value.

5 It is misleading to believe that non-royals were excluded from having funerary texts and to think of a process of democratisation of funerary customs in the Middle Kingdom instead. As long as the possibility of an oral tradition of funerary texts for upper and middle-class deceased can not be ruled out, there is no need to believe that funerary texts were of a restricted nature. Moreover, inscriptions that date 200 years earlier than the Pyramid Texts mention the recitation of glorifications (šd.t s:3ḫ. w) in front of tombs (*e.g.* in the tomb of Debeheni, Giza, see Hassan 1943, fig. 122).

6 Losing body control during rituals is based on social experience, as shown by Douglas (1973, ch. 5).

7 A personal constituent.

8 *E.g.* mtn.y jrj.w m jrj.t n=f M3ʿ.t pw ḥr.y-jb nṯr, incompletely cited by Assmann (1990, 65, n. 25).

9 The god discussed in this text is Osiris of Abydos for whom Pharaoh Neferhotep wants to create a statue according to the ancient inscriptions of the temple of Osiris, see Kahl (1999, 276f.).

10 Assmann (1990, 54) follows Bergmann (1972, 80–102) and argues that the ideology of Ma'at arose in parallel to the emergence of the Egyptian state.

11 The earliest instance of the word Ma'at can be found in the name of Chasechemui's wife Nj-ma'at-hap ("Belonging to the oar of Ma'at") although it seems to be unlikely that in this name Ma'at denotes order/justice instead of a Ma'at-ship that is well attested as an euphemism for the barque of Sokar (De Buck 1961, 42a and 282f.). The chronology of the concept of Ma'at has not yet been undertaken as a research topic; see Helck (1980, 1110–1119; not mentioned in Assmann 1990).

12 This development of Ma'at is to a great extent politically driven. Nonetheless, the texts in question underline the perception and knowledge of Ma'at as belonging to everyone, which is believed to be true by some scholars, *e.g.* Lichtheim (1997, 12).

13   Source B, 17.4–6; Quack's (1994, 289–290) transcription as well as his translation leave out the rubrum.

14   Jansen (1980, 149) lists five *ostraca* which describe wȝḥ mw on particular days. For a specific day, see: pCairo 86637 vs. 8,8, Bakir 1966, 48, Pl. 38 A and B; Leitz (1994, 406*f.*) thinks of rising Nile water where the manuscript shows a lacuna. Possibly the early inundation water was taken to the tombs as a token of rejuvenation.

15   For the social meaning of exchanging goods already during the Old Kingdom see Müller-Wollermann (1985, 121–168).

16   Funerary texts used by the living is a phenomenon widely discussed and recently re-investigated by Gee (2006 73*f.*), who equates funerary literature with funerary texts.

17   Burials of children within inhabited houses, such as on the island of Elephantine during the Middle Kingdom (Bommas 1995, 144, figs 17 and 146), must be excluded from this concept.

18   This convincing reconstruction was first brought forward by Römer (2000, 141–161); Borg (1998, 77–79) thinks of private homes as places where portrait-mummies were initially displayed. For the Egyptian sources see Quaegebeur (1978, 238).

19   On this passage see the brief remarks of Lloyd (1988, 87–88).

Bibliography

Andrews, C. A. R. and Faulkner, R. O. (eds) (1985) *The Ancient Egyptian Book of the Dead*. London, British Museum Press

Antes, P. (1978) Religion einmal anders. *Temenos* 14, 184–197.

Assmann, J. (1975) *Ägyptische Hymnen und Gebete*. Zurich/Munich, Vandenhoeck & Ruprecht.

Assmann, J. (1990a) Egyptian Mortuary Liturgies. In S. Israelit-Groll (ed.) *Studies in Egyptology Presented to Miriam Lichtheim*, 1–45. Jerusalem, Magnes Press.

Assmann, J. (1990b) *Ma'at. Gerechtigkeit und Unsterblichkeit im Alten Ägypten*. München, Beck.

Assmann, J. (1995) Geheimnis, Gedächtnis und Gottesnähe: zum Strukturwandel der Grabsemantik und der Diesseits-Jenseitsbeziehungen im Neuen Reich. In J. Assmann *et al.* (eds) *Thebanische Beamtennekropolen. Neue Perspektiven archäologischer Forschung.* Internationales Symposion Heidelberg 9.–13.6.1993, Studien zur Archäologie und Geschichte Altägyptens 12, 281–293. Heidelberg, Heidelberger Orientverlag.

Assmann, J. and Bommas, M. (2002) *Totenliturgien in den Sargtexten des Mittleren Reiches*, Altägyptische Totenliturgien, vol. I. Heidelberg, Universitätsverlag Winter GmbH Heidelberg.

Assmann, J., Bommas, M. and Kucharek, A. (2005) *Totenliturgien und Totensprüche in Grabinschriften des Neuen Reiches*, Altägyptische Totenliturgien, vol. II. Heidelberg, Universitätsverlag Winter GmbH Heidelberg.

Austin, J. L. (1962) *How To Do Things With Words*. Oxford, Oxford University Press.

Baines, J. (1991) Society, Morality, and Religious Practice. In B. E. Shafer (ed.) *Religion in Ancient Egypt. Gods, Myths, and Personal Practice*, 147–160. Ithaca, Cornell University Press.

Bakir, A. (1966) *The Cairo Calendar No. 86637*. Cairo, Government Printing Office.

Bergmann, J. (1972) "Zum Mythus vom Staat" im Alten Ägypten. In H. Biezais (ed.) The Myth of the State, 80–102. Stockholm, Almqvist & Wiksell.

Bommas, M. (1995) Nordoststadt: Siedlungsbebauung der 1. Zwischenzeit und des Mittleren

Reiches nordwestlich des Inselmuseums. In W. Kaiser *et al.* (eds) Stadt und Tempel von Elephantine, 21./22. Grabungsbericht. *Mitteilungen des Deutschen Archäologischen Institutes Kairo* 51, 141–147.

Bommas, M. (1999) Zur Datierung einiger Briefe an die Toten. *Göttinger Miszellen* 173, 53–60.

Bommas, M. (2003) Schrein unter. Gebel es-Silsilah im Neuen Reich. In H. Guksch, E. Hofmann and M. Bommas (eds) *Grab und Totenkult im Alten Ägypten, Festschrift Jan Assmann*, 88–103. München, Beck

Bommas, M. (2005a) Sepolture all'interno di corti templari in Egitto: il rinovamento del rituale di sepoltura all'inizio del I millenio a.C. *Aegyptus* 85, 53–68.

Bommas, M. (2005b) Situlae and the Offering of Water in the Devine Funerary Cult: A New Approach to the Ritual of Djeme. In A. Amentam, M. Luiselli and M. N. Sordi (eds) *L'acqua nell' antico Egitto, Proceedings of the First International Conference for Young Egyptologists, 15th–18th of October 2003 in Chianciano Terme*, 257–272. Rome, "L'Erma" di Bretschneider.

Bommas, M. (2006) Review: Willems, H (ed.) (2006) *Social Aspects of Funerary Culture in the Egyptian Old and Middle Kingdoms*, Orientalia Lovaniensia analecta 103. Leuven. *Bibliotheca Orientalis* 68, 50–55.

Bommas, M. (2009) The Legacy of Egypt in Early Christian Thought According to the Epitaph of Alcuin of York. In *Festschrift A. M. Fadda Luiselli*. Rome, in press.

Borg, B. (1996) *Mumienportraits, Chronologie und kultureller Kontext*. Mainz, Philipp von Zabern.

Borg, B. (1998) „*Der zierlichste Anblick der Welt …*". *Ägyptische Portraitmumien*. Mainz, Philipp von Zabern.

Bosticco, S. (1959) *Le stele Egiziane dall'antico al nuovo regno, Museo Archeologico di Firenze*. Rome, Istituto Poligrafico dello Stato.

Caminos, R. A. and James, T. G. H. (1963) *Gebel es-Silsilah I, The Shrines*, Archaeological Survey of Egypt 31. London, Egypt Exploration Society.

Clère, J. J. (1968) Deux statues "Gardiennes de Porte" d'époque ramesside. *Journal of Egyptian Archaeology* 54, 135–148.

Clère, J. J. (1969) Dur un corpus des statues sistrophores égyptiennes. *Zeitschrift für ägyptische Sprache* 96, 1–4.

Corcoran, L. (1995) *Portrait Mummies from Roman Egypt*. Chicago, Oriental Institute of the University of Chicago.

de Buck, A. (1935) *The Egyptian Coffin Texts*, vol. I. Chicago, Oriental Institute of the University of Chicago.

de Buck, A. (1956) *Ancient Egyptian Coffin Texts*, vol. VI. Chicago, Oriental Institute of the University of Chicago.

de Buck, A. (1961) *The Egyptian Coffin Texts*, vol. VII. Chicago, Oriental Institute of the University of Chicago.

Demarée, R. (1983) *The #X |qr n Ro-Stelae. On Ancestor Worship in Ancient Egypt*. Leiden, Nederlands Instituut vor het Nabije Oosten.

Dioxiadis, S. and Thompson, D. (1995) *The Mysterious Fayum Portraits, Faces from ancient Egypt*. London, Thames & Hudson Ltd.

Douglas, M. (1973) *Natural Symbols. Explorations in Cosmology*. London, Pelican Books.

Franke, D. (1984) *Personendaten aus dem späten Mittleren Reich (20.–16. Jahrhundert v. Chr.)*, Ägyptologische Abhandlungen 41.Wiesbaden, Harrassowitz.

Gardiner, A. H. and Sethe, K. (1928) *Egyptian Letters to the Dead*. London, Egypt Exploration Society.

Gee, J. (2006) The Use of the Daily Temple Liturgy in the Book of the Dead. In B. Backes, I. Munro and S. Stöhr (eds) *Totenbuch-Forschungen. Gesammelte Beiträge des 2. Internationalen Totenbuch-Symposiums 2005*, Studien zum Altägyptischen Totenbuch 11, 73–86. Wiesbaden, Harrassowitz.

Guksch, H., Hofmann, E. and Bommas, M. (eds) (2003) *Grab und Totenkult im Alten Ägypten, Fs Jan Assmann*. München, Beck

Hassan, S. (1943) *Excavations at Giza 4, 1932–1933*. Cairo, Government Press.

Helck, W. (1958) *Urkunden der 18. Dynastie*, vol. IV. Berlin, Akademie der Wissenschaften

Helck, W. (1980) Maat. *Lexikon der Ägyptologie* III, 1110–1119. Wiesbaden, Harrassowitz.

Herodotus. *The Histories*. R. Waterfield, trans. (1998). Oxford/New York, Oxford University Press.

James, T. G. H. (1985) Preface. In C. A. R. Andrews and R. O. Faulkner (eds) *The Ancient Egyptian Book of the Dead*, 7–8. London, British Museum Press.

Jansen, J. J. (1980) Absence from work by the necropolis workmen of Thebes. *Studien zur altägyptischen Kultur* 8, 127–152.

Kahl, J. (1999) *Siut-Theben. Zur Wertschätzung von Traditionen im alten Ägypten*, Probleme der Ägyptologie 13. Leiden/Boston/Cologne, Brill.

Kucharek, A. (2000) Die frühe Persönliche Frömmigkeit im Fest. Über ein Lied in Gebel es-Silsilah. *Göttingen Miszellen* 176, 77–80.

Leitz, C. (1994) *Tagewählerei*, Ägyptologische Abhandlungen 55. Wiesbaden, Harrassowitz.

Lewis, N. (1983) *Life in Egypt under Roman Rule*, Classics in Papyrology. Oxford, Oxbow.

Lichtheim, M. (1980) *Ancient Egyptian Literature III, The Late Period*. Berkeley, University of California Press.

Lichtheim, M. (1992) *Maat in Egyptian Autobiographies and Related Studies*, Orbis Biblicus Orientalis 120. Fribourg/Göttingen, Universitätsverlag Freiburg Schweiz.

Lichtheim, M. (1997) *Moral Values in Ancient Egypt*, Oriens Biblicus et Orientalis 155. Fribourg/Göttingen, Universitätsverlag Freiburg Schweiz.

Lloyd, A. B. (1988) *Herodotus, Book II, Commentary 99–182*. Leiden/New York/København/Köln, Brill.

Luiselli, M. M. (2004) *Der Amun-Re Hymnus des P.Boulaq 17 (P.Kairo CG 58038)*, Kleine ägyptische Texte 14. Wiesbaden, Harrassowitz.

Luiselli, M. M. (2006) *Gottesnähe. Die persönliche Teilnahme an der Religion in Ägypten im Mittleren und Neuen Reich*. Unpublished PhD dissertation, University of Basel.

Mariette, A. (1869) *Abydos II*. Paris, Librairie A. Franck.

Mauss, M. (1990) *Die Gabe. Form und Funktion des Austausches in archaischen Gesellschaften*. Frankfurt, Suhrkamp.

Müller, Ch. (1975) Anruf an Lebende. *Lexikon der Ägyptologie* I, col. 293–299. Wiesbaden, Harrassowitz.

Müller-Wollermann, R. (1985) Warenaustausch im Ägypten des Alten Reiches. *Journal of Economic and Social History of the Orient* 28, 121–168.

Parkinson, R. B. (1998) *The Tale Of Sinuhe And Other Ancient Egyptian Poems, 1940–1640 BC*. Oxford, Oxford University Press.

Pinch, G. (1993) *Votive Offerings to Hathor*. Oxford, Griffith Institute, University of Oxford.

Quack, J. F. (1992) *Studien zur Lehre für Merikare*, Göttinger Orientforschungen IV. 23. Wiesbaden, Harrassowitz.

Quack, J. F. (1994) *Die Lehren des Ani. Ein neuägyptischer Weisheitstext in seinem kulturellen Umfeld*, Orbis Biblicus Orientalis 141. Freiburg/Göttingen, Vandenhoeck & Ruprecht.

Quaegebeur, J. (1978) Mummy labels: an orientation. In E. Boswinkel and P. W. Pestman (eds) *Textes grecs, démotiques et bilingues*, 232–259. Leiden, Brill.

Riggs, C. (2005) *The Beautiful Burial in Roman Egypt. Art, Identity, and Funerary Religion.* Oxford, Oxford University Press.

Ritner, R. K. (1988) Uninscribed Mummy Bandage. In S. d'Auria *et al.* (eds) *Mummies & Magic,* catalogue Museum of Fine Arts Boston, 226–227. Hong Kong, Museum of Fine Arts, Boston.

Ritner, R. K. (1993) *The Mechanics of Ancient Egyptian Magical Practice*, Studies in Ancient Oriental Civilization 54. Chicago, Oriental Institute of the University of Chicago.

Römer, C. (2000) Das Werden zu Osiris im römischen Ägypten. *Archiv für Religionsgeschichte* 2.2, 141–161.

Sabbatucci, D. (1988) Kultur und Religion. In H. Cancik, B. Gladigow and M. Laubscher (eds) *Handbuch religionswissenschaftlicher Grundbegriffe*, vol. I, 43–58. Stuttgart, Kohlhammer.

Schott, S. (1953) *Das schöne Fest vom Wüstentale, Festbräuche einer Totenstadt.* Abhandlungen der Mainzer Akademie der Wissenschaften 11. Mainz, Akademie der Wissenschaften.

Schultz, M. and Schmidt-Schultz, T. (1993) Erste Ergebnisse der osteologischen Untersuchung an den menschlichen Skelettfunden der 16.–20. Kampagne. In W. Kaiser *et al.* (eds) Stadt und Tempel von Elephantine, 19./20. Grabungsbericht. *Mitteilungen des Deutschen Archäologischen Instituts, Kairo* 49, 182–187.

Seidlmayer, S. J. (2003) Vom Sterben der Kleinen Leute. Tod und Bestattung in der sozialen Grundschicht am Ende des Alten Reiches. In H. Guksch, E. Hofmann and M. Bommas (eds) *Grab und Totenkult im Alten Ägypten, Fs Jan Assmann*, 60–74. München, Beck.

Sethe, K. (1908) *Die altägyptischen Pyramidentexte*, vol. I. Leipzig, J.C. Hinrichs'sche Buchhandlung.

Sethe, K. (1983) *Ägyptische Lesestücke zum Gebrauch im akademischen Unterricht.* Darmstadt, J.C. Hinrichs'sche Buchhandlung.

Shillingsburg, P. L. (2006) *From Gutenberg to Google.* Cambridge, Cambridge University Press.

Spencer, A. J. (2007) The possible existence of Third Intermediate Period elite tombs at el-Ashmunein. *British Museum Studies in Ancient Egypt and Sudan* 8, 49–51.

Strudwick, N. and Strudwick, H. (1999) *Thebes in Egypt*. Ithaca, Cornell University Press.

Strudwick, N. C. (2005) *Texts From the Pyramid Age*. Atlanta, Society of Biblical Literature.

Verhoeven, U. (2003) Post ins Jenseits. Formular und Funktion altägyptischer Briefe an Tote. *Nordostafrikanisch-Westasiatische Studien* 4, 31–51.

Vogelsang, F. and Gardiner, A. H. (1908) *Die Klagen des Bauern*, Hieratische Papyrus Berlin, vol. IV. Leipzig, J.C. Hinrichs'sche Buchhandlung.

Wiebach, S. (1986) Die Begegnung von Lebenden und Verstorbenen im Rahmen des Thebanischen Talfestes. *Studien zur altägyptischen Kultur* 13, 263–291.

Willems, H. (1996) *The Coffin of Heqata (Cairo JdE 36418): A Case Study of Egyptian Funerary Culture of the Early Middle Kingdom*, Orientalia Lovaniensia analecta 70. Leuven, Peeters.

Willems, H (ed.) (2006) *Social Aspects of Funerary Culture in the Egyptian Old and Middle Kingdoms*, Orientalia Lovaniensia analecta 103. Leuven, Peeters.

Yoyotte, J. (1960) Les pèlerinages dans l' Égypte ancienne. In J. Yoyotte and others (eds) *Les pèlerinages, Sources Orientales 3*, 17–74. Paris, Éditions Seuil.

9

Innocent X, *Pontifex Optimus Maximus*, and the church of Sant' Agnese: A mausoleum for the Pamphilj 'forum'

Susan Russell

A recent guide to the church of Sant' Agnese in Piazza Navona (Figs 9.1 and 9.2) observes that 'the quantity and size of Pamphilj-commissioned works in and around the Piazza Navona, abounding in symbolic references to the Pope and his family, led to its being nick-named the Pamphilj "forum"' (Studio Forme n.d., 12; Boesel 2000, 391–409). But this was more than a nickname, it represented a serious campaign by Giovanni Battista Pamphilj (1574–1655), who ascended the papal throne as Innocent X in 1644, to create a visual signature for his reign that deliberately manipulated the connections between ancient Rome, the Pamphilj family and the Papacy. The area is, indeed, formally referred to as the '*foro Agonali*' in the section on Innocent X's medals in the *Numismata Pontificum Romanorum* of 1699 (Fig. 9.8), where the construction of Sant' Agnese is celebrated, and a view of the square from 1773 is similarly called the *Prospectus Fori Agonalis* (*Prospectus Fori Agonalis* 1773; Bonanni 1699, 2, 630). The aim of this essay is to show that Innocent's resting place, the church of Sant' Agnese in Piazza Navona, although a late addition to the so-called forum was, in both form and function, an integral part of this campaign.

The inscription on Innocent X's tomb monument designed by Giovanni Battista Maini (1690–1752) is telling in its brevity: *Innocentius X Pamphilius Romanus Pontifex Optimus Maximus* (Fig. 9.3). It records his family name, his place of birth and his status as pope, the three most important attributes by which he would be remembered for posterity. *Pontifex Optimus Maximus*, the ancient title of Rome's high priest, was traditionally applied to the occupant of St. Peter's throne, but took on a renewed significance under Innocent X, for it was used to emphasise not only its longevity in Christian custom but also its Classical origins. This 'Romanness' stemmed from two main circumstances: that Giovanni Battista Pamphilj was the first Roman-born pope in nearly a hundred years, and that the Pamphilj claimed descent from the very founders of Rome. The following brief outline of the iconography of key monuments of Innocent's reign will show how important the Roman tradition was to its visual identity and will provide a context for the site, style and meaning of the church of Sant' Agnese.

Figure 9.1 S. Agnese in Piazza Navona (photo, Author).

In 1662 Niccolò Angelo Cafferri, the secretary of Don Camillo Pamphilj (1621–
1666), Innocent X's nephew, published a genealogy of the Pamphilj family entitled *Numa*
Pompilio disceso dalla Famiglia Pamphilia di Sparta, in quelle Città fondata da Pamphilio

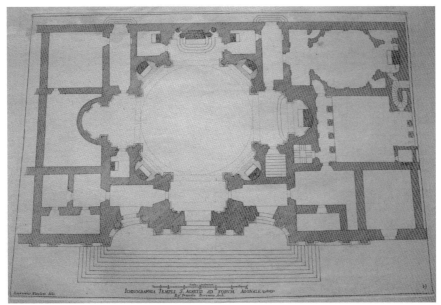

Figure 9.2 Plan of S. Agnese in Piazza Navona. Giovanni Battista Falda, after Francesco Borromini, etching (G.G. De Rossi, 1665, Rome) (photo, Author, courtesy of the British School at Rome).

Figure 9.3 Giovanni Battista Maini, Funerary monument of Innocent X, 1729, marble, S. Agnese in Piazza Navona (Rome, Istituto Centrale per il Catalogo e il Documentazione).

Rè de' Dorici 350 anni prima dell'edificazione di Roma (Cafferri 1662, 3–9). It was the culmination of years of genealogical research that had begun with Innocent X's uncle, Cardinal Gerolamo Pamphilj (1544–1610) and, as the title declares, relates the Pamphilj to Romulus's successor, Numa Pompilius (Cafferri 1662, 3–4, 8). Numa, second king of Rome and first *Pontifex Maximus* in the late eighth and early seventh centuries BC, was understood as a conventional forbear of Rome's popes: the biographer of Gregory XIII Buoncompagni (reigned 1572–85), placed his patron in a direct line from Numa, not only because of their similar activity in reforming the Calendar, but also because the ancient king was Rome's head priest (Courtright 1990, 57; Cartari 1647, 170). Innocent X's place in this traditional line of succession could, consequently, be claimed even more authoritatively because of the Pamphilj's genealogical pretensions, which were made manifest in at least three important building projects: the Pamphilj complex in Piazza Navona (comprising the Palazzo Pamphilj, the Biblioteca Innocenziana and Sant' Agnese), the Villa Pamphilj and the church of S. Andrea on the Quirinal Hill. All these were built on sites associated with Numa's legend.

In the 1660s, Don Camillo Pamphilj would commission Bernini to build the church of San Andrea where it was believed that Numa had lived (Cafferri 1662, 6; Gijsbers 1996), so there is no doubt that a similar idea was already in the minds of the family when, in 1630, Camillo's father, Pamphilio, bought a farmhouse on the Janiculum Hill, not far from where antiquarian maps and classical literary sources posited both ancient villas and Numa's tomb. Cicero (*Republic* 2.56) placed Numa's tomb on the Janiculum near an altar dedicated to Fontus the son of Janus, and Plutarch (*Parallel Lives* 22.2), one of Cafferri's sources, says that Numa was buried 'under the Janiculum' (Ambrogi 2001, 13; Cafferri 1662, 4). Archaeology has proved that antiquarians were right to suspect the presence of ancient dwellings here, for remains of a late Republican villa have been uncovered beneath the necropolis located between the new Casino del Bel Respiro and the old farmhouse at Villa Pamphilj (Ambrogi 2001, 14; Ciancio & Virgili 1993, 50–20; Virgili 1986, 760).

When Giambattista Pamphilj ascended the Papal throne in 1644 the building of the elegant Casino del Bel Respiro began. The model of antiquity is evident in its design, for the Casino resembles a Triumphal arch, concomitantly decorated with sculpture that artfully synthesised classical fragments with seventeenth-century additions (Benocci 2005; Benocci 1999; Benocci, 1998; Benocci 1998b; Benocci 1996; Calza *et al.*, 1977; Hoffmann 1976). It was also situated near what was believed to be the ancient Via Triumphalis on antiquarian maps of Rome. In Marco Fabio Calvo's 1527 view of Rome in the time of Pliny – a map in the Pamphilj's possession – the tomb is placed on the Janiculum within the walls (ADP Arch. 306 f. 354r; Frutaz 1962, 2, pianta X, tav. 19). Pirro Ligorio located the Pons Triumphalis near the Porta Aurelia on his 1553 map, and on his 1561 map relocated it behind the gate, inserting the Campus Triumphalis directly in front (Frutaz 1962, 2, pianta XVI, tav. 25 – 1553; 2, pianta XVII, tav. 31 – 1561). Etienne Du Pérac, in his 1574 map, designated the Via Triumphalis as the road which borders the Campus Triumphalis to the west, leading from the Porta Aurelia, and Mario Cartaro in his 1579 map has the Via Aurelia and the Via Triumphalis meet at the gate, a confluence followed by Giacomo Lauro, *c.* 1612 (Frutaz 1962, Du Pérac: 2, pianta XXII, tav. 42; Cartaro: 2, pianta XXIII, 3, tav. 54; Lauro: 2, pianta XXVII, tav. 59; also Marshall 2003). The latter conjunction neatly provides a boundary for the territory subsequently occupied by the Villa Pamphilj.

These reverberations of ancient Rome in the area occupied by the Casino del Bel Respiro are reinforced by the iconography of its interior decorations, where an Augustan *pax romana* is suggested. In the Gallery of Roman Customs scenes of good government are represented through depictions in low-relief stucco of victory, sacrifice, triumphs, temples, arches, mausolea and medals of emperors, designed by the architect of the Casino, the sculptor Alessandro Algardi (*c.* 1598–1654) (Benocci 1996, 86–101; Montagu 1986; Raggio 1971). The images were derived from an eclectic range of sources, including ancient marble reliefs, coins (such as those found in Francesco Angeloni's *Historia Augusta*, published in 1641) and from reconstructions of ancient buildings in Giacomo Lauro's *Antiquae Urbis Splendor*, published in 1637. Both these books were held in the Pamphilj library (ADP Archviolo 106, f. 356r.; Benocci 1996, 86–101; Lauro 1651; Angeloni 1641). The Augustan atmosphere of the sequence is encapsulated in a relief of the *Pietas Augusti*, which shows Marcus Aurelius sacrificing, and in two relief medallions, the *Aequitas Augusti* and the *Pax Augusta*, the latter two images also derived from coins in Angeloni's *Historia Augusta* (Benocci 1999, 43–49; Benocci 1998a, 458–468; Benocci 1996, 86–103; Hoffmann 1976, 220–221, 258–264).

The Imperial references were elsewhere echoed by the waters that fed the extensive fountains of the new villa. These issued from an aqueduct abutting the site on the Via Aurelia Antica. An inscription on the arch, dated 1609, marks its reconstruction under Paul V Borghese (1605–21), and states that the Pope 'restored and enlarged the aqueduct built by the Emperor Augustus', although in fact the aqueduct – virtually a new construction – occupied the site of two ancient waterways of the late first century BC and second century AD, Augustus's Aqua Alsietina and Trajan's Acqua Traiana. Scholars of the period were unaware that Trajan had reconstructed the old Augustan aqueduct, relying for their information about Roman aqueducts on Sextus Iulius Frontinus's treatise, *De Aquae Ductu Urbis Romae*, which was written before Trajan's aqueduct was built *c.* 109 AD (Bruun 2001, 299–315; Ashby 1935, 183–189, 299–307). The error, nevertheless, could hardly have been more suited to Pamphilj pretensions because Augustus, who famously brought peace to the empire, was a suggestive model for a family whose major heraldic device, the dove with an olive branch in its beak, is the symbol of peace.

Yet, significantly, the zone where the Casino was to stand was also strongly connected with early Christian tradition. Another book in the Pamphilj's possession, Paolo Aringhi's annotated version of Antonio Bosio's *Roma Sotterranea*, which appeared in 1635 not long after the Pamphilj obtained the land on the Via Aurelia Antica, states that in the

Figure 9.4 View of Piazza Navona with Palazzo Pamphilj, S. Agnese and Four Rivers Fountain (photo, Author).

area between the Via Aurelia and the Via Trionfale many martyrs were buried who died under the Emperor Commodus (ADP Archiviolo 106, f. 343v.; Ditchfield 1997, 344; Bosio 1635, 15, 23). These included, amongst numerous others, Saints Eusebius, Vincenzo, Peregrino and Pontiano and two Popes, Felix I and Felix II (Bosio 1635, 23, 115). The Casino's proximity to St Peter's – the entrance façade is situated directly opposite St Peter's dome – reinforces the site's connection with early Christianity. This pagan/christian duality is also evident in the works that Innocent set in motion to refurbish Piazza Navona, most notably the extensively renovated and enlarged Palazzo Pamphilj and the church of Sant' Agnese.

The first stage of this project, begun in 1644, was the extension of the family's small, fifteenth-century palace into the splendid new building that now occupies a large part of the western side of the piazza and abuts the church of Sant' Agnese (Fig. 9.4) (De Gregori n.d.; Preimesberger 1976; Romano and Partini 1947; Gerlini 1943). Many of the new frescoes, painted between the late 1640s and early 1650s were inspired by Augustan literature. Vergil's *Aeneid* was the source for Pietro da Cortona's magnificent ceiling fresco in Borromini's Gallery: according to Cafferri's genealogy, the hero Aeneas was Numa's forbear, and by implication the Pamphilj descend through Aeneas and his mother, the goddess Venus, who is invariably accompanied by doves, the dominating emblem of Pamphilj heraldry (Scott 1997, 90–91; Cafferri 1660, 3–9). Vergil's bucolic poetry also inspired the pastoral scenes, reminiscent of ancient Roman landscapes that were painted by Gaspard Dughet (1615–1675) in the Sala dei paesi. In the Sala di Ovidio and the Sala della storia romana, painted by Giacinto Brandi (1621–1691) and Giacinto Gimignani (1611–1681) respectively, the fresco-friezes show episodes drawn from two further Augustan literary sources, Ovid's *Metamorphoses* and Livy's *Early History of Rome* (Russell 2007b; Russell 2006; Simonetta *et al.* 2003/04, 1: 55–57; Russell 1999a, 177–235; Boisclair 1986, 99–200; Pampalone 1973; Redig De Campos 1970, 168–173; Di Domenico Cortese 1968). Yet these classical scenes were juxtaposed with Christian subjects: Giacinto Gimignani's scenes of Old Testament heroines in the Camera delle donne illustri, painted in 1648, reflect episodes from stories of the Old Testament patriarchs Moses and Joseph that were painted during the 1630s (Russell 2006; Simonetta *et al.* 2003/04, 1: 53–54; Russell 1999b; Russell 1997; Redig de Campos 1970, 161–63, 184–85).

Outside, at the centre of the new Piazza Navona precinct, Bernini's Four Rivers Fountain formed the base of an obelisk that Innocent X had had transported from the fourth-century Circus of Maxentius on the Via Appia, and the waters that fed the fountain revived the Aqua Vergine, both of which were celebrated with medals struck during Innocent's reign (Marder 2000, 140; Bonanni 1699, 2, 634–39). At the very core of Piazza Navona one finds the pervasive presence of the Pamphilj's legendary ancestor, Numa Pompilius, as Giacomo Lauro tells us in his reconstruction of the '*Circo Agonale*': "In this Circus were celebrated the games called Agonali, that were instituted by Numa Pompilius: and from these games called Agonali, is called Piazza Nagona, or Agone, which in Greek signifies combat or fighting, because in this circus fights and battles were played…." (Lauro 1651, plate 81 with Latin inscription and translations of the Latin text in Italian, German and French, plate 81 verso). This connection is also recorded in Filippo Bonanni's description of the *Abluto Acqua Virgine Agonalium Cruore* in the Pope's *Numismata* (Bonanni 1699, 2, 634). Ovid (*Metamorphoses,* lines 161–93, 357; 474–99, 366), writing in the late first century BC and early first century AD, tells us that the most important of all the civilized practices that Numa brought to Rome were 'the arts of peace', and given the Augustan overtones of the decorative programmes at Palazzo and Villa Pamphilj it is evident that Innocent was, in Piazza Navona, attempting to convey the idea of a *Pax Romana* in a public arena at the very centre of the Pamphilj 'forum'. Reinforcing the idea of secular peace is the dove with the olive branch in its beak – not the Papal arms or a cross – surmounting the obelisk. The message was highly suitable to the Holy Year of 1650, promising the peace Innocent X hoped to bring not only to a warring Europe but also to the restive Papal States (Preimesberger 1998, 619–627; Benocci 1998: 458–59). At the same time, by placing an obelisk in the very centre of the square, its original function as a circus or stadium was deliberately recalled, because the obelisk occupies the same place that it would have in the middle of a circus's *spina* in antiquity – or at least where obelisks were usually placed in reconstructions by, notably, Pirro Ligorio (*c.* 1513–1583), then by imitators like Onofrio Panvinio (1530–1568), whose book on circuses the Pamphilj owned, and by Giacomo Lauro (1584–1637), a new edition of whose *Antiquae Urbis Splendor* appeared in 1651, the year in which the building programme of the new church of Sant' Agnese began (ADP. Archiviolo 106: 348r; Coffin 2004, 22–23; Lauro 1651, plate 81 and verso; Panvinio 1600; Ligorio 1553, 20v.–21r: *Circo Agonale*).

    The site of the new Pamphilj church was previously occupied by the small, early Christian church of Sant' Agnese (De Gregori n.d.; Romano and Partini 1947; Gerlini 1943). Beneath it, during the construction of the church that now dominates the square, a stone was purportedly found inscribed '*Aulo Vulturgio Pamphilio*', giving rise to the claim that the Pamphilj had lived there in ancient times; Bonnani (1699, 2, 630) refers to the remains as '*Avita Pamphiliorum Domus*' (Simonetta *et al.* 2003/04, 1, 7–81; Brusoni 1664, 18). The new church became a monument to this circumstance and its command of the square imparted an incontrovertibly Christian authority to the pagan arena. The old church of S. Agnese had, like most early Christian churches, a basilical plan, and was built on the vaults of Domitian's stadium where Agnes, the teen-aged virgin saint, was believed to have died in AD 304. She was buried, however, in the catacomb under the church that bears her name in the Via Nomentana, outside the walls of Rome (Simonetta *et al.* 2003/04, 1, 73–77; Sciubba and Sabatini 1962). The chapels situated underneath the ancient church in Piazza Navona were, nevertheless, considered relics in their own right in the seventeenth century (Studio Forme n.d., 12). While not exactly a martyrium, Sant' Agnese still manifested something of the mystery of a cemetery church and therefore burial on the site promised almost the same hope for resurrection as did being buried close to the saint herself. From the start, the new building was intended to function as a tomb for Innocent X and his family, a mausoleum that equally performed the function of a private chapel (Sciubba and Sabatini 1962, 25). The Pamphilj had a particular devotion for Sant' Agnese, having lived in Piazza Navona since 1470 when Antonio Pamphilj arrived from Gubbio and became tax agent (*procuratore fiscale*) to Innocent VIII (reigned 1484–92), in whose honour Giovanni Battista Pamphilj took his Papal name (Chiomenti Vassalli 1979, 22–23; Freiherr von Pastor 1940, 23). It was under Innocent X that Sant' Agnese's cult was renewed when, in the Holy Year of 1650, a large altar was erected in front of the old church for Easter celebrations (Studio Forme n.d., 12; Sciubba and Sabatini 1962, 25).

    In 1651 plans for a new church to be integrated into the Pamphilj complex were begun. The commission saw several changes of architects. Initial ideas were sought from Giambattista Mola (1585–1665). Further plans were provided by Girolamo Rainaldi (1570–1655), the architect at work on Palazzo Pamphilj and by his son, Carlo (1611–1691). However, both architects were eventually replaced by Francesco Borromini (1599–1667), who modified the preceding designs in order to create a façade that was less rigid than that of the Rainaldi. What finally resulted was a combination of designs by Borromini and the two Rainaldi. With Innocent's death in 1655 the project lost focus and momentum as various members of the family took over its supervision, with differing degrees of enthusiasm and success. In 1657 Borromini was removed by Don Camillo Pamphilj (1621–1666) and the project was returned to Carlo Rainaldi, who completed the façade; the interior was finished by Bernini, who was brought in by Camillo's widow, Olimpia Aldobrandini Borghese Pamphilj (1623–1681). Restorations and additions were made by Andrea Busiri Vici in the nineteenth-century. The bibliography on Borromini and Sant' Agnese is too extensive to be included here; I refer the reader to key publications cited (Simonetta *et al.* 2003/04, 1, 81–97; Huemer 2001; Clancy 2000, 148–150; Eimer 1971, 58–65; Sciubba and Sabatini 1962, 39–40).

With so many hands at work it is difficult to establish what the original vision might have been. What is clear, however, is that from the very beginning a central plan church was envisaged, in complete contrast to the basilical plan of the original structure. Modestly-sized, central plan churches were, by the middle of the century, emerging as a solution both for restricted sites and for the remodelling of earlier structures. In the 1630s, Borromini had created a new ideal with San Carlo alle Quattro Fontane, transforming a small, narrow piece of land into one of the jewels of Baroque architecture (Blunt 1979, 52–84; Steinberg 1977). Around the same time, Pietro da Cortona (1597–1669) reworked the early Christian church of SS. Luca e Martina which overlooks the Roman Forum (Noehles 1969). Both architects used a central plan, and in both cases emphasised height, using punctured domes to exploit light and its symbolism. Sant' Agnese follows in this tradition. Mola's initial idea for the 1652 plan bears distinct similarities to that of San Carlo, while Carlo Rainaldi's plan has more in common with Cortona's design. Yet of the Pamphilj architects, neither Mola, nor the younger Rainaldi, nor still the ageing Girolamo, seem to have attempted this type of plan previously, so it appears likely that the initial idea for a central plan church came from the Pamphilj themselves, or one of their agents such as Virgilio Spada (1596–1662), the Pope's almoner and supporter of Borromini, whose antiquarian interests he shared (Raspe 2000, esp. 85–86; Finocchiaro 1999). For it was not only in the context of contemporary architectural practice that Borromini developed his plans for Sant' Agnese, but also from his knowledge of ancient structures, their form and function.

As early as *c.*1650 Borromini had drawn up a plan for a Pamphilj mausoleum (Fig. 9.5) that was to be attached to Santa Maria in Vallicella, the 'Chiesa Nuova', San Filippo Neri's Oratorian church (Clancy 2000, 146; Raspe 1996, 318–21). Innocent was personally devoted to San Filippo Neri. As a young man he had probably met him through his uncle Gerolamo Pamphilj, who was buried in the church: his monument, a large, black marble wall plaque with the Pamphilj dove clearly delineated in white marble, is situated at the altar end of left aisle. Moreover, Virgilio Spada, allied both with the Pamphilj and Borromini, had effected commissions for the architect with

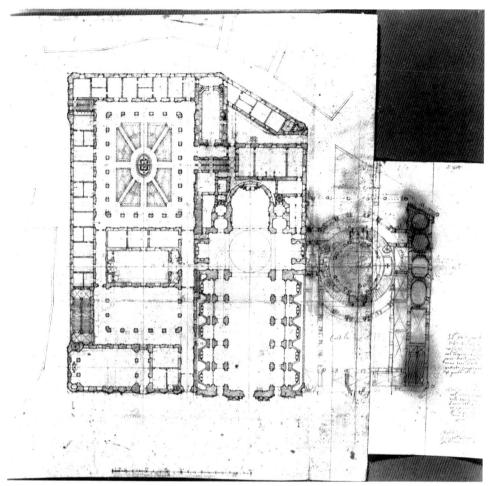

Figure 9.5 Francesco Borromini, Plan for a Pamphilj mausoleum attached to Santa Maria in Vallicella, c. 1651, Vienna, Albertina (Vienna, Albertina).

the Oratorians (Clancy 2000, 146; Connors 1980). The Chiesa Nuova project was abandoned when the more suitable site became available in the Pamphilj precinct, but Borromini's circular plan was undoubtedly a cherished concept that may have been suggested to Mola and the Rainaldis, the motivation clearly being to create a link between a Pamphilj tomb and the mausolea of ancient Rome. It is germane to this discussion to mention Karl Noehles' suggestion that Cortona probably referred to the plan and elevation of a mausoleum on the Via Appia Antica reproduced by G.B. Montano for SS. Luca e Martina (Noehles 1997, 142). It seems evident that Borromini's ideas for Sant' Agnese, ultimately unrealised because of the vicissitudes of the commission, but recorded in a series of drawings, similarly derived from an understanding of ancient architectural types which were well known from extant examples, antiquarian literature and prints and drawings.

Innocent X's proposed tomb, with its circular plan, stood in a long line of Roman rulers' burial monuments beginning, perhaps most significantly given Pamphilj interests, with that of Augustus, whose mausoleum, completed in 23 BC, was known in both its contemporary form and in reconstructions such as those by Ligorio and Montano (Rausa 1997, 114–123). Similarly Hadrian, himself looking back to Augustus, created a circular mausoleum between AD 135 and 139, which had more recently had been a papal residence that dominated the Tiber on the opposite bank. Formal echoes of Michelangelo's San Pietro that have been observed in Sant' Agnese reinforce the notion of a Pope's burial place whose origins lie in the central plan mausoleum of antiquity, and by an architect that Borromini undoubtedly hoped to emulate (Huemer 2001). As Maria Luisa Madonna and Marcello Fagiolo (1972, 383) have observed in the context of another Augustan revival, that of Julius II (1503–13), "La Basilica di S. Pietro sarebbe stata insieme cappella palatina e mausoleo imperiale [Saint Peter's Basilica would have been simultaneously a palatine chapel and an imperial mausoleum]."

Circular or central plan tombs were to be found in abundance on the Appian Way, amongst the best known of which today is the Augustan-period tomb of Caecilia Metella, but as a manuscript by Pirro Ligorio shows, there was a strong graphic tradition recording numerous others on the ancient road, from Rome to as far away as Naples. Dealing solely with tomb monuments, Ligorio's manuscript, entitled *De Luoghi delle sepulture delle fameglie Romane et degli huomini illustri*, dates from the early 1560s (Rausa 1997, 1–2). It had been available in the Vatican Library since 1600 in a copy made by Onofrio Panvinio (1530–1568) and Fulvio Orsini (1529–1600) and was well known to members of the scholarly circle of Cassiano dal Pozzo (1588–1657) and Cardinal Francesco Barberini (1597–1679), a circle that included Borromini (Russell 2007a; Raspe 2000, 85–86; Rausa 1997, 19–20). The copy, BAV Vat. lat. 3439, is a rich source of plans and elevations of well-observed, measured and reconstructed tombs of the ancient nobility, such as the Tomb of the Calventii, with its circular plan, pedimental façade and dome (Rausa 1997, 82–87). Further examples include the Tomb of the 'Calatini', the Tomb of the 'Servilii' and the so-called 'Carceri Vecchie' which can still be seen, well-preserved, in the Via Nazionale at Santa Maria Capua Vetere near Naples (Rausa 1997, 97–98). Some of these tombs were also known through the published treatises of Sebastiano Serlio (1475–1554) – a book owned by the Pamphilj – and of Giovanni Battista Montano (*c.* 1545–1621), who has often been cited as a source for Borromini's architecture (ADP Archiviolo 106 f. 349; Rausa 1997; Raspe 1996, 317–322).

It is clear, nevertheless, that the plan for the projected Pamphilj mausoleum at the Chiesa Nuova, with its paired columns and circular ambulatory, was based on the early Christian mausoleum church of Santa Costanza, the burial-place in the mid-fourth century of Constantine's daughter, which is situated right next to the church of Sant'

Figure 9.6 Montano, Reconstruction of S. Costanza and enclosure (photo, Author, courtesy of the British School at Rome).

Agnese fuori le mura, in the Via Nomentana (Fig. 9.6). When it came to providing designs for Sant' Agnese in Piazza Navona, however, Montano's reconstruction of the complex, showing its original, circus-like enclosure (Fig. 9.6), may have been instrumental in promoting the idea to create a central plan building on a site where a

Figure 9.7 S. Agnese in Piazza Navona (detail) (photo, Author).

circus-like arena already existed (Raspe 1996, 317–322). It is certainly tempting to make analogies between Sta Costanza and the juxtaposition of the church-mausoleum and 'circus' at Piazza Navona, especially given that the veneration of Sant' Agnese was at the heart of both the Via Nomentana site and the city square. Apart from Sant' Agnese fuori le mura, several other Constantinian *martyria* and mausolea were similarly central-plan structures, connected to stadia-like enclosures: S. Lorenzo fuori le mura, the Basilica of the via Prenestina (Tor de' Schiavi), the Basilica of SS. Pietro e Marcellino, the Basilica of the via Ardeatina and the Basilica of SS. Apostoli

Figure 9.8 Bonnani, S. Agnese medal (photo, Author, courtesy of the British School at Rome).

Figure 9.9 Pirro Ligorio, La Conocchia BNN XIII. Book 10, etc. (Naples, Biblioteca Nazionale di Napoli).

(S. Sebastiano *in Catacumbus*) (Bisconti 2005; Brandenburg 2004, 55–92; La Rocca 2000, 213; 204–220; Frutaz 1976, 40–45; Krautheimer 1960). Richard Krautheimer considered that the Christian cemetery-basilica did not derive from Roman circuses, for him the similarity was in plan only (Krautheimer 1960, 39–40). Yet it seems clear that these so-called circus-basilicas must have appropriated something of the late imperial custom of building a stadium to celebrate funeral games for the defunct, for example the Circus of Maxentius that abuts the circular tomb (AD 309) of Maxentius's son, Romulus, on the Via Appia. The institution of games at Piazza Navona, the *Circo Agonale,* by their putative ancestor, Numa Pompilius, may have had particular meaning for the Pamphilj in this context.

Martin Raspe (1996, 315–68) considered that with Sant' Agnese Borromini managed to combine a façade in the form of an antique temple front with an early Christian central-plan mausoleum, yet the façade design Borromini eventually adopted could have derived equally from a pagan building that was, in fact, a tomb monument, thus enriching the iconographic decorum of the church as a mausoleum (Huemer 2001, 16). Borromini's façade design for Sant' Agnese was altered in the execution once the commission was handed back to Rainaldi, Borromini's aim to create a more organic façade for Sant' Agnese being frustrated by Rainaldi's subsequent alterations, which tended to flatten it out. However, the cornice of Sant' Agnese viewed from below gives a good idea of the effect that was achieved, even given Rainaldi's alterations (Fig. 9.7). Something of Borromini's original intentions can be seen in Bonanni's (1669, 2, 630) print recording Innocent's 1654 Jubilee medal made after Borromini's 1653 drawing in the Albertina, Vienna (Fig. 9.8; Huemer 2001, figs 1a, 1b). Dramatic convex and concave rhythms are an idiosyncratic aspect of Borromini's architecture which, as numerous commentators have observed, owe a great deal to unusual prototypes from antiquity. There is a direct relationship, for instance, between the 1654 medal design and a mausoleum from the Flavian period (AD 69–98) that is recorded in Ligorio's manuscript (Fig. 9.9). Known as *La Conocchia* (the distaff), it can still be seen at S. Maria Capua Vetere, albeit much restored, and is particularly suggestive as an inspiration for Borromini (Frommel 2000, 52–53; Rausa 1997, 97–98). Borromini certainly knew the monument, or representations of it, such as those found in Vat. Lat. 3439, because his design for the tribune of S. Andrea della Fratte, as has been noted elsewhere, is particularly reminiscent of it, even to the use of unadorned brick, which became a Borromini trademark. S. Andrea della Fratte was begun around 1653, the same year that Borromini also started work on Sant' Agnese, so these undulating forms were clearly in his mind at this time (Blunt 1979, 196; D'Onofrio 1971, 12).

Sant' Agnese also has certain similarities to yet another tomb monument, the monument of the freedmen of the Lucretii (*Monumentum Lucretianorum Lib*) that comprises part of the *Monumentum Deciorum,* with its dome, curved façade and symmetrical wings on the *Anteiquae Urbis Imago accuratissime ex vetusteis monumenteis formata,* Pirro Ligorio's 1561 map of ancient Rome reconstructed (Fig. 9.10). The

Figure 9.10 Pirro Ligorio, Anteiquae Urbis Imago accuratissime ex vetusteis monumenteis formata, 1561, detail: Monumentum Lucretianorum Lib (photo, Author, courtesy of the British School at Rome).

building, invented as it may be, relies, nevertheless, on Ligorio's deep knowledge of ancient architecture, based both on observation and on information derived from coins, reliefs, inscriptions and literary descriptions. It is likely that Borromini aimed at a similarly imaginative construction for Sant' Agnese, referring to models from antiquity that would be suitable to the decorum of death and commemoration but transforming them into contemporary baroque architectural idioms. It is not my intention to suggest that Borromini preferred one or another antique model, but that his designs for Sant' Agnese represent a synthesis of ancient types that aimed at evoking a building both formally and iconographically appropriate to a pope who wished in death, as in life, to be identified with Rome's glorious past and its ancient virtues. The interior chapels, although finished well after the Pope's death, nevertheless completed the ancient character of the church: with the exception of S. Filippo Neri (1515–1595) and Sta. Francesca Romana (1384–1440), the dedications were to early Christian saints (Agnes, Alexis, Cecilia, Emerenziana, Eustace and Sebastian) whose renewed veneration confirmed the authority of Rome through the longevity of its classical tradition, in which the Christian grew from the pagan (Simonetta, *et al.* 2003/04, 1, 100–159).

The Pope's desire to be buried in his mausoleum church was not honoured immediately. His corpse lay unburied for several days after he died, his closest relatives refusing to act. Donna Olimpia Pamphilj, his sister-in-law, pleaded a widow's poverty and her son, Don Camillo, denied that it was his responsibility; eventually Monsignor Segni, a canon of St. Peter's, paid the miserable five *scudi* required and the Pope was buried in St. Peter's. It was not until January 1677 that the remains were moved to Sant' Agnese by Innocent's great-nephew, another Camillo, where he was buried opposite the altar of Santa Francesa Romana (Sciubba and Sabatini 1962, 100; Ciampi 1878, 176–181). His tomb monument, placed immediately above the doors on the interior of the entrance façade (Fig. 9.3), was not completed until 1729, but it continued to encapsulate the twofold nature of Pamphilj iconography that had characterized his reign. The centrally placed Pope is flanked to his right by Religion, bearing cross, chalice and host, and to his left by Justice, who grasps her sword and holds aloft the *fasces*, symbols of ancient Roman power and authority. Whatever the failings of Innocent's reign may have been – and they were many – his vision of a Pamphilj 'forum' to rival the emperors of ancient Rome succeeded magnificently, for with Sant' Agnese as its focus, Piazza Navona still stands as a monument to the Pamphilj, Roman Catholicism, and the enduring authority of Classical Rome.

Bibliography

Abbreviations
ADP   Archivio Doria Pamphilj
BAV   Biblioteca Apostolica Vaticana

Ancient Sources
Cicero. *De Re Publica, De Legibus*. Trans. C. Walker Keyes, 1959. London, Heinemann and Cambridge, Mass., Harvard University Press.
Ovid. *Metamorphoses*. Trans. A. D. Melville, 1987. Oxford, Oxford University Press.
Plutarch. *Plutarch's Lives*, vol. 1. Trans. B. Perrin, 1959. London, Heinemann and Cambridge, Mass., Harvard University Press.

Ambrogi, A. (2001) Il territorio della Villa Doria Pamphilj. In B. Palma Venetucci (ed.) *Villa Doria Pamphilj, storia della collezione*, 13–25. Rome, Edizioni de Luca.
Angeloni, F. (1641) *La Historia augusta da Giulio Cesare infino à Costantino il Magno. Illustrata con la verità delle antiche medaglie da Francesco Angeloni.* Rome, Andrea Fei.
Ashby, T. (1935) *The Aqueducts of Ancient Rome*. I.A. Richmond (ed.). Oxford, Oxford at the Clarendon Press.
Benocci, C. (1996) *Villa Doria Pamphilj*. Rome, Editalia.
Benocci, C. (1998a) La Fortuna di villa Adriana a Tivoli e della cultura classica nel seicento: il caso della villa Doria Pamphilj a Roma. In M. Cima and E. La Rocca (eds) *Horti Romani*, 453–468. Rome, 'L'Erma' di Breschneider.
Benocci, C. (1998b) Camillo Pamphilj e la grande villa barocca: le componenti culturali. In C. Benocci (ed.) *Le virtù e i piaceri in Villa. Per il nuovo museo comunale della Villa Doria Pamphilj*, 36–51. Milan, Electa.
Benocci, C. (1999) *Algardi a Roma: il Casino del Bel Respiro a Villa Doria Pamphilj*. Rome, De Luca.
Benocci, C. (2005) *Villa Doria Pamphilj* (Realizzato dal Municipio Roma XVI e curato da Carla Benocci). Rome, Archivio Storico Culturale del Municipio Roma XVI.
Bisconti, F. (2005) 'Basilicam fecit'. Tipologie e caratteri degli edifici di culto al tempo dei Costantinidi. In A. Donati and G. Gentili (eds) *Costantino il Grande, La civiltà antica al bivio tra Occidente e Oriente,* 82–91. Milan, Silvana Editoriale.
Blunt, A. (1979) *Borromini*. Cambridge, Massachusetts, Harvard University Press.
Boesel, R. and Frommel, C. L. (2000) *Borromini e l'universo barocco.* Milan, Electa.
Boisclair, M.-N. (1986) *Gaspard Dughet, sa vie et son oeuvre (1615–1675)*. Paris, Arthéna.
Bonnani, F. (1699) *Numismata Pontificum Romanorum quae a tempore Martini V useque ad annum M.DC.XIX,* 2 vols. Rome, Ex Typographia Dominici Antonii Herculis.
Bosio, A. (1935) *Roma sotterranea di Antonio Bosio romano*. Facsimile edition, Rome, Quasar (1998).
Brandenburg, H. (2004) *Le prime chiese di Roma IV–VI secolo, l'inizio dell'architettura ecclesiastica occidentale*. Milan, Jaca Book.
Brusoni, G. (1664) Ristretto della Vita di Papa Innocenzo Decimo. In G. Brusoni, *Supplemento all'historia d'Italia*, 9–153. Frankfurt, S. Scouerth.
Bruun, C. (2001) Frontinus, Pope Paul V and the Aqua Alsietina/Traiana confusion. *Papers of the British School at Rome* 69, 300–315.
Cafferri, N. A. (1662) Numa Pompilio disceso dalla Famiglia Pamphilia di Sparta, in quelle Città fondata da Pamphilio Rè de' Dorici 350 anni prima dell'edificazione di Roma.

In G. Brusoni (ed.) *Degli Allori d'Eurota, Poesie diverse all'Eccellentiss. Sig. Principe D. Camillo Pamphilio,* 3–7. Rome, Valvasense.

Calza, R., *et al.* (1977) *Le antichità di Villa Doria Pamphili.* Rome, De Luca Editore.

Cartari, V. (1647) *Imagini delli dei degl'antichi,* facsimile of 1647 edition. Genoa, Nuova Stile Regina Editrice (1987).

Chiomenti Vassalli, D. (1979) *Donna Olimpia e del nepotismo nel Seicento.* Milan, Mursia.

Ciampi, I. (1878) *Innocenzo X Pamfili e la sua corte, storia di Roma dal 1644 al 1655.* Rome, Galeati.

Ciancio, P. and Virgili, P. (1993) Un frammento del suburbio romano: il sito di villa Doria Pamphilj in epoca romana. In C. Benocci (ed.) *Le virtù e i piaceri in Villa. Per il nuovo museo comunale della Villa Doria Pamphilj,* 15–20. Milan, Electa.

Clancy, B. C. (2000) Borromini e i Pamphili: una riconsiderazione della cappella funeraria di Innocenzo X alla Chiesa Nuova. In C. L. Frommel and E. Sladek (eds) *Francesco Borromini. Atti del convegno internazionale Roma 13–15 gennaio 2000,* 146–151. Milan, Electa.

Coffin, D. R. (2004) *Pirro Ligorio, The Renaissance Artist, Architect and Antiquarian, with a Checklist of Drawings.* University Park, Pennsylvania, The Pennsylvania State University Press.

Connors, J. (1980) *Borromini and the Roman Oratory, Style and Society.* New York, The Architectural History Foundation; Cambridge, Massachusetts and London, The MIT Press.

Courtright, N. M. (1990) *Gregory XIII's Tower of the Winds in the Vatican.* Unpublished thesis, New York University.

De Gregori, L. (n.d.) *Piazza Navona prima d'Innocenzo X.* Rome, Fratelli Palombi.

Di Domenico Cortese, G. (1968) Percorso di Giacinto Gimignani. *Commentari,* 18, 186–204.

D'Onofrio, M. (1971) *S. Andrea della Fratte* (Le Chiese di Roma Illustrate, n. 116). Rome, Edizioni 'Roma'.

Ditchfield, S. (1997) Text before trowel: Antonio Bosio's *Roma Sotterranea* Revisited. In R. N. Swanson (ed.) *The Church Retrospective,* Studies in Church History 33, 343–360. Woodbridge, The Boydell Press.

Eimer, G. (1971) *La Fabbrica di S. Agnese in Navona* 2 vols. Stockholm, Almquist and Wiksell.

Fagiolo M. and Madonna, M. L. (1972) La Roma di Pio IV: La 'Civitas Pia', La 'Salus Medica', La 'Custodia Angelica'. *Arte Illustrata* V, 383–402.

Fasolo, F. (1960) *L'Opera di Hieronimo e Carlo Rainaldi (1570–1655 e 1611–1691).* Rome, Edizioni Ricerche.

Finocchiaro, G. (1999) *Il museo di curiosità di Virgilio Spada, una raccolta romana del Seicento.* Rome, Palombi Editori.

Frommel, C. L. and Sladek, E. (2000) *Francesco Borromini. Atti del convegno internazionale Roma 13–15 gennaio 2000.* Milan, Electa.

Frommel, C. L. (2000) Borromini e la tradizione. In C. L. Frommel and E. Sladek (eds) *Francesco Borromini. Atti del convegno internazionale Roma 13–15 gennaio 2000.* 51–63. Milan, Electa.

Frutaz, A. P. (1976) *Il complesso monumentale di Sant'Agnese,* 3rd edition. Vatican, Tipografia Poliglotta Vaticana.

Gerlini, E. (1943) *Piazza Navona.* Catalogo delle Mostre de 'Il Volto di Roma nei secoli', 2nd edition. Rome, Reale Istituto di Studi Romani, Rome.

Gijsbers, P.-M. (1996) *Resurgit Pamphilj in Templo Pamphiliana Domus:* Camillo Pamphilj's

Patronage of the Church of Sant'Andrea al Quirinale. *Mededelingen van het Nederlands Instituut te Rome*, 55, 293–335.

Hempel E. (1921) *Carlo Rainaldi.* Biblioteca d'Arte Illustrata, Sei e Settecento Italiano, Series I, 2. Rome. Unione Editrice.

Heumer, F. (2001) Borromini and Michelangelo, II: Some preliminary thoughts on Sant'Agnese in Piazza Navona. *Source* 20, 12–22.

Hoffmann, P. (1976) *Villa Doria Pamphilj.* Roma, Edizione Capitolium.

Krautheimer, R. (1960) 'Mensa-Coemeterium-Martyrium'. *Cahiers Archéologiques fin de l'Antiquité et Moyen Âge* 11, 15–40.

La Rocca, E. (2000) Le basiliche cristiane "a deambulatorio" e la sopravvivenza del culto eroico. In S. Ensoli and E. La Rocca (eds) *Aurea Roma dalla città pagana alla città cristiana*, 204–220. Rome, "L'Erma" di Breschneider.

Lauro, G. (1651) *Antiquae Urbis splendor: hoc est praecipua eiusdem templa, amphitheatra, theatra, circi, naumachiae, arcus triumphales, mausolea aliaque sumptuosiora aedificia, pompae item triumphalis et colossaearum imaginum descriptio / opera & industria Iacobi Lauri Romani in aes incisa atque in lucem edita.* Rome, G. Lauro.

Ligorio, P. (1553) *Libro di M. Pyrrho Ligori Napoletano, delle Antichità di Roma, nelquale si tratta de' Circi, Theatri, & Anfitheatri. Con le paradosse del Medesmo autore,quai confutano le commune opinione sopra varii luoghi della città di Roma.* Venice, Michele Tramezino.

Marder, T. A. (2000) Borromini e Bernini a piazza Navona. In C. L. Frommel and E. Sladek (eds) *Francesco Borromini. Atti del convegno internazionale Roma 13–15 gennaio 2000*, 140–145. Milan, Electa.

Marshall, D. R. (2003) Piranesi, Juvarra and the Triumphal Bridge Tradition. *Art Bulletin* 85, 321–352.

Martin Raspe, R. (2000) Borromini e la cultura antiquaria. In R. Boesel and C. L. Frommel (eds) *Borromini e l'universo barocco*, 83–94. Milan, Electa.

Montagu, J. (1985) *Alessandro Algardi*, 2 vols. New Haven and London, Yale University Press.

Noehles, K. (1969) *La Chiesa dei SS. Luca e Martina nell'opera di Pietro da Cortona.* Rome, Bozzi.

Noehles, K. (1997) Cortona architetto, Osservazione sull'origine Toscana e la formazione romana del suo fare architettonico. In A. Lo Bianco (ed.) *Pietro da Cortona, 1597–1669.* Exhibition catalogue, 133–149. Milan, Electa.

Pampalone, A. (1973) Per Giacinto Brandi. *Bollettino d'Arte* 58, 123–166.

Panvinio, O. (1600) *De ludis circensibus libri II. De triumphis liber unus, quibus universa fere Romanorum veterum sacra ritusque declarantur.* Venice, I.B. Giottus.

Freiherr von Pastor, L. (1940) *The history of the Popes from the close of the Middle Ages, drawn from the secret archives of the Vatican and other original sources, etc.* Vol. 30. Trans., Dom Ernest Graf, O.S.B. London, Routledge & Kegan Paul, Trench, Trubner and Co.

Preimesberger, R. (1998) Images of the Papacy before and after 1648. In K. Bussmann and H. Schilling (eds) *1648 War and peace in Europe/Veranstaltungsgesellschaft 350 Jahre Westfälischer Friede*, 619–627. Munich, Bruckmann.

Preimesberger, R. (1976) 'Pontifex Romanus per Aeneam Praesignatus'. *Römisches Jahrbuch fur Kunstgeschicte* 16, 169–187.

Raggio, O. (1971) Alessandro Algardi e gli stucchi di Villa Pamphilj. *Paragone – Arte*, 251, 3–38.

Raspe, M. (1996) Borromini und Sant'Agnese in Piazza Navona, von der Päpstlichen Grablege zur Residenzkirche der Pamphili. *Römisches Jahrbuch der Bibliotheca Hertziana* 31, 313–367. *Prospectus Fori Agonalis*, Roma apud Carolum Losi, 1773.

Rausa, F. (1997) *Pirro Ligorio, Tombe e Mausolei dei Romani.* Rome, Quasar.

Redig de Campos, D. (1970) Palazzo Pamphilj, La Decorazione Pittorica. In F. Spinosi (ed.) *Piazza Navona Isola dei Pamfilj,* 157–192. Rome, Franco Spinosi Editore.

Romano, P. and Partini, P. (1947) *Piazza Navona nella storia e nell'arte.* Rome, Fratelli Palombi.

Russell, S. (1996) L'Intervento di Donna Olimpia Pamphilj nella Sala Grande di Palazzo Pamphilj a Piazza Navona. *Bollettino d'Arte* 95, Series VI, 111–120.

Russell, S. (1997) Frescoes by Herman van Swanevelt in Palazzo Pamphilj in Piazza Navona. *The Burlington Magazine* 169, 171–177.

Russell, S. (1999a) *The fresco friezes of Palazzo Pamphilj in Piazza Navona, Rome.* Unpublished thesis, University of Melbourne.

Russell, S. (1999b) Virtuous Women: the decoration of Donna Olimpia's audience room in the Palazzo Pamphilj in Piazza Navona, Rome. *Melbourne Art Journal* 3, 14–24.

Russell, S. (2006) Giovan Battista Pamphilj (1574–1655) mecenate della pittura di paesaggio come cardinale e come papa. In F. Cappelletti (ed.) *Archivi dello sguardo. Origini e momenti della pittura di paesaggio in Italia, Atti del Convegno Ferrara, Castello Estense 22–23 ottobre 2004, Quaderni degli annali dell'Università di Ferrara, Sezione Storia,* 4, 265–284. Firenze, Le Lettere.

Russell, S. (2007a) Pirro Ligorio, Cassiano dal Pozzo and the Republic of Letters. *Papers of the British School at Rome,* 75, 239–274.

Russell, S. (2007b) Rape, Ritual and the Responsible Citizen: the *Sala della storia romana* at Palazzo Pamphilj in Rome. *Storia dell'Arte,* 118 (n.s. 18), 57–72.

Sciubba S. and Sabatini, L. (1962) *Sant'Agnese in Agone* (Le Chiese di Roma Illustrate, n. 69). Rome, Marietti.

Scott, J. B. (1997) Strumenti di potere: Pietro da Cortona tra Barberini e Pamphilj. In A. Lo Bianco (ed.) *Pietro da Cortona, 1597–1669,* 87–98. Exhibition catalogue. Milan, Electa.

Simonetta, G., Gigli L. and Marchetti, G. (2003/04) *Sant'Agnese in Agone a Piazza Navona* 2 vols: 1 (2003), 2 (2004). Rome, Gangemi Editore.

Steinberg, L. (1977) *Borromini's San Carlo alle Quattro Fontane: a study of multiple form and architectural symbolism.* New York, Garland.

Studio Forme, (n.d.) *A brief guide to the church of St Agnese in Agone.* Rome, Edigraf Editoriale Grafica.

Virgili, P. (1986) Villa Pamphilj Necropoli. *Bulletino della commissione archaeologica comunale di Roma* 91, 760–761.

Index

necropolis 170, 173, 174
  see also cemeteries
neglect (of funerary monuments) 65, 71, 84
netherworld 169

obelisk 189–190
offerings, *see* food offerings/remains; funerary gifts; funerary ritual; grave goods; libations; plant remains
oikoumene (Greek) 24, 25
os resectum x, 92, 93–95, 98–99, 100, 102–106
Osiris 162–164, 166, 170, 171, 176

Pamphilj, Giovanni Battista, *see* Innocent X
Pamphilj family 184, 186, 188–189, 190, 191, 197, 199
  tomb 192, 193
Parilia festival 100–101
Pausanias 5–6, 8, 9, 13
Pausanias the Regent xii, 9, 10, 11, 12, 15
perfume/perfumed oil 111, 122, 126, 129, 131
  see also unguent flasks
Persians xi, xii, 1, 3, 8, 13
  Wars 5, 6, 9, 11–12, 13–16
pit burials 34, 37
plant remains (in burials/cremations) 53, 124, 127, 129, 131
  see also food offerings/remains
Pliny the Younger 67, 68, 71, 84
pollution, *see* death pollution
Pompeii 65, 69–70, 84, 111, 112, 118, 137
poor burials 71
Porta Nocera cemetery, Pompeii x, 111–123, 126, 132

portraiture 68–69, 71, 72, 74, 75, 79, 83, 85, 86, 113, 141, 176, 177
  see also death masks; sculpture
prayers/praying (Egyptian) 164, 166, 171–172, 173
priests (Egyptian) viii, 159, 161, 174
processions (Egyptian) 159, 171, 173–174
purification 92, 93, 100, 101, 102, 105, 106, 111
  see also death pollution; lustration; *Parilia* festival; ritual cleansing
pyre 92, 93, 103, 111, 119, 121, 124, 126

recitations (Egyptian) 161, 162, 163
recycling/re-use 56, 65, 83, 84, 85, 86, 122, 131, 139, 140, 142, 147
religion
  Egyptian 160, 164
  Roman x, 91, 93, 100
remembrance x, xi, 65, 68, 86, 91, 92, 101, 105, 106
  see also memory
repatriation xii, 8–9, 10, 16, 95
resurrection 190
ritual cleansing x, 100, 101, 102, 103, 105–106
royal burials 8, 9, 11, 21, 26, 40, 174

sacrifices 93, 110, 129, 161, 166, 177, 187
San Andrea, Rome (church of) 186
San Cesareo, Rome 95–100, 101, 102, 103, 106
Sant'Agnese, Rome (church of) xi, 183, 188, 190, 191, 192, 193–194, 197, 199
sarcophagi 26, 30, 33, 35, 70, 71, 96, 135, 140, 143

Digital Watermarking for Digital Media

Table of Contents

Foreword

Digital watermarking is an important topic because of the many illegal copies of images, music titles, and video films. This is strengthened by the digitalization of media assets, the rapid growth of the Internet, and the speed of file transfers. Therefore, it is necessary to have mechanisms to protect these digital assets and associated rights. This book gives an overview on storage formats of different media types, data compression, and mechanisms and techniques to protect these media types.

This book is an effort to give a comprehensive overview on different aspects of media asset and digital rights management. The book aims to provide relevant theoretical frameworks and the latest research findings in the area. It is written for students, researchers, and professionals who want to improve their understanding of the role of digital watermarking to protect media assets.

Dr. Juergen Seitz
University of Cooperative Education
Heidenheim, Germany

Preface

Digital media, like audio, video, images, and other multimedia documents, can be protected against copyright infringements with invisible, integrated patterns. Such methods are based on steganography and digital watermarking techniques. Most watermarks are inserted as a plain-bit or adjusted digital signal using a key-based embedding algorithm. The embedded information is hidden (in low-value bits or least significant bits of picture pixels, frequency, or other value domains) and linked inseparably with the source data structure. For the optimal watermarking application a trade-off between competing criteria such as robustness, non-perceptibility, non-detectability, and security have to be made. Most watermarking algorithms are not resistant to all attacks and even friendly attacks such as file and data modifications can easily destroy the watermark.

The features of the digital world lead to economical chances such as cheap distribution and also to serious risks in simplifying unauthorized copying and distribution (Rosenblatt, Trippe, & Mooney, 2002). In order to solve intellectual property problems of the digital age, two basic procedures are used: "buy and drop," linked to the destruction of various peer-to-peer solutions and "subpoena and fear," as the creation of non-natural social fear by specific legislations. Although customers around the world are willing to buy digital products over networks, the industry is still using conventional procedures to push such a decisive customer impulse back into existing and conventional markets.

The importance and the supposed economical thread for copyright holders are clarified by initiatives of the entertainment industry, such as VIVA (Visual Identity Verification Auditor) (VIVA, n.d.) and SDMI (Secure Digital Music Initiative) (SDMI, n.d.). Although distributors and artists already recognize the advantages in making their material available online, they will not go further into the online business until their content can be protected by technical and wide law regulations. As new intellectual property changes became new European law in 2003 and begin to fit the proposals of the World Intellectual Property Organi-